DINKUM DIGGERS

DINKUM DIGGERS

An Australian Battalion at War

DALE BLAIR

MELBOURNE UNIVERSITY PRESS

MELBOURNE UNIVERSITY PRESS
PO Box 278, Carlton South, Victoria 3053, Australia
info@mup.unimelb.edu.au
www.mup.com.au

First published 2001

Designed by Melissa Graham
Typeset by Syarikat Seng Teik Sdn. Bhd., Malaysia in 10 point FF Scala
Printed in Australia by Australian Print Group

National Library of Australia Cataloguing-in-Publication entry

Blair, Dale James.
   Dinkum diggers: an Australian battalion at war.
   Bibliography.
   Includes index.
   ISBN 0 522 84944 X.

   1. Australia. Army. Battalion, 1st. 2. Australia. Army. Australian Imperial Force (1914–1921). 3. World War, 1914–1918—Australia. 4. National characteristics, Australian. I. Title.

940.394

Contents

Illustrations

Acknowledgements

This book, as with most work, owes its completion to the input of many people. First and foremost of these people whom I wish to thank is Associate Professor Phillip Deery at Victoria University. Phillip's encouragement, advice, criticisms and direction were crucial to the completion of my doctoral thesis from which this book is adapted. His enthusiasm and availability throughout were (and continues to be) greatly appreciated. Mr Colin Hassal of the Department of Veterans' Affairs provided much-appreciated assistance in gaining special access to the repatriation files of ex-1st Battalion soldiers held in the Sydney repository of Australian Archives. Also, the prompt attention and service provided by the staff of the WWI Personnel Section at Australian Archives' Mitchell repository in Canberra ensured that no undue delays were encountered in the gathering of data from the soldiers' personnel dossiers. I would also like to acknowledge the many people with whom I have had association at the Australian War Memorial, particularly those of the Historical Research Section and Official Historians, who have shown interest in my work since my time as a summer vacation scholar at the Memorial in 1994. It was, in fact, during that time that the seeds of this book were planted when the then Director of the War Memorial, Brendan Kelson, suggested a battalion as a worthy subject for postgraduate enquiry.

I am also grateful to the men and women—the children of 1st Battalion soldiers—who allowed me the opportunity to share their memories through interviews and questionnaires. The hospitality that many of these people extended to me in their homes made the task of research all the more enjoyable. Ms Joy Stacy, daughter of the 1st Battalion's last commanding officer, was especially helpful in providing contact with several other people whose fathers had served in the Battalion and who, in turn, provided information. Similarly, Miss Nancy Joyce and Mrs Heather Cooper made available many photographs that contributed a valuable pictorial dimension to my research. A cherished memory from this exercise was the rendition provided by Mrs Barbara Fitzherbert of the French song, *Madelon* (learnt from her father). Finally, an especial and heartfelt thanks is due to my wife, Noelene (Non), whose patience and practical support across a range of family and academic chores was pivotal to my ability to complete this book. *Merci beaucoup, mesdames.*

Abbreviations

AIF	Australian Imperial Force
AWM	Australian War Memorial
Bde	Brigade
BEF	British Expeditionary Force
Bn	Battalion
CO	Commanding Officer
Coy	Company
Div	Division
Dvr	Driver
Maj.	Major
Maj.-Gen.	Major-General
NCO	non-commissioned officer
OC	Officer Commanding
OIC	Officer-in-Charge
PUO	pyrexia of uncertain origin
RSM	Regimental Sergeant-Major

It does not matter where one goes or what paper one reads, there seems to be hardly anything but Anzac and the Anzacs. Anzacs this and Anzacs that until we have become sick of the word. We cannot do anything especially raid the Hun trenches without a great column in the papers concerning the wonderful facts of the famous 'Anzacs'. I don't reckon we are any better than the English Tommy for we are all British.

Pte F. J. Gales
1st MG Battalion

INTRODUCTION

Though time renders the First World War an increasingly distant historical drama, events such as the celebration of the major anniversaries of Australian participation ensure its currency in our popular memory. Eighty-five years have elapsed since Australian soldiers rushed ashore at Anzac Cove and lay the foundations for what was to become the centrepiece of the nation's remembrance of war. The Australian soldiers who waded ashore at Gallipoli on 25 April 1915 represented the apotheosis of Australia's national identity.

The events of that historic morning proved the catalyst for the establishment of the Anzac legend. The legend that emerged from the bedlam and mayhem of battle unleashed across the scrubby knolls and ravines at Anzac that day was one of national affirmation. It asserts that Australia came of age when the blood of its sons was spilled and stained upon the altar of sacrifice.[1] With that consecration the nation declared itself a worthy defender of the ideals that sustained the British Empire. Entwined in this remembrance is the assertion of a distinct national character and code of behaviour. Although writings about a distinct Australian character can be traced as far back as the early decades in colonial New South Wales, it was the Australian soldier of the First World War who was to provide the most emphatic model for Australian manliness. It was in the furnace of the front line that the national character would be forged into its most enduring form.

The 'digger' stereotype that emerged during the war and cemented itself in the nation's post-war iconography remains with us today. The image, of course, is singularly masculine. According to the nation's myth-makers the 'digger' was an uncomplicated common man whose behaviour was regulated by a simple set of values. Paramount among these was his desire for a 'fair go' and his willingness to stick by his mates. This notion of mateship was to become a powerful ideal for those propagating a distinct Australian character. So much so that Prime Minister John Howard could seriously consider the term 'mateship' as reasonable and worthy for inclusion in a proposed preamble to an Australian Constitution. The public outcry that followed suggests that the concept had become so tainted by the excesses of cronyism among politicians and businessman as to be somewhat invidious as well as irrelevant to a large portion of the population.

The post-war period saw a concerted effort by conservative forces to enshrine, mythologise and sanitise Australia's sacrifice. The Australian Labor Party, at least in Victoria, suggested that all articles extolling the battles and heroes of past wars be banned from school texts.[2] The sanctioning of a public holiday on Anzac Day, however, ensured that the events commemorated by that day, whatever they stood for, remained a part of the national calendar. It also provided another forum for the staging of the values of the victorious Right. The pomp and ceremony that fronted proceedings at the various shrines of remembrance on Anzac Day were as much a celebration of the established order of authority as they were of the nation's manhood. Importantly, as Lloyd Robson observed, ceremonies such as 'the annual school Day services . . . steadily inculcated the digger stereotype in the minds of the impressionable young' so that by the eve of the Second World War, 'the stereotype of the Australian soldier was confirmed and embedded in the Australian consciousness'.[3]

Of equal importance to the formation of this stereotype, and those with which this book is most concerned, were the qualities that the 'digger' allegedly displayed on the battlefield. Descriptions of the 'digger'—as a good-natured larrikin out of the line but both highly skilled and uncompromising in battle—proliferate in the celebratory writings about the Australian soldier. Furthermore, attributes of resourcefulness and initiative are universally applied to the Australian soldiers' exploits both on the battlefield and behind the lines. These qualities of independent action, coupled with the soldiers' humour and anti-authoritarian outlook, have combined to produce an indefatigable defender of democracy and worthy representation of Australian manhood. The merging of the individual qualities of the Australian soldier with the national ideal is where the legend gains most potency. The words used by Australia's official historian of the First World War, C. E. W. Bean to describe the evacuation from the Anzac position at Gallipoli exemplify this: 'But Anzac stood, and still stands, for reckless valour in a good cause, for enterprise, resourcefulness, fidelity, comradeship, and endurance that will never own defeat'.[4] Indomitable individual characteristics of the Australian soldier sustain the 'good cause'.

Prime Minister Paul Keating's eulogy delivered at the entombment of the Unknown Soldier revealed that the essence of the Anzac legend in 1993 had changed little since its inception:

> It is legend not of sweeping military victories so much as triumphs against the odds, of courage and ingenuity in adversity. It is legend of free and independent spirits whose discipline derived less from military formalities and customs than from the bonds of mateship and the demands of necessity. It is a democratic tradition, in which Australians have gone to war ever since.[5]

This stereotyping of the 'digger' has served to obscure much of the reality of the experience of Australian soldiers in the First World War. Its perpetuation deflects attention from the sometimes horrific realities of individuals' variegated experiences, and thereby limits our understanding of Australian experience in the First World War. It implies a uniformity of experiences and responses by Australian soldiers. All assume the same identity in the khaki of the Australian Imperial Force (AIF). We need only reflect on our own experiences to doubt the veracity of this assumption. As individuals we are all innately different and our perceptions are shaped by biases and prejudices that dictate our responses at any given time or place. Do we really expect that Australian soldiers drawn from different age-groups, from different workplaces and social environments, religious denominations and national backgrounds would respond to their collective experience in exactly the same manner? Yet this is exactly what the Anzac legend asks of us. The legend purports to transcend class, and so descriptions of the AIF as 'egalitarian' and 'democratic' have become axiomatic. In reality, class *was* a factor in the shaping of the AIF and democracy *was not* a concept that particularly underpinned or informed martial control in either the British or Australian armies.

That the stereotypical image of the Australian soldier has persisted for so long is a testament to the power of the legend. The 'digger' has evolved through a series of historical and fictional works, ceremonial eulogies and portrayals on television and film, to the point that *he* is now fixed in the popular imagination.[6] Given the prominence of the Anzac legend (and the 'digger') in Australian society, it is appropriate that it be placed under historical scrutiny. It is necessary to test the validity of the myths that surround the Australian soldier of the First World War, to examine and understand the soldiers' experience as it occurred in the front line and how that experience was transmitted into the corpus of history and public memory.

This study, then, arises from a desire to broaden the context in which we have traditionally viewed the Australian soldier. More importantly, though, the misrepresentation of the soldiers' experience through false eulogy is bad history. Joan Beaumont has suggested that 'What matters is not so much whether the legend was true as why it was believed by Australians to be so'.[7] While accepting the importance of inquiring into the nation's belief system, to neglect the veracity or otherwise of something so central to that belief system would be to ignore an equally important role of the historian, namely, *to confront myths*. History that perpetuates myths and falsehoods (as truth) particularly when of national significance, borders on propaganda. Arthur Marwick considered that 'one of the purposes of serious historical study is, in advancing understanding of the past, to challenge and deflate myths, while at the same time, perhaps, explaining their origins and significance'.[8] If we make false claims in advancing the memory of Australian soldiers then, ultimately, we are committing a disservice to the integrity of the men who fought and died. In addition, we run the risk of causing their real achievements to be doubted.[9]

The Anzac legend has tended to be exceedingly chauvinistic in its portrayal of the Australian soldier. The 'digger' has been depicted as a superior soldier when matched against the men of other nations, enemy and allies alike. Two types that have been particularly vilified in this respect are the British officer and the English soldier or 'Tommy'. If our degree of self-worth is still predicated, in part, by the denigration of others then it is surely desirable to jettison such mean-spirited vanity in favour of a more equitable and honourable appreciation of the Australian experience. Inherent to the chauvinism of the legend is its fundamental dependence on the values and code of behaviour of the fighting man. Its approval of things of worth often revolves around acts of physical endeavour, violence, and comradeship peculiar to an extraordinary male world. This is hardly surprising, given that the nature of war in the front line was an overwhelmingly male experience. This experience does not, however, need to be evaluated exclusively in a masculine manner. Although the legend is intrinsically masculine, a more modest approach—as opposed to the use of overblown rhetoric—and a concentration on aspects of the soldiers' experience other than the 'heroic' ought to be encouraged. Attention to the civilian links of family and class, coupled with an examination of the emotional dilemmas presented by homesickness, fatigue (physical and mental) and fear, can dilute the masculine emphasis to some degree. If the Anzac legend is to maintain its prominence in a society that is presumably developing a more inclusive and increasingly globalised outlook, then it, too, must broaden its scope. Myopic and xenophobic nationalism ought not sustain it.

The quality and character of the Australian soldier has been the subject of uneven treatment over the years, with a general tendency toward a celebratory outlook. Press journalism has consistently eulogised the Australian soldier as a means of portraying desirable national characteristics. Historians, too, have at times embraced the celebratory generalisations of Australian soldiers. Revisionist historians have emerged over the past three decades to challenge and scrutinise some of the revered characteristics of the nation's First World War soldiers. Their findings, however, continue to struggle against the popular manifestation of the Anzac legend.

This book adds to the body of revisionist works about Australia and the First World War. Revision is a natural and necessary process of history. Most historians engage in it, if only for the plain fact that as new documents and other source materials are uncovered, our assumptions of the past can be influenced by fresh evidence. Revisionism is not an inherently destructive process, and historians reassessing the Anzac legend and its myths ought not be seen as possessing some gratuitous urge to destroy it.

It is appropriate to acknowledge some of the important revisionist works that have broadened understanding of the period. Robin Gerster's book *Bignoting* revealed the alarming trend of self-aggrandisement that had run rampant through both fictional and non-fictional Australian war writings and invited new questions as to the real experience of Australian soldiers. Alistair Thomson also disputed the veracity of some written accounts, in particular C. E. W. Bean's use of language to dilute negative views of the Australian experience.[10] Furthermore, in his book *Anzac Memories*, he explored the changes and evolution in the recording of soldiers' experiences through oral testimony. Clearly both written and oral testimony contain pitfalls which make for a cautious pursuit of an elusive truth.

Peter Cochrane's *Simpson and the Donkey* is another insightful work that showed how a life and symbol could be appropriated by a society and sustained in the public consciousness. Simpson's real story was quickly lost to a simplified and preferred public version and was symptomatic of the treatment of the 'digger' for many decades.

In regard to specific military campaigns, Robin Prior and Trevor Wilson have also broadened the context in which we view Australian endeavour.[11] Campaigns encompassed a far greater breadth of planning and logistics beyond the immediate sphere of Australian operations than has generally been acknowledged by many Australians. These writers and others, referenced throughout the text, have extended the perimeters of research in the field of Australian First World War studies. In doing so, they have illuminated the way and made easier the writing of this book.

The vehicle for this study is the 1st Australian Infantry Battalion, a unit raised in Sydney which saw service at Gallipoli and later in France and Belgium. The 1st Battalion has been selected for a number of reasons. It is one of the best-represented units in the Australian War Memorial's collection of diaries and letters of the First World War and provides a solid body of empirical data for study of a single battalion. Bean accompanied the Battalion, along with the Divisional Headquarters, on the journey from Egypt to Lemnos and again during the voyage to Anzac. Through this association, Bean may have fostered a closer relationship with the officers of the 1st Battalion that was tapped into during the collection of papers for the War Memorial. As one of the AIF's original units the 1st Battalion participated in the key battles that are central to any discussion about the development of the Anzac legend. Also, the Battalion's primacy in the AIF's order of battle supposedly carried some prestige that set it apart from other units. Depiction of the 'digger' stereotype is manifest in works that present an overview of the AIF or paint the battles, campaigns and the national response with a broad brush. By narrowing the focus of Australian war experience to a single battalion, nuances in behaviour that have been previously undiscovered will be revealed, particularly in relation to how the men viewed and reacted to their own officers and how both men and officers behaved in combat.

The battalion provides fertile ground for investigation into the behaviour and character of Australian soldiers. After all, the infantry battalion is arguably the most distinct unit pertinent to the majority of Australian soldiers' war service. The paucity of academic battalion studies suggests that battalion histories are regarded as a specific genre within military history. However, with the deepening of academic interest in the nation's military involvement, it is appropriate that we look afresh at the study of a battalion as a means of broadening our understanding of Australians in war.

Analysis of a single battalion offers the prospect, denied to wider-ranging general studies, of examining the minutiae of a soldier's experiences, some of which might offer contrary images to those celebrated within the legend. As the stock unit of the AIF, the battalion provides a compact formation upon which to focus. As Richard White noted of John McQuilton's study of enlistment in the shire of Yackandandah: 'The microcosm might well prove to be far more revealing than the macrocosm'.

A battalion's function, in the context of the front line, was to provide for the army a manageable formation in which men could be brought to the point of action in a cohesive and effective manner. The battalion was, in effect, a self-contained community. It was responsible for providing for the basic needs of its men. Food, clothing, recreation and religious instruction were all largely catered for at battalion level. As well, the unit had to provide weapons and support specialists that, through their variety, enhanced the sense of community generally attached to a battalion. Bombers, machine-gunners, signallers, snipers, stretcher-bearers, bandsmen, cooks and transport drivers all contributed to a rich tapestry of professions. Across this was overlaid the divisions in rank inherent to military systems that imposed a hierarchical order, as existed in most communities, upon the lives of the men. A battalion normally comprised four companies, which in turn were divided into four platoons, divided, again, into four sections. A company comprised about 240 men, a platoon sixty and a section fifteen. Commissioned officers commanded the platoons and companies while non-commissioned officers (NCOs) commanded the sections. Within these sub-units strong friendships and cliques were often formed as the men became dependent upon one another for support, moral and physical, both in and out of battle. This community sentiment and camaraderie contributed to the battalion's *esprit de corps*.

Australian battalions of the First World War are generally accepted as possessing a dedication to the unit that bordered on fanaticism. The standard proof offered for the existence of this bond in Australian soldiers is the disbandment mutinies involving eight Australian battalions in 1918.[12] The refusal on the part of the officers and men of those battalions to disband, a measure introduced because of the attrition rate and lack of reinforcements, is widely accepted as representing the intensity of a soldier's affiliation to his unit throughout the AIF. The actions of the soldiers within these units appear to provide compelling support for Bill Gammage's assertion that this attachment was strengthened through 'years of battle . . . until a man's battalion was the centre of his existence'.[13] Similarly, John Laffin stated: 'The disbandment crisis proved, if nothing else, that battalion *esprit de corps* was the greatest binding force in the AIF'.[14]

Australian soldiers' attachments to battalions spring, most likely, from two sources. First, the powerful tradition of the British regiment, which was such a potent symbol in the maintenance and defence of the British Empire, was ever present in the society to which Australian volunteers for the First World War belonged. A sense of mimicry suggests itself. Second, loyalty to the battalion provided an emphatic formality to the strong bonds of friendship that were sometimes formed within the smaller unit formations. This special *esprit de corps* is of particular interest given the occurrence of a serious mutiny in the 1st Battalion in 1918. That mutiny suggests that not all Australian soldiers were willing to submit themselves slavishly to the ideal of the regiment. The 1st Battalion was unique in another critical way: it (or rather a large portion of it) was the only Australian unit to have walked out of the front line and that fact alone marks it as being a unit of particular interest. That act, too, contradicts one of the most fundamental (if not the central) elements of the Anzac legend, the Australian creed of mateship. The nation's mythical 'digger' would never have turned his back on his mates.

Because of the tendency to examine Australian soldiers mainly in the general context of the achievements of the AIF, there has been little examination of the attitudes and behaviour within the smaller unit formations. Such analysis is, for example, virtually non-existent in Bean's writings in the official histories. From a small unit viewpoint, the official histories give only a disconnected history of the actions of Australian battalions. Issues such as the officer–man relationship are not adequately examined.

The life of the front-line infantryman was lived in an extremely volatile environment, and his immediate opinions and perceptions often reflected his anger and suspicion. Lieutenant A. W. Edwards made the important observation, and one pertinent throughout the war in all theatres of operation, that: 'we often went into and came out of the front line with our horizon and objective obscure. We were too close to events to see them in perspective'.[15] Front-line soldiers lived a confused and fragmented existence. In such an environment rumours gained easy acceptance. It was through this myopic and distorted prism that soldiers experienced the war.

The treatment of the diaries and letters of two 1st Battalion men, Reg Donkin and John Gammage, for example, provides some proof as to how important war experiences can be ignored in general studies.[16] The writings of both of these soldiers were referenced by Bill Gammage, *The Broken Years,* and John Robertson, *Anzac and Empire,* yet neither made mention of the ongoing and strident criticisms that those soldiers made about their officers.[17] Although overlooked, the attitudes of the two soldiers have significant implications for the relations between officers and men within the 1st Battalion particularly and, more generally, to the notion of egalitarianism that underpins the majority of writings about the AIF.

This book seeks to identify some of the junctures at which reality and myth diverged. Particular emphasis will be given to the myths of egalitarianism and individualism that are synonymous with the stereotypical 'digger'. It is important that we address these themes since egalitarianism and individualism are two attributes central to the indices upon which our national character continues to be measured. It will be argued that the actual experience of the 1st Battalion provided significant contradictions to the 'digger' image that has been contemporarily and historically constructed.

Within those general experiences there also existed a degree of anti-British sentiment that contributed to the establishment of the 'digger' image. Criticism of British generals and English soldiers was evident during the Gallipoli campaign and continued to feature in written descriptions by Australian soldiers about the fighting in France. By the end of the war the notion that the English were particularly poor soldiers had become widely accepted within the AIF. That such a view prevailed and was general throughout the AIF appears incontrovertible. A post-war American report observed that a 'lack of respect on the part of the Australian enlisted man for the English soldier of whatever rank . . . was the subject of general comment'.[18] It was a view founded principally on the belief that the English, when compared against the Australians, lacked—in particular—the same qualities for resourcefulness and initiative. The legitimacy of this view will be explored since the negative perception of English soldiers, in all likelihood, fortified the positive view that Australian soldiers held of themselves.

Before entering a full discussion of the 1st Battalion's war experience it is necessary to acknowledge some of the bias in the evidence and problems encountered in researching this book. It was Bean's judgement that the diaries and letters of soldiers needed to be treated with circumspection. He did not consider them as reliable sources for the reconstruction of the operations that he wished to describe. However, while soldiers' diaries and letters may not be the most reliable source for operational studies, they do provide a revealing insight into the hearts and minds of soldiers and of the environment within which they lived. Diaries and letters provide some of the most compelling and poignant avenues we have for exploring and understanding the world of Australian soldiers. In addition to the archival material held in the War Memorial's collection, this study also uses letters published in newspapers. It was the view of some soldiers that these letters were largely humbug. It was certainly true that the headlines that introduced such letters spouted standard patriotic jargon of the time, but careful scrutiny suggests that the majority of these letters were honest accounts (when compared with what we already know of some of the events they described) and, except where editors provided selected extracts only, provide many illuminating insights into attitudes held by the soldiers. These personal archives are a crucial contribution to gaining '*intimate* knowledge' of tactical appreciations and social interactions of units in battle.[19] The honesty of these accounts, their descriptions of what the soldiers actually experienced in the front line, is central to the reconstruction and assessment of Australian performance contained in this book.

The major problem in using soldiers' letters and diaries as a basis for research is that as a group the authors are not necessarily an accurate representation of the men who served in a battalion. Numerically, they are only a small fraction of the men who served. This study has examined the written records of approximately one hundred men who served in, or whose service pertained, to the 1st Battalion.[20] This represents 1.66 per cent of the Battalion; it compares favourably with Bill Gammage's *The Broken Years,* which relied on approximately one thousand diary and letter writers, or 0.303 per cent of Australian soldiers serving abroad with the AIF. Also, chroniclers were more likely to come from the more articulate within the ranks. Many of these men occupied the officer ranks. Officers provided 31.16 per cent of writers, NCOs 41.55 per cent (over half of whom were sergeants), and the other ranks 25.97 per cent. The rank of 1.29 per cent could not be positively identified. Desmond Morton, in his study of the Canadian forces, has warned of the dangers of relying on the descriptions of soldier writers:

> It is easy for historians to see all soldiers as replicas of the relative handful of articulate diarists, letter writers, and memoirists . . . Whatever common sense tells us, we trust our own tribe, particularly when they reinforce our own admirable ideas. However right writers might have been, they are untypical.[21]

Diaries and letters for the Gallipoli campaign provide a disproportionate body of data when compared to those held for the French and Belgium campaigns. Descriptions of the later stages of the Battalion's service (1917–18) suffer from a tailing off in the number of diarists and letter writers for the period. This reflects the growing rate of attrition and downturn in the reinforcement numbers. As a consequence, the book at times must rely on the voice of a select few. However, the voice of these men is genuine. For instance the reliability of the accounts by Reg Donkin, who was a prominent contributor during the Gallipoli phase and one critical of his superiors, withstands historical scrutiny. Donkin, a particularly emotive individual, provides many insightful comments. The Battalion's offences book records him as being of 'bad' character and 'insubordinate' during the voyage to Egypt.[22] Similarly, Archie Barwick's diaries (also) reveal grievances and insights that are generally overlooked in more sanitised accounts of the 1st Battalion's experiences. His views were sometimes volatile and inconsistent but there exist no reasonable grounds on which his accounts can be rejected as untruthful. Incidents he comments upon are, in fact, corroborated in other diaries and letters. He was also a competent soldier. By the war's end he was a senior NCO, the award of a Belgian *croix de guerre* a reflection of his soldierly qualities. On that basis, his views on military matters are all the more pertinent. There is, too, variation in the quality and quantity of the soldiers' writings. For example, Barwick provides sixteen diaries, while Private P. Q. J. Collins has left a single postcard.[23]

Those who submitted diaries and letters to newspapers or various collections, whether the soldiers themselves or family and friends, did so because they derived some positive fulfilment and saw their war service as worthwhile. These possibilities need to be considered as, similarly, the content of their diaries and letters might be inspired by similar biases that were not necessarily shared by others. On this point, it is worth recollecting what Lloyd Robson wrote in his review of *The Broken Years*:

> Gammage cites some 400 letters and diaries; nearly half the number of their authors died on active service, whereas about one fifth of the AIF who embarked were killed. In more ways than one, then, his evidence comes from a select source. These letter-writers form a most atypical example of the Force. Is it further possible that their propensity to have been killed is related to their particular assumptions about the war? These letters and diaries, indeed, were officially appealed for in the 1920s and 1930s, and it seems unlikely that many parents or relatives or returned soldiers would have lodged with the Australian War Memorial any documents which were markedly discreditable. Too often one has the impression that these men are indulging in rhetoric and playing a role, explaining their motives and conduct in ideological terms because they feel that is required of them. What were the thoughts of that vast majority of soldiers who are not represented?[24]

The bias evident in Gammage's research also intrudes into this study. However, the bias is less dramatic. Of the 1st Battalion diary and letter writers, a little more than one-third (36.84 per cent) died on active service, still more than the percentage for the AIF but considerably less than the chroniclers used by Gammage. Identifying the views of the silent majority, however, remains a largely insurmountable problem. Nevertheless, the letters and diaries bring an intimacy and authentic voice to the narrative.

The letters and diaries of the soldiers form only part of the data of this book. Unit diaries—battalion, brigade and divisional—and relative operational records were also examined. Service and repatriation records of the men provide a further dimension and reveal some of the personal problems that arose from the on-going effects of the war. However, some difficulties were encountered in obtaining these records. In the case of the soldiers' personnel dossiers, direct access was denied due to public health concerns over the existence of white powder (possibly asbestos) throughout many of the files. As a consequence, information was gathered by supplying lists of the records required, which were then identified and forwarded by Australian Archives. Because of this, it is possible that some useful information contained in the correspondence section of the file between a soldier's next-of-kin and the military authorities has been ignored. For the most part, information extracted from a soldier's personnel dossier has been drawn from two main sources: the attestation papers and casualty/record of service forms. Information gathered from the repatriation files was also hampered due to the method by which records of pensions granted by the Repatriation Department (later Veterans' Affairs) were compiled. War pension recipients were not identified by unit, nor were they listed in alphabetical order in the Department's registers. It was therefore decided to concentrate the search on a sub-group within the 1st Battalion—the original E Company. Despite these problems, the repatriation records have provided insights into the post-war realities of the Battalion's members.

This book does not claim to be the definitive history of the 1st Battalion or of Australian soldiers generally. The themes it addresses, however, have lain dormant in much of the earlier Australian First World War writings: the history of the 1st Battalion, published in 1931, is a good example.[25] It was through this history that the 1st Battalion Association contributed to both the nation's early Great War historiography and the purifying process applied to the deeds of its soldiers, in which the behaviour of Australian soldiers was interpreted in a suitable manner for an exemplar of the national character.

The book was written principally by senior officers of the Battalion and was based on the war diaries of the unit supplemented by diaries and letters submitted by some of the officers and men who had served. Not surprisingly the history is top-heavy, in that it is officer-oriented, and echoes the pro-Empire rhetoric of the press, pulpit and parliaments of the day. The most salient criticism of this history is the near total absence of critical comment. Admittedly, officers whose reputations were tied closely to the performance of the unit were hardly likely to accentuate anything other than the positives or interpret events in a way that would bring discredit upon themselves or their men. As a consequence some important aspects of the unit's war experience are neglected: officers are never criticised, and relationships between officers and men are invariably depicted as excellent. As a consequence the view of a happy and united family is projected. Never is the spectre of the dysfunctional family raised.

That such a veneer was applied to battalion histories is not surprising. One of the main reasons for the absence of critical discussion lies in the style or formula of that particular *genre* of military history. The content and intent of the 1st Battalion history was described by one of its authors, Lieutenant-Colonel B. V. Stacy:

> The greater part of it deals with the military doings of the battalion; the various engagements are shortly described from the battalion point of view, and where possible, some mention is made of any outstanding personal deeds. There will be a short diary—of the dates—of the main movements and events in which the battalion was concerned. A roll of those who belonged to the battalion at any time will be included;

this roll was made available by the military authorities and should prove interesting to those who will be able to recall from it many old friends. It was thought also that such a roll would interest those whose friends and relations were in the battalion, and enable them to follow to some extent their movements over the 'other side'. An endeavour will be made to include a few simple maps . . . also . . . a few photographs. It is proposed to publish the book at as low a price as possible without sacrificing reading matter.[26]

The book's aims were essentially benign. It did not seek to advance the Battalion's reputation over other units with which it served and so its language is generally passive, though peppered with the odd humorous anecdote and recollection. Its purpose was essentially to commemorate those who served in the unit. It also contained the underlying message of triumph in adversity. Here it is pertinent to note Barbara Tuchman's comment about the British ability to extract positives from military reverses:

No nation has ever produced a military history of such verbal nobility as the British. Retreat or advance, win or lose, blunder or bravery, murderous folly or unyielding resolution, all emerge alike clothed in dignity and touched with glory . . . Everyone is splendid: soldiers are staunch, commanders cool, the fighting magnificent. Whatever the fiasco, aplomb is unbroken. Mistakes, failures, stupidities, or other causes of disaster mysteriously vanish. Disasters are recorded with care and pride and become transmuted into things of beauty . . . Other nations attempt but never quite achieve the same self-esteem.[27]

Australia was not one of those nations. It had inherited the literary skills of its parent and created its own object of veneration—the Australian soldier. An incident during the Battle of Lone Pine recounted in the foreword to the *First Battalion* provided by Major-General Sir Nevill M. Smyth[28] is indicative of the manner in which the war experiences of Australian battalions have generally been depicted and a good example of the 'verbal nobility' to which Tuchman refers. More importantly, when compared with some accounts of 1st Battalion soldiers, it demonstrates how ennobling rhetoric can obscure the realities of combat experience:

I well remember . . . a reinforcement of a hundred men of the 1st Battalion, conspicuous for their stature and physique, had just been landed and was sent straight into the hand-to-hand fight which was raging in the maze of trenches and tunnels. A corporal with a fair beard, stripped to the waist and covered with wounds, staggered out into the open and said to them, 'The boys are keeping up the name grandly in there'. The new-comers heard his words. They, too, would 'keep up the name'; I could see that. They marched calmly on, entered the fray and took a terrible toll on the enemy; but in a short time many of them were carried out with severe wounds which actually seemed to them a subject for joking and hilarity, so persistent was their courage.[29]

That this event occurred is not in dispute. What is questioned is the interpretation placed upon it. Accounts by some members of these reinforcements (cited in Chapter 3) depict an experience not entertained by the Brigadier: one of dread, terror, and costly inexperience. Smyth's description depicts the warrior of the Anzac tradition. The 1st Battalion, he concluded, were enamoured by the discipline of 'regular veterans whose whole being was concentrated on the all-absorbing object of fighting for the right, and in the hour of victory they were, as always, cheerful, honourable, chivalrous and merciful'.[30]

The 1st Battalion history, in fairness to its authors, did not raise itself completely to Smyth's lofty rhetoric. They were, in fact, quite conscious of achieving balance in their descriptions of the Battalion's actions, particularly in the final year in France (a mark of the contribution of the Battalion commander, Lieutenant-Colonel Stacy). Nevertheless they did give way to euphemisms that clouded judgements about the unit's war experience that have contributed to the uncritical perpetuation of the stereotypical Australian soldier.

Accounts of the Battalion's war experience also found expression in the New South Wales RSL journal *Reveille*. This journal, apart from the articles submitted, also acted as a bulletin board for the Battalion Association. The articles published in *Reveille*, even more than the Battalion history, promoted the stereotypical Australian soldier through their focus on the character traits and moral fortitude of the men. The articles were also inspired by a desire to ensure the 1st Battalion's war service was not overshadowed by that of other units, as indicated by Sergeant Norman Langford in a preface to an article on his reminiscences:

> My reason for venturing these reminiscences is to spur on other former members to do likewise, for the 1st Battalion did very good work and possessed many fine officers and men who deserve a niche of the glory of the AIF. I appeal to all 1st Battalion Diggers to join their association and maintain the spirit and traditions of the old Battalion. The fame of other units and of their personnel have been chronicled in "Reveille" by various writers. Let it not be said that the 1st Battalion lags behind.[31]

Langford's reminiscences followed the pattern of many other returned soldier contributors: an uncritical chronological narrative of war service, with a smattering of humour based on near-misses experienced. Other articles did little to enlighten readers about the experience of the Battalion and frequently resorted to platitudes and cliches. Brigadier-General J. Heane, the Battalion's CO in 1916 and the Battalion Association's patron, wrote of the sacrifice of the unit's dead 'whose deeds had built up the traditions that the Battalion had won—traditions that had given Australia a place as a nation among the nations of the world'.[32] Fred Davison contributed an article about the death of Private C. B. Storm, titled *Storm of the 1st Bn*, which tells of an incident late in the war that saw the unlucky private wounded along with two others in front of the Battalion's line. Suffering a severe wound, he insisted that the stretcher-bearers take his mates first. When Storm was finally brought in, a doctor pronounced his case hopeless with the lament: 'If we'd got him ten minutes ago we might have saved him'. Storm braced himself for death and died an hour later. Davison concluded reverently: 'Storm was a Jew. So was that other Christ.'[33] Another less holy snippet was provided about the rat cunning or 'nishitive' of Australians in procuring extra coal over the measly rations allotted in a training camp.[34] In keeping with that light-hearted vein, an anecdote appeared of two 1st Battalion diggers dressed in evening attire, frock coat and dress, during a hop-over in 1918.[35] More serious was a reflection on some of the Battalion's officers by Lieutenant-Colonel F. J. Kindon. The title of the article, *Swannell and Others: 1st Bn Braves,* was in keeping with the advancement of the warrior tradition.[36] Other articles pertaining to the 1st Battalion followed in similar style. Their overriding tone was laudatory and humorous with an emphasis on the comradeship and sacrifice involved with the men's war experience. In providing such superficial accounts of their war experience the writers were employing, perhaps unconsciously, a tactic common among ex-servicemen: one that obscured and protected their real experience from public scrutiny.

As the alleged qualities of the Australian soldier were woven into the commemorative services on Anzac Day and national literature, it became less likely that alternative experiences would be aired, much less considered. Returned soldiers who held contrary views were placed in an invidious position. Criticism would be construed as unpatriotic and disrespectful to the sacrifice of their fallen comrades. Overall, these works have advanced an uncontroversial and conservative interpretation of Australian soldiers that deliberately support and perpetuate the key characteristics of the Anzac legend's 'digger' stereotype.

This book does not cast itself as a military history. It recognises that military history is a *genre* governed by its own conventions and, understandably, its focus is more often on uncovering the reasons for victory or defeat. In such studies battalions are examined for their functional process, what they contributed to an outcome. They are a tool of war, and casualties sustained are an inevitable outcome of the military process. Histories that are concerned with establishing a unit's place in the annals of war are almost universally celebratory in nature. This commemorative tradition of battalion histories is evident in number of recently published works on Australian First World War battalions, all written with an intention to 'perpetuate the spirit of the men . . . which inspired them to serve faithfully and cheerfully, to strive to endure, and to sacrifice even life itself for a cause'.[37] They continue to describe the horror and heroism of the battalions in the context of the legendary qualities of the stereotype. The introduction to Ron Austin's history of the 8th Battalion (dedicated to the memory of his father who served in the unit) asserts that his book features 'true heroes', unlike the modern heroes of Australian society (tv/pop stars and sportsmen).[38] The foreword of Austin's book, written by Major Peter Ainslie, OAM, compliments perfectly the author's underlying assumption: '*Cobbers in Khaki* should be read by all Australians, the fundamental keys to the formation of our national character are here'.[39]

The fact that at the close of the twentieth century, preposterous descriptions can still find expression in major daily newspapers of Australian soldiers being 'mostly country-bred . . . grown up on sunshine and steaks', running fast, bounding over barbed wire and capable of shooting jam tins off fence posts at one hundred yards, suggests that the beginning of a new century is both an appropriate and necessary time to review our understanding of the character of Australian soldiers of the First World War.[40]

The sycophantic back-slapping triumphalism that politicians and media displayed in relation to the Australian military intervention in East Timor is a timely reminder that, as a nation, we have still not outgrown our penchant to uncritically equate nationalism with military endeavour. It was with similar public exaltation that the Australian experience in the First World War was appropriated and shaped. The reality of the experience from which the legend was hewn, in many of its aspects, is something quite different. It is hoped that this book will show that greater awareness needs to be applied if the truth of military experience is to be preserved from the indulgences of vainglorious nationalism.

I

FORMATION OF THE 1ST BATTALION

In the euphoria of Great Britain's declaration of war on Germany, many of the men who rushed the recruitment offices and filled the early battalions were responding to personal rather than national stimuli. C. E. W. Bean was certainly under no illusion about the type of volunteer that besieged the recruitment stations in the first weeks following the declaration of war, describing them, in part, as comprising some of the 'romantic, quixotic, adventurous flotsam that eddied on the surface of the Australian people'.[1] In this respect the formation and composition of the 1st Battalion was unremarkable when compared to other Australian units.

Notwithstanding the difficulties of attributing responses to any one group, there did exist a variety of reasons that dispel idealistic sentiments of the original Anzacs going 'off to war with the purest of hearts'.[2] Unemployment was one factor that influenced the decision of some within the 1st Battalion to enlist, and coalminers out of work since the outbreak of the war were reported among those presenting themselves for service in the first contingent.[3] For some British-born, such as Henry Angel (and the 'man with the donkey', John Simpson Kirkpatrick), the war presented a roundabout opportunity to return home. Angel, who had been working as a bushman, had hoped to return to England to see his family after the fighting but had his hopes dashed when he contracted pneumonia before the Gallipoli landing and was repatriated to Australia.[4] Members of New South Wales' Syrian community, whose ill-feeling for the Turks was little concealed, also offered their personal and communal support for the war.[5] Others, like Henry Lanser, were inspired by intensely personal reasons. By participating in the war, Lanser intended to dispel any doubts that people held over his family's nationality and loyalty due to its Germanic name.[6] John Reid, a school-teacher from Dubbo, wrote to his parents a few days prior to the landing at Gallipoli and recalled the dramatic shift in his motive for enlistment:

> My first idea of enlistment was born of a spirit of adventure; but on hearing Dr. Long, the Bishop of Bathurst, deliver an appealing address on the war and its causes, of the tragic fate of gallant Belgium crushed beneath the heel of Prussian militarism, of the grasp for world dominion by a power that respects not the right of small nations nor its own plighted word—then, unconvincing adventure gave way to an irresistible appeal of Duty.[7]

Providing a meaningful account of the men's enlistment motives is difficult because of their intangible and often emotive nature. It is an aspect little mentioned in the men's diaries.

One of the qualities of the AIF that is said to have sustained it and marked it as distinct from the British, European and American armies was its unique composition. The boast that it was the only volunteer army is often advanced as a reason for its high morale and performance. A point often overlooked by such statements is the fact that the Irish divisions of the British army were also complete volunteer organisations. The British government had considered the political climate in Ireland too volatile to attempt to introduce conscription. In Australia, this voluntaryism was underpinned by a sense of egalitarianism and strong democratic ideal that characterised the radical Australian nationalist traditions prior to the war. The view that Australia was an especially egalitarian society and, as such, distinct from other nations had been espoused by many in pre-war Australia. It had been particularly promulgated in the 1880s and 1890s through the press, especially in jingoistic publications such as the *Bulletin* and *Boomerang*.[8] It was not surprising that commentators sought to interpret the formation of the AIF in familiar terms. However, such an unbridled expectation of civilian life did not readily transfer to military life, nor could it be (realistically) expected to flourish in the regimented environment of an army. If the AIF were truly egalitarian, it could be expected that a strong sense of equality would be reflected in the composition of the force.

Topsyturvydom: the great leveller?

After the war many returned Australian soldiers believed that egalitarianism had been a reality of the AIF's war experience, despite entries in diaries and letters that depict a somewhat different view of military life. Reality was no match for the power of myth surrounding the Anzac legend. Australian volunteers did, however, carry to war a specific idea of what egalitarianism entailed. It represented an equality they expected to see displayed in their relationships in the army, particularly with their officers. Officers, NCOs and other soldiers who were seen as speaking plainly, squarely or man to man were regarded approvingly. This aspect of 'digger' egalitarianism carried the potential of being a formidable bonding force within the AIF; indeed, Australia's military myth-makers have said it was. Observers were keen to find examples of the existence of Australia's imagined egalitarianism. War was a great leveller, according to one account in the *Sydney Morning Herald*. It claimed that just as one could not distinguish between the beggar and millionaire in the Coogee surf nor could one discern any difference in the military camps: 'The uniform has made them all equal. There are no social distinctions.' The case of Sergeant Larkin of the 1st Battalion was offered as an example. Larkin was a NSW state parliamentarian and Labor politician representing the seat of Willoughby, and of him it was noted:

> Sergeant Larkin, according to what one hears in talking to the men, is proving that members of the Parliament can sometimes do more than talk. Over him is an officer who comes from one of the Government departments. The member of Parliament is now taking his orders from a Civil Servant. It is one more example of topsyturvydom.[9]

An example of topsyturvydom Larkin may have been, but he certainly did not subscribe to the notion of class within the army being as indistinguishable as in the Coogee surf. In practice it was not such a compelling force, certainly not within the early experience of the AIF. Its absence was suggested by Larkin himself in a letter written while training in Egypt: 'Suffice it to say that there would be very few here if the men were free to leave or had anticipated how they would be treated'.[10]

'Digger' prototypes

Two other aspects seized upon by the press as being important to the development and essence of a national army were, first, the presence of Boer War veterans whose experience and fighting ability were deemed to be valuable assets and, second, the quality of recruits drawn from the compulsory military training scheme that had been introduced in 1911. It was within descriptions of these two recruitment pools that the existence of natural-born martial qualities of Australia's youth and past-soldiery was advanced.

The desire to extol the virtues of Australia's volunteers was born, in part, from a need to compensate for the shallowness of the nation's military tradition. Prior to the war volunteer militia regiments had been the mainstay of the nation's military endeavours. Although they had been able to excite the population with colourful marches on occasions, the militia's public standing had been subject to fluctuations in interest over the years. Residents of Australian towns and cities could not cite long and rich histories of the deeds of their local regiments. Australian military history contained no charge of the Scots Greys, no 'Charge of the Light Brigade' or bloody defence of Hougoumont, although those events figured in the public mind by the very nature of Australia's British heritage. No Australian actions stood among the deeds that won the Empire. Indeed, New South Wales' contribution to the nation's military tradition had almost a comical edge. The overthrow of the notorious Governor Bligh was reportedly achieved only after he was dragged from beneath a bed by arresting soldiers. Although the story is probably apocryphal, it gained popular currency. Nevertheless, his arresters—the equally notorious New South Wales Corps—were later disbanded and the officers returned to England in disgrace. During the Sudan conflict the colony had been quick to respond and raise a volunteer force. The Sudan contingent was despatched overseas, arrived too late to see any substantial action and had three men wounded by sniper fire near Tamai. One man was shot in the foot and hopped some distance before he realised what had occurred. Another, shot in the shoulder, took issue with the soldier next to him who he thought had struck him. Three men also died from typhoid and dysentery.[11]

It was the Boer War rather than the Sudan expedition that was to provide the nation's most concrete and substantial military foray prior to the Great War. The small size of the colonial and Commonwealth contingents and the manner in which those units were used did not allow for any outpourings of public emotion to match that which followed the Gallipoli landing. In fact, the conduct of the war carried with it accusations of inhumane treatment of Boer women and children confined in British concentration camps, which, added to reports of misbehaviour by Australian troops and the execution of two Australian soldiers, Morant and Handcock, left a distaste in the public's memory of the war. One important impression did emanate from the Boer War and it was crucial to the shaping of perceptions about Australian soldiers in the conflict to follow. Australian soldiers had impressed with their horsemanship and enthusiasm for the fight, but not with their discipline.[12] This supported the dichotomy that existed in one perception of the Australian soldier, that he was a good fighter but a poor soldier. Supplementing this perception was an urge toward self-fulfilment of a national type. A definite self-image already existed before the war of an idealised Australian man. He was a robust, resourceful individual engaged with the land, combating the perils of the bush as he carved out a living. The outline was there, it remained only to be 'sketched in'.[13] As Russel Ward has suggested, such self-image had the potential to modify men's behaviour of 'how they ought "typically" behave'.[14]

Other than the Boer War, the most significant military event in pre-war Australia was the introduction of a system of compulsory training for the nation's youth in 1911. The scheme was territorial and divided Australia into

219 training areas. Ideally it would furnish 92 infantry battalions, 56 field artillery batteries and 28 light horse regiments.[15] The purpose of the scheme was to provide the nation with a pool of trained men to be called to its defence if necessary. On the eve of the war an army of some 50,000 trainees was available for service.[16] The large number of trainees and the veterans of Australia's previous military sortie were of obvious interest to those who keenly monitored the composition of the expeditionary force. Visitors to the military camps inevitably were moved to comment on the fine physique of the men and their soldierly bearing, while the *Sydney Morning Herald,* one of the keenest observers, promulgated an image of the men being 'young, active, born soldiers'.[17] Early portrayals of the typical recruit were dotingly positive. What the public were told often bore little resemblance to the calibre of recruit whom military authorities had to shape into a soldier. The Boer War was seen as a focal point for creating a military prototype to underpin the fledgling force and to boost its standing. Many Boer War veterans were reported to be among the ranks of the recruits, and the majority of volunteers were said to have undergone some form of previous military service and to be in need of 'little training'.[18] The creation of a soldier type worthy of the nation's admiration and of upholding Australia's name in the international arena was important to the fuelling of support for the war and for the esteem of the nation.

As much as reporters imagined that Boer War veterans would provide the linchpin of the nation's new force, they were mistaken. It is difficult to assess accurately the number of Boer War veterans within the ranks of the 1st Battalion as not all necessarily advised of their South African experience when signing their attestation papers. Figures for the 1st Division reveal that of the original embarkations 42.7 per cent were either currently serving in the Australian Military Force (AMF) or had previous experience in the militia, while 41.5 per cent had never before served in any military capacity. The remainder were men who had experience with the British regular and territorial forces.[19] Certainly some of the expeditionary force's senior commanders had seen service in South Africa. Of the 1st Division's 631 officers, 104 (16.48 per cent) had served in the 'South African or *other wars'.[20]

Fourteen years had elapsed since the Boer War and the initial age restriction on recruits, 18 to 39 years, excluded most veterans though some no doubt lowered their age. A further hurdle, though only a temporary one, was a decision to debar married men from enlisting. That decision proved unpopular and was revoked soon after being implemented. On 3 September it was reported that the upper age limit for volunteers was to be extended to 40 years.[21] This hardly addressed the problem, and the *Sydney Mail* rightly dismissed it as a measure that merely played with the question, pointing to the fact that a one-year extension still excluded many of the South African vet-erans as well as many fine militia officers and NCOs.[22] The following day age restrictions of a proposed second contingent were announced and set at 18 to 45 years.[23] It was a clear concession to Boer War veterans as well as an indi-cation that military minds had begun their grisly equations. Despite these acknowledgments, the *Newcastle Morning Herald* was able to report: 'The large element of old campaigners in the ranks has tended to bring the forces up to a great degree of efficiency, and the division while on the march, looked very workmanlike'.[24]

While the plight and helpful contributions of Boer War veterans were being reported, it was noted with concern that few of the militia were among the early volunteers. This absence was believed to be the result of a mis-apprehension on their part as to their eligibility. As militia they could not be despatched from Australia, but that did not preclude them from volunteering for service abroad. Official notification to this effect was made public, and trainees over the age of twenty who wished to enlist were asked to present themselves at the barracks.[25] The number of current serving AMF men who enrolled in the 1st Battalion was not high: it amounted to only 177 or 17 per cent of the originals who embarked, although the numbers of those who had undergone previous military service was considerably higher, figuring at about 50 per cent.[26] More obvious reasons existed than misapprehension for the low number of volunteers from the militia. First was that throughout the initial period of recruitment for the expeditionary force the militia regiments were involved in serious military duties, in theory, to defend Australia against invasion from an eastern power—a thinly veiled reference to Japan. That threat, real or imagined, evaporated with Japan's entry into the war on the Allied side on 23 August 1914, and thereafter only a small militia force was required. Of the Battalion's 177 AMF men, 45 per cent (79 men) enlisted after Japan's position became known. It is impossible to know whether these men held off enlisting because of a commitment to their militia duties or other-wise. Certainly those duties were not an impediment to those who enlisted before Japan's position became known.[27] In fact the service of the AMF men was actively sought by the 1st Battalion commander, Lieutent-Colonel Dobbin. A serving soldier of the militia recorded in his diary on 15 August 1914: 'Lieut.Alexander receives word from Colonel Dobbin to enrol volunteers for active service abroad'.[28] Another factor that must certainly have affected the enlistment of some militiamen was their age. Many of the trainees were under the age of twenty-one and required parental permission to enlist. That age group would come to represent nearly 20 per cent of the Battalion by the embarkation date. While many parents acceded to the demands of their eager sons, others were more resolute and refused permission. Ben Champion's father had refused his son's request to enlist in the Rabaul force and relented only when news of the losses at Gallipoli swept the nation.[29]

An Australian 'officer-type'

As much as commentators advanced the notion of egalitarianism and celebrated the martial qualities of the nation's Boer War veterans and militia-trained youth, the reality was somewhat different. The men's demographic background is measurable and reveals a number of biases that cast considerable doubt on the supposed egalitarianism of the AIF, biases that have been ignored through a general reliance on broad figures to define the character of the AIF. Bean asserted that the selection of Australian officers stood in marked contrast to the British preferment to social position and education and wrote: 'Anyone watching an Australian battalion on parade felt that in this year's corporals he saw the next year's sergeants and the following year's subalterns'.[30] Such a smooth and natural progression through the ranks was not always the case in the 1st Battalion. Closer to the truth was General John Monash's declaration in relation to the officers of his Third Division: 'The officers (the great majority of whom I have promoted from the ranks) represent the cream of our professional and educated classes, young engineers, architects, medicals, accountants, pastoralists, public-school boys, and so on.'[31] Some salient differences are indeed evident within the 1st Battalion between the occupations of the Battalion's commissioned officers and other ranks.

Table 1 clearly demonstrates a bias in selection according to occupational background of the Battalion's officers. Figures for the original battalion are based on examination of 982 of the 1030 men listed on the 1st Battalion embarkation roll. Records for thirty-two of the Battalion's original officers and fifty-eight reinforcement officers were identified from the embarkation rolls. However, as the reinforcement embarkation rolls are incomplete that figure represents the majority, not all, of the commissioned officers attached to the reinforcement groups. The majority of unstated cases were students. Where the type of 'student' was stated an appropriate category was chosen. For example a 'law student' would be categorised as a 'professional' and a 'farm student' as rural. Seventeen (53.12 per cent) of the officers were drawn from professional or clerical occupations, a figure completely out of proportion to the overall representation of the Battalion, in which those two categories combined accounted for only 16.27 per cent of all occupations. The three most labour-intensive categories of 'tradesmen', 'labourers' and 'industrial/manufacturing' accounted for over half (52.23 per cent) of occupations in the

Battalion. These figures are reinforced by a comparison of the Battalion's sergeants and, at the next level of command, lieutenants (Table 2). More than half (57.14 per cent) of the lieutenants came from professional and clerical occupations while 48.32 per cent of sergeants came from labour-intensive occupations.

Table 1: Comparison of the occupations of 1st Battalion officers against occupations of the original 1st Battalion

Occupation	Original Battalion (including officers) (%)	Officers of the Original Battalion (%)	Officers of the 1st to 26th Reinforcements (%)
Professional	5.39	21.87	25.86
Clerical	10.38	31.25	29.31
Tradesman	17.00	12.5	12.06
Labourer	22.40	0	0
Industrial and manufacturing	12.83	3.12	1.72
Transport	8.75	0	3.44
Commercial	5.60	9.37	12.06
Rural	7.73	0	5.17
Seafaring	3.66	0	1.72
Mining	2.64	0	0
Domestic	2.54	0	0
Other/Unstated	1.00	21.87	8.61
Total	99.92	99.98	99.95

Table 2: Comparison of the occupations of 1st Battalion lieutenants and sergeants[32]

Occupation	Lieutenants (%)	Sergeants (%)
Professional	22.22	11.66
Clerical	34.92	5
Tradesman	4.76	15
Labourer	3.17	16.66
Industrial and manufacturing	1.58	16.66
Transport	4.76	13.33
Commercial	6.34	8.33
Rural	12.69	11.66
Seafaring	0	0
Mining	0	0
Domestic	4.76	1.66
Other/Unstated	4.76	0
Total	99.96	99.96

Of further interest to the background of both sergeants and lieutenants is the fact that nearly double the Battalion percentage, 11.66 per cent and 12.69 per cent respectively, came from rural occupations. This may indicate that a bush ethos (in this instance that the bush cultivated better soldiers) was believed and applied in the selection of junior officers and NCOs. Men of rural or bush backgrounds may have been regarded as ideal types to lead small groups in combat. These figures suggest that the independence of thought associated with rural occupations was viewed as a valuable attribute for the selection of section leaders. Overall, however, the occupational background of the 1st Battalion's sergeants was overwhelmingly blue-collar. Although the occupational background of sergeants did not debar them from promotion, it does seem to have inhibited the likelihood of further advancement. Despite this bias there existed some sound reasons for selecting officers from professional and clerical backgrounds. Literacy and clerical skills were essential to the conduct of an officer's duties, with the ability to understand manuals, write orders and compose reports being important requirements.

Table 3: Religion as a percentage of various sub-groups of the original 1st Battalion, as represented on 1st Battalion embarkation roll

Religious denomination	Whole Battalion (1030 men) (%)	Officers (32 men) (%)	NCOs (156 men) (%)	AMF Volunteers (177 men) (%)
Church of England	61.26	78.12	62.82	58.19
Roman Catholic	17.80	3.12	14.10	20.90
Protestant/Presbyterian	12.71	15.62	14.10	11.86
Methodist	4.27	3.12	1.92	5.64
Other/Unstated	3.88	0	7.05	3.38
Total	99.92	99.98	99.99	99.97

While previous military experience and occupation contributed to the selection of officers within the 1st Battalion, Table 3 shows a further bias in the religious background of officers, most notably in the lack of Catholic officers. A compelling fact that gives some poignancy to the speculation of bias is that of the Battalion's original thirty-two officers only one was Catholic. That figure is a disproportionate one when one considers that 17.86 per cent of the Battalion was Catholic and of those men 20.10 per cent, a figure higher than the Battalion average, had been serving in the AMF. One would have expected a higher ratio of Catholics within the commissioned ranks, especially given that previous military service was a preferred prerequisite for officers of the expeditionary force; twenty-seven of the thirty-two officers who embarked in 1914 had served in the militia. One would expect, in an egalitarian force, that the distribution of commissions would be proportionate to the main religious denominations, particularly given that figures for the occupations held by the Battalion's Catholics are comparable with those of the Battalion overall: 11.95 per cent held professional and clerical positions while 48.91 per cent came from labour-intensive categories. Yet Catholic professional and clerical workers were not reflected proportionately in the composition of the Battalion's officers.

Of 184 Catholics in the Battalion only one was a commissioned officer and twenty-three non-commissioned, representing 0.5 and 12.5 per cent of that group respectively. Presbyterians and Protestants form a comparative group, numbering 131, of whom five were commissioned officers and twenty-three non-commissioned, representing 3.8 and 17.5 per cent respectively. The relative percentages for Anglican officers were 3.9 and 15.8. The trends of these figures seem to confirm Lloyd Robson's query as to the veracity of claims about the egalitarian nature of the AIF and of the democratic character of Australian society.[33] These figures, when viewed in conjunction with Robson's findings, appear to support the notion that a deliberate bias existed in preventing Catholics entering into the commissioned ranks. The one Catholic who was appointed was Lieutenant Geoffrey Street, a student of the University of Sydney and clearly a young man of some ability.[34] He was to hold the position of Australia's Minister for Defence during the Second World War until his tragic death in an aeroplane crash on 1 August 1940. Exceptional ability, it seems, was recognised and counted for something. Yet even Street's appointment appears to have been tailored for the company to which he was assigned. F Company, to which he belonged, had the highest Catholic representation among its AMF men. Of its eighteen AMF men, eight were Catholics, eight Anglicans, one was a Presbyterian and another a Baptist. In all other companies Anglican representation was clearly in the majority, with the exception of H Company which could claim only eight militiamen.

The system of preferment and bias that was evident in the selection of officers at the outset of the war was perpetuated throughout the war. A bias in terms of occupation and religion against Catholics was still evident in the selection of the commissioned officers of the Battalion's reinforcements, 55.17 per cent of whom came from professional and clerical backgrounds while only 8.62 were Catholic, a marked improvement on the original Battalion but still well below the percentage of Catholics enrolled in the Battalion (see Table 4).

Table 4: Religion as a percentage of 1st Battalion Reinforcement officers

Religious denomination	Officers of the 1st to 26th Reinforcements (58 men)
Church of England	51.72
Catholic	8.62
Protestant/Presbyterian	24.13
Methodist	8.62
Other/Unstated	6.88
Total	99.97

The lower percentage of Catholics selected as officers may have reflected a suspicion about Catholic loyalty toward Britain and the Empire. However, Catholic response to enlistment as evidenced by the records of the 1st Battalion was consistent throughout the war; Table 5 shows that neither charges of disloyalty leveled at Catholics during the conscription referendas, nor resentment over the British treatment of Irish rebels following the Easter Uprising in Dublin, had any effect on the number of Catholic enlistments. In relation to the uprising, the volunteers most likely to have reflected any signs of Catholic disaffection would have been those found in the 19th and 20th reinforcement groups. These two groups were recruited during the period of the rebellion and execution of the rebel leaders. They, and those who followed, contributed a higher percentage of Catholic volunteers than the original Battalion. In fact, generally, the percentage of Catholic volunteers in the reinforcement groups was higher than in the original Battalion.

Table 5: Level of Catholic representation within 1st to 26th Reinforcements for 1st Battalion

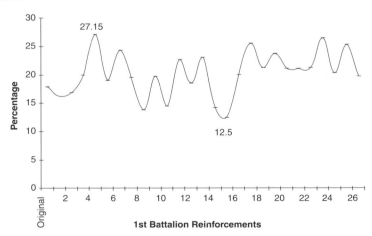

One other consideration in the selection of officers, and one that has been ignored in Australia's Great War literature, was a man's physical stature. A comparison of the height of officers and sergeants reveals that they differed considerably from the other ranks. Officers were generally taller, and it is within that group that notions of the tall bronzed Anzac are more likely to be evident than among the ordinary soldiers. This is demonstrated in Table 6.

Table 6: Comparison of the height of 1st Battalion officers, sergeants and other ranks

Height	Officers (%)	Sergeants (%)	1st Battalion (%)
6'0 and over	11.59	10.16	1.78
5'9" and over	49.27	33.89	24.10
5'6" and over	33.33	33.89	46.87
5'3" and over	5.79	20.33	20.08
5'0" and over	–	1.69	4.91
Total	99.98	99.96	97.74

Of the officers, 60.86 per cent were over 5'9" as opposed to 44.05 per cent of sergeants and 25.88 per cent of the Battalion overall. In fact, 72.22 per cent of the Battalion were under 5'9", a figure that suggests the legendary tall Anzac type represented, in reality, a significant minority. These figures are based on the examination of the heights provided on the attestation papers of 224 1st Battalion soldiers represented by the following groups: mutineers, non-mutineers and non-commissioned diary and letter writers (including sergeants) used in this study. In addition, the heights of forty-four 1st Battalion soldiers who formed part of 'the Waratahs' are also incorporated.[35] The heights of 69 commissioned officers of the 1st Battalion and 59 sergeants were examined separately.

The height difference may, in fact, have had a basis in class bias. One would expect that men from the middle and upper classes would have been the beneficiaries of physical growth resulting from better diet and living conditions. A comparison of these figures with those of British recruits for the period up to 1916 reveals that height differences between Australian and British soldiers were not as dramatic as has generally been imagined. Differences were no doubt exaggerated by comparison of Australian troops with British 'bantam' battalions and some territorials, particularly those from heavily industrialised towns and cities who were notably smaller. However, the mean heights for British recruits aged 18 years, 21 to 23, and 24 to 29 years old, at least up until 1916, were approximately $5'7\frac{1}{4}"$, 5'8" and 5'6" respectively.[36] Nearly three-quarters of the 1st Battalion fell within (46.87 per cent) and below (24.99 per cent) the mean figures for British recruits.

It is an inescapable fact that there existed a definite predilection toward an 'officer-type' in the selection of the 1st Battalion's officers. A man's physical size appears to have had some influence, even if unconscious, in the selection of officers. This physiognomic aspect, coupled with the consideration of occupation and religion in the appointment of officers within the 1st Battalion (and the first contingent of the AIF) reveals the emergence of a distinct 'officer-type'. Officers of the 1st Battalion were likely to be tall, Anglo-Celtic, educated at a private school or university, and/or from the professional classes residing in one of the more affluent suburbs of Sydney. In effect the Australian 'officer-type' embodied the very characteristics of the stereotypical British officer. This similarity is little considered in descriptions of the AIF officer corps, which, in the main, are based on the premise that most AIF officers rose through the ranks and were therefore more egalitarian. A recent example of this generalisation is provided in a comparison of the psychology of British and Anzac officers:

> The fact that many Anzac officers were promoted from the ranks may have meant they were less likely to experience the psychological pressure of honour and duty, which was ingrained in the British officer class during their years in public schools and military academies. Anzac officers were volunteers, often from humble backgrounds, who by force of their personality and leadership were promoted to the higher rank, while British officers, at least in the early years of the war, were a distinct caste, inculcated with military ideals from an early age.[37]

Other biases

Biases were not confined to the commissioned ranks: they existed in the next level down in the chain of command. It was here that the most influence needed to be wielded to transform the volunteers into soldiers. Military authorities recognised that if the new battalions were to be moulded into a competent force, the key lay in the quality of training and leadership that could be instilled in the units at their formative stage. To meet this requirement great care was taken in the selection of the senior non-commissioned officers. General Bridges, commander of the expeditionary force, insisted that all regimental sergeant-majors, quartermaster-sergeants and those belonging to machine-gun and signal sections were to be drawn from the warrant-officers and non-commissioned officers of Australia's permanent forces. Bean believed that in newly raised British battalions a good regimental sergeant-major (RSM) was more important than the colonel to the discipline of a battalion during its infancy, a fact he attributed to the 'considerable awe' with which the RSM was viewed by the privates. Yet Bean, in attempting to highlight Australian adaptability, downplayed this influence, suggesting it was less a factor in the formation of the Australian battalions.[38] The RSMs were, in fact, as crucial to the Australian regimental infrastructure as they were to the British.[39]

RSMs shaped a soldier's formative experience. Peter Bourne, in his study of American soldiers during the Vietnam War, has described the process of basic training as 'a masculine initiation rite that often has particular appeal to the late adolescent struggling to establish a masculine identity for himself in society'.[40] Obscene or colourful language was a part of this rite but, as Richard Holmes notes, it was often tempered by a paternalistic form in gentler moments, with the terms 'lads' and 'boys' employed to encourage a sense of belonging to a group.[41] RSMs through their closer contact with the other ranks were more likely to cultivate this relationship than higher-ranking officers who by nature of their positions were more detached from the men.

The age and marital status of the senior sergeants selected in the 1st Battalion reflect the paternal role that was expected of them. Of the sixteen senior and specialty sergeants, twelve were between 31 and 40 years of age, ten were married, and nine were serving in the AMF on enlistment.[42] As well, throughout the course of the war, 30 per cent of the 1st Battalion's sergeants were British-born (compared to 22.62 per cent of the original Battalion) a fact that suggests, if those NCOs were culturally attuned to the mores of the British Army, that the Battalion may have been styled more closely along the lines of British martial control than is generally imagined. The image of American drill sergeants and British sergeant-majors abusing, cajoling and belittling recruits is a familiar one to the post-Second World War television generation. In the 1960s audiences watched with amusement the over-the-top performance of the exasperated Sergeant Carter as he attempted to mould the gormless Gomer Pyle into a United States marine. The 1st Battalion recruits, while presumably not as inept as Gomer Pyle, could nevertheless exasperate their instructors, as Archie Barwick recalled:

> What a crowd we were, I suppose there were 9 out of 10 who had never formed fours in their life before and I was one of them, it was flimsy to see us trying to get through the most simplest movements and getting completely boxed up, it was about 3 weeks before I mastered the form fours properly, I could never remember whether it was the odd or the even numbers who had to move. We were enough to break any drill instructor's heart and when some of them were spoken to they used to get quite shirty about it, however they knocked us into some sort of shape by the time we left Randwick to go to Kensington.[43]

Although education and previous military service were definite factors that figured in the selection of officers and NCOs, such criteria were largely irrelevant to the selection of the other ranks, where physical health and stature were of prime importance. Nevertheless a particular character was envisaged for the fledgling national force. General Bridges had instructed the commandants of the military districts to establish the battalions on a territorial basis, and as a consequence the battalions of the 1st Brigade were allotted specific areas within the 2nd Military District. In theory the 1st Battalion was to represent the western suburbs of Sydney, but in reality it proved a heterogeneous representation of the city.[44] The regimental areas allocated to the Battalion were 29 through to 36 and concentrated on Sydney's 'inner west', an area bound by Balmain to the north, Haberfield and Glebe to the west and east, and Marrickville to the south.[45] The Battalion history records the affiliation of its companies with those of the militia occurring in the second week of September—nearly a month after the core of the Battalion had been formed. Examination of the embarkation rolls for the Battalion reveals the limitations that the low number of AMF trainees imposed upon the attempt to comply within the eight companies that formed the Battalion. A concentration of 29th Infantry militia existed in A company, commanded by Major Dawson, a renowned crack shot and former commander of the old Australian Rifles; C Company was home to a number of the 31st Infantry, D Company to the 33rd, and E Company the 34th. No discernible trend can be detected in the remaining companies. B and H companies could lay claim to only seven and eight AMF men within their ranks. The overwhelming statistic of the AMF volunteers was their youth: 77 per cent were 25 years or under, and 64 per cent between 18 and 20 years of age.[46] Generally, it appears that the selection of men for the various companies resembled that of schoolyard football sides. Barwick, who was to become a member of H Company, recollected the men being formed in two ranks on arrival at the racecourse from which the officers 'picked so many men out' for their companies.[47] It seems to have been the system that prevailed throughout the war. Ben Champion, a reinforcement at Gallipoli, wrote that the men were split into companies on the beach and he was 'claimed' by the Company Sergeant-Major of A Company.[48] The seemingly *ad hoc* manner in which the men were selected for the original companies hardly seemed conducive to the establishment of a special *esprit de corps* based upon the territorial model of the militia. Yet this is exactly what was hoped for.

The distribution of country and city men throughout the original battalion appears to have been fairly even. However, this was not always the case with the volunteers after 1914. One area that did provide a sizeable portion *en bloc* to the Battalion was the Southern Districts of New South Wales, and a number of men from that region filled the ranks of the 17th Reinforcements. The recruiting officer for the district had urged that the area raise a thousand men. Such a feat could be assisted, he argued, through the creation of four territorially designated companies to appeal to the various areas within the district. It was his opinion that the district was graced with the 'finest type of manhood in the Commonwealth', and consequently was beholden to supply the men.[49] Another area that provided a similar number of men was the South Coast. This area had been thrust into prominence by 'the Waratahs' recruitment march that commenced on 30 November 1915 and concluded two and a half weeks later in Sydney on 17 December. The Waratahs had been promised they would be kept together where feasible. They were subsequently distributed between the 15th and 16th Reinforcements of the 1st Battalion.[50] The value of maintaining an *esprit de corps* based on locality was obvious. Unfortunately this benefit was diluted once the reinforcements reached the front where they were split up among the existing companies.

Using the federal electoral boundaries as a geographical guide, it is possible to determine the extent to which particular areas of Sydney contributed to the composition of the original Battalion. Six electoral divisions could be said to represent the inner to outer western suburbs (including Liverpool) of Sydney: West Sydney, Dalley, Lang, Cook, Parkes and Nepean. Of the 1030 names listed on the Battalion's embarkation roll only 324 can be identified as originating from the western suburbs. Ninety-one came from the north side of the harbour; the eastern divisions of East Sydney and Wentworth accounted for 120; South Sydney and Illawarra, which included Kogarah, provided 69 men. Those giving their addresses as Sydney numbered 81, and there were 74 men whose address was unstated. As a combined total the metropolitan area represented two-thirds of the Battalion, slightly more if the unstated cases are distributed evenly. The other one-third came from throughout the state, with a small percentage from interstate and overseas. Clearly the Battalion fell well short of attaining its allotted territorial identity, but with nearly one-third of its personnel emanating from the west the original battalion, at least, could claim to have had a territorial flavour to it.

Some salient differences emerge about the type of recruit drawn from some of the suburbs within those boundaries. Marrickville, Newtown and Annandale provided the youngest recruits and were well represented by AMF trainees, which suggests that the youth from some of the most entrenched working-class suburbs were keen supporters of the war effort either by natural inclination or through the inculcation of military ideals through compulsory training. Drummoyne and Kogarah provided only single men and Redfern could boast only one married man among its twenty-three volunteers, while

Chippendale contributed no men to the original Battalion. Volunteers from Mosman were predominantly from white-collar occupations, ten of thirteen being from professional, clerical and commercial backgrounds. They also supplied 10 per cent of the Battalion's commissioned officers. If a tangible identity existed at this early stage it lay not in the preferred territorial model but in more general terms. The majority of the Battalion resided in Sydney and its suburbs, and most worked in blue-collar occupations. Seventy-two per cent were Australian-born and 22.62 per cent hailed from the British Isles (which included the whole of Ireland at this time), with 3.78 per cent originating from other countries. The origins of 1.55 per cent were unstated. The significant minority of British-born within the ranks, most of whom were English (17.47), poses a problem to any stereotyping of Australian soldiers in regard to a national type. The British-born were not Australian, although many may well have considered themselves to be so, and one wonders how they subsequently reacted to the strong anti-British thread that runs through the Anzac legend. The British-born reaction is ambiguous. The comments of some of the men and observers suggests that in the early stages of the AIF's existence ex-Imperial soldiers enlisted in the AIF as a convenient stepping stone to return to Britain. On the other hand, some British-born embraced the AIF and Australia as their own.

In his confidential report, MacLaurin stated that after the first three weeks of recruiting, 60 per cent of the 1st Brigade were British-born, but by the time the first contingent sailed 73 per cent were Australian-born.[51] This statistic is not supported by the enlistment dates given on the 1st Battalion's embarkation rolls. Examination of records with an enlistment date up to and including 21 August 1914 show that 78.5 per cent were Australian-born and 18.6 per cent British-born. Many of the British-born were residing in the hostels and hotels in the heart of the city and were members of ships' companies. These figures may reflect a greater degree of unemployment among the Australian-born of the 1st Battalion, who saw the war as a convenient solution to their predicament or, conversely, may suggest that they were inspired by a strong sense of patriotism. However, a distinct trend of the second contingent figures was that a higher proportion of the British-born volunteers were found in the first five reinforcement groups, 34.26, 31.80, 34.42, 16.54 and 24.99 per cent (see Table 7). The high proportion of British-born in the first drafts of the second contingent suggests the likelihood that many of those men had been unable to meet the selection criteria of the first contingent or were not preferred over Australian-born volunteers. Thereafter those figures fell away to around 10 per cent and under.

Table 7: Rise of Australian-born volunteers and decline of British-born volunteers within 1st to 26th Reinforcements of the 1st Battalion

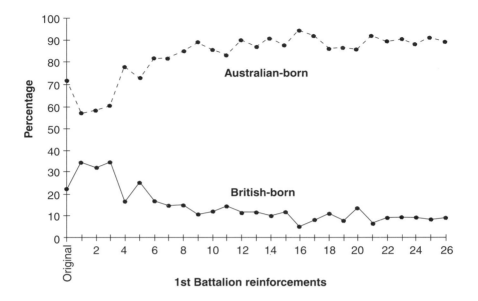

Figures for British-born soldiers varied within particular battalions: for instance, 34 per cent of the ranks of Western Australia's 11th Battalion were British-born, as were 32 per cent of the 28th Battalion.[52] Other battalions within the 1st Brigade may have contained a higher proportion of British-born than the 1st Battalion. Scotsmen who wished to join the expeditionary force were asked to report to the 4th Battalion headquarters.[53] Whether they did or not and whether there existed any correlation between a higher ratio of Scotsmen and that unit's sobriquet, the drunken fourth,[54] falls beyond the purview of this study. The high number of British in the ranks did draw comment at the time. One correspondent who commented was Banjo Paterson. His description reflected the incongruity that the British presence suggested in the newly formed national army:

> A topsy-turvy force this, for the Brigadier, General MacLaurin, has never seen any active service, while the ranks are full of English ex-service men, wearing as many ribbons as prize bulls. These . . . by the way, volunteered to a man when the war broke out, and the Australian ranks were full of Yorkshiremen, Cockneys, and Cousin Jacks . . . Any one of them would sooner be shot as a private in the Coldstream Guards than get a decoration in a nameless Australian force.[55]

J. G. Fuller has suggested that British-born volunteers, whose numbers were proportionately higher in the original contingents of Dominion troops, would have played a large part in the initial establishment of the character of units within the national armies of the various Dominions. However, regarding the Australians, Fuller concluded that the lower proportion of British-born within the AIF probably reduced the likelihood of their influence (particularly in regard to restraining ill-disciplined behaviour) having much effect, although as we have seen they did form a higher proportion of the 1st Battalion's sergeants.[56] In fact, a perception existed within the ranks that it was the old British soldiers who were among the worst offenders when it came to discipline. In that respect, if true, their influence was a negative rather than a positive one.

The composition of the 1st Battalion reveals that the perceived egalitarianism of the AIF was not evident in the command structure of the Battalion. Although examination of the various sub-groups indicates that the 1st Battalion was a relatively heterogeneous outfit, it was so in only the most general sense. Throughout the historiography of the AIF, this heterogeneity has generally been advanced as a proof that the AIF was egalitarian, it being assumed that volunteers, irrespective of their occupational or social backgrounds, had the same opportunities for promotion. On the contrary, the composition of the 1st Battalion was influenced by the backgrounds of its men and by social cliques. The occupational and social backgrounds of the officers were, overall, distinct from those of the other ranks. Volunteers who shared similar backgrounds to the Battalion's existing officers were favoured for advancement. It is impossible to measure whether those men were, in fact, better suited for command than those who were passed over. The reading and writing skills associated with higher education and white-collar occupations were certainly an advantage in the administrative aspects of command but held little relevance in combat. This plain fact was recognised by the military authorities. In an attempt to prevent the selection of men ill-equipped for the business of war, each military district subsequently appointed a board, comprising the district commandant and three senior militia officers, to deal with future selections.[57] Despite this, biases continued to be evident within the composition of 1st Battalion officers throughout the war. Occupation and education continued to influence selection. For many NCOs, the highest rank they could realistically hope to achieve was that of sergeant. As well, there was a bias against the selection of Catholics for command. The higher ratio of Methodist officers, compared to their overall representation within the Battalion, stands in stark contrast to the lower ratio of Catholic officers. Of course, differing religious attitudes toward community and duty may have been a factor in the discrepancy between these two groups. Catholic soldiers may have been more attuned to social values that expressed greater community accord and equality. They may not have been forceful in seeking advancement. Methodist soldiers, on the other hand, may have been more wedded to notions of duty and sacrifice and might have been more active in seeking leadership roles. The statistics provided in this chapter reveal that social divisions, based on demographic categories, did exist. Although they clearly differentiate the officers from other ranks, they do not reveal the extent to which these differences were translated into attitudes and behaviour that further defined the relationships of officers and men. That aspect forms the basis of the next chapter.

2

'CLASS IS EVERYTHING':
THE OFFICER—MAN RELATIONSHIP

There exists a popular apocryphal anecdote about an Australian colonel that epitomises the nature of Australian egalitarianism inherent in the Anzac legend. In the story the colonel appeals to his men as the brigadier approaches for an inspection: 'Here he comes! Now boys, no coughing, no spitting, and for Christ's sake don't call me Alf!' This egalitarianism represents one of the central themes of the Anzac legend. It implies a cohesive relationship and even-handed treatment of both officers and men within the AIF.

Australians certainly viewed themselves as being part of a democratic army. It was a view shared by many soldiers within the British army who looked upon the seemingly carefree ways of their antipodean comrades as marking an invidious contrast, in what seemed to them a feeling of mutuality between Australian officers and men, to the oppression that they themselves felt in their own officer—man relationships.[1] The 'Alf' anecdote was clearly enjoyed by Australians and has been repeated to successive generations through a variety of publications. Its apocryphal nature has been lost and it sometimes thrives as an undisputed factual account, as it did in a major city daily's souvenir edition celebrating the seventy-fifth anniversary of the Anzac landing.[2]

As much as Australian soldiers came to believe in the egalitarianism of the AIF, they believed, also, that they were victims of their officers' officiousness. Moreover, as a number of overseas studies have shown, egalitarianism was not the sole preserve of Australian troops within the British armies. For instance, the 22nd Battalion Royal Fusiliers, under the inspired and enlightened tutelage of its commanding officer, Barnett-Barker, encouraged close relationships between officers and men.[3] Furthermore, the practice of this unwritten contract was evident in the conduct of a number of British divisions, particularly those of the new armies. The egalitarianism practised within some of those divisions appears to have been a purer form than that practised by the Australians, exemplified by 'pals' battalions needing to select, not only their own NCOs but also, owing to the lack of regular officers assigned to them initially, their own commissioned officers as well. 'Pals' was a term used to describe the battalions in Kitchener's new armies that had enlisted from the same towns or workplaces. Those assigned to commissioned ranks in such battalions were generally given only a probationary status until the War Office could find replacements who were considered to possess the necessary gentlemanly qualities of an English officer. While this hardly benefited the new battalions in the long term, its short-term effect was positive.[4] This was certainly not true of the 1st Battalion, where the commissioning of aspiring officers often followed preferential selection by senior officers. In a letter home to a colleague, Sergeant Larkin revealed that the principles of 'equal opportunity and recognition of merit' that underpinned his and the labour movement's ethics were not much in evidence within the army:

> We have been silly enough to think that the Australian Army had been democratised. There was never a greater delusion. *Class* is everything for advancement. There have been three glaring cases—or rather four—and you can bet that someone will get a rough time over them one of these days.[5]

Even though Larkin's perspective was coloured by his political leanings, his concerns were not without foundation. The nature of the inequities in the system of advancement will be discussed later in this chapter, revealing that the 1st Battalion experience does not particularly support a defining egalitarianism within the AIF.

The response of Australian soldiers to military authority is generally viewed in the context of the high rate of indiscipline within the AIF. This indiscipline is interpreted as an expression of the Australian soldier's individualism, a sign that he was unwilling to buckle under the regimen of the army. It celebrates his anti-authoritarian attitude. The importance of this indiscipline to the officer–man relationship has been largely neglected. The extent of indiscipline in the 1st Battalion's formative stages was significant to the formation of that relationship because it created a culture of dissidence that officers had to confront throughout the war. Difficulties would arise as officers attempted to impose their own and the army's will upon men accustomed to the protections of civil liberties. How military ceremony and discipline were enacted depended upon the personalities of those in authority, and this could at times, as T. J. Richards noted, translate into a 'low-down humiliation and curtailment of the spirit so essential to the success of any—and all—forms of warfare'.[6] The men's belief in a civilian-type democracy was largely unchallenged in the first months of the Battalion's life as the overburdened military infrastructure had first to struggle with the formation, training and despatch of the first contingent, rather than the eradication of ideals synonymous with their civilian identity.

In his study of combat identity of First World War soldiers, Eric Leed suggested that the transition from citizen to soldier heralded the beginning of a new identity whereby the recruit engaged in a series of initiations that marked a distinctive rite of passage. Leed contended that a soldier's identity is both separate from his civilian identity and unique in that it is formed beyond the margins of normal society.[7] The first stage of this process—and the first act of separation—was the soldier's entry into camp. Ideally this process would bring to an army what the Prussian soldier General Carl von Clausewitz, in his famous treatise *On War*, termed 'military virtue'. Clausewitz described war as a 'special business . . . different and separate from the pursuits which occupy the life of man'. To successfully enter this business a man needed to be 'imbued with a sense of the spirit and nature' of the business and assimilated to the powers active in it until he was 'completely given up to it'. When the recruit had reached that state and was able to 'pass out of the man' into the part assigned to him in war, then he had acquired what Clausewitz called 'the military virtue of an Army in the individual'. Importantly, Clausewitz acknowledged that it was impossible to 'do away with the individuality of the business', and as a consequence those participating saw themselves as members of something resembling a 'guild'. At this point was established what Clausewitz termed a 'corporate spirit' or *esprit de corps* so critical to the performance of an army.[8] Aspiration to such a military condition was one thing, attainment was another. The formative experience of the 1st Battalion exemplifies how circumstances and a strong civilian identity could thwart such military idealism.

The problems, derived from both civilian and military causes, that affected the discipline and early organisation of the expeditionary force were addressed by Colonel H. N. MacLaurin, commanding officer of the 1st Brigade, in a confidential report on the raising and equipping of the Brigade. Many of MacLaurin's complaints emanated from poor administrative procedures and ranged from difficulties in the acquisition and distribution of uniforms, to shortages in tents and camp equipage, to delays in pay. There were also too few qualified staff to cope with the burden of clerical work and the battalion commanding officers found themselves embroiled in the paperchase. By far the greatest of MacLaurin's concerns was the closeness of the Brigade encampments to the city with its obvious distractions. He maintained that this had contributed to many absences from the camp, undermined discipline, and contributed to the contraction of venereal disease by some of the men. The majority of NCOs responsible for the enforcement of discipline among the sections and platoons were inexperienced and appointed on a provisional or temporary basis. This posed problems not only for the discharge of discipline but for the conduct of basic military drills. In addition, some 700 men who had enrolled in the Brigade (and been issued uniforms) remained unaccounted for by the Brigade's embarkation date. Presumably they had decided that a military life was not for them. Between 15 August and 17 October (the day before embarkation), 1258 men had been attested in the 1st Battalion yet 245 of that number did not embark, representing a wastage of nearly 20 per cent.[9]

'Mutiny, rank mutiny'

Some of the same problems that confronted the original force would resurface in the training of later reinforcements. The most infamous of these was the soldier unrest that occurred at Liverpool camp, on Sydney's western outskirts, among the reinforcement groups. These men represented the AIF's New South Welsh battalions. The riot or strike of 15 February 1916 that occurred at Liverpool shows how a territorially based *esprit de corps,* as envisaged by General Bridges but not universally applied throughout the AIF battalions (including the 1st), could resist the pressures of group indiscipline. It also serves as an example of how civil industrial unrest was interpreted as having penetrated military life. The decision to shift the volunteer encampments to Liverpool was made as a result of problems that had afflicted the training of the early volunteers. The camp lay twenty miles west of the city. The distance provided a useful, though not an insurmountable, barrier that deterred recruits from attempting to savour the fruits of the city. Entertainment in the camps was restricted and centred upon the many bands that played there. Occasionally fights among the recruits punctuated what was usually a mundane existence.[10] The boredom in the camp was exacerbated by the constant delays in providing firm embarkation dates. This often brought embarrassment to soldiers who had farewelled friends and relatives only to have to later inform them that the date of embarkation had been deferred.[11] The chief reason for such delays lay in the difficulties that the government had in acquiring transports. Apart from the boredom, many of the men harboured complaints about the conditions and their treatment at the camp.

Complaints about the Liverpool Camp predated the war and trouble was not unknown to it. Conditions were spartan, consisting of the most rudimentary barracks and material. On 29 November 1913 a riot of sorts had broken out among Compulsory Service trainees, which resulted in the matter being investigated by a court of inquiry. Of particular interest in that event was that the trouble was caused mainly by the behaviour of the 14th Battalion, a unit drawn largely from the mining towns of Newcastle and districts, from men not unaccustomed to militancy in the acquiring of working rights. Poorly trained men and poor officers who lacked common sense combined to cause a breakdown in discipline and inflame the trainees' feeling of injustice when they were confined to camp while the officers, in full mess dress, readied themselves for dinner. The incident concluded with an abusive and rock-throwing mob of several hundred soldiers dispersing before a resolute guard of twenty-five men standing firm at the bridge over which the men had to pass if they were to leave camp.[12] The incident served as a warning as to what might happen on a larger scale if military authorities did not adjust their attitude to the treatment and conditions of civilians undergoing military training.

The use of the camp to train volunteers also brought complaint to the floor of the New South Wales parliament. Mr Orchard, the Member for Nepean, raised criticisms of the camp, chief among them being a lack of uniforms and decent bedding, a shortage of overcoats, a lack of rifles for training, and an inadequate system for the dispensing of medicines and treatment of the sick. Of particular disgust to the troops was the fact that German internees at the internment camp, also in Liverpool, suffered none of these shortages.[13] Orchard's criticism appears to have had a positive effect and in the inquiry that followed a number of soldiers stated that overcoats were only issued following the politician's comments. Despite parliamentary intervention, trouble persisted at the camps. A disturbance was reported on the night of 26 November 1915 when soldiers without leave passes attempted to pass sentries on the bridge leading out of the camp. Several thousand men were drawn to the scene. Stones were thrown and three or four police tents were set alight. The incident was not considered, by the camp's commandant, to have assumed serious proportions.[14] That the situation at Liverpool finally dissolved into a general strike (or mutiny) was hardly surprising. The action that inflamed the men's grievances was a decision to extend training hours by an hour and a half.

The decision to lengthen training hours had followed a recommendation by Major-General McCay, who had recently toured the camp; it had provoked much ill-feeling among the men. Trouble first began at the light horse camp at Casula, and when those men, numbering approximately 500, marched across to the infantry camp at Liverpool the number of strikers swelled to about 10,000. This mass of men marched out of camp, and two representatives from each battalion were sent as part of a large delegation to the camp commandant, Colonel Miller. Miller told the men that the matter should have been brought to him without striking; he asked that they return to work under the old hours and he would approach the state commandant to see what could be done. This was considered unsatisfactory by the men, who by this time were emotionally intoxicated by participation in such a large demonstration, and they marched to the railway station at Liverpool. The cellar of the Commercial Hotel was raided and barrels of beer were rolled into the street and their contents consumed by some of the excited mob. A small force of local police were on hand but powerless to halt what was described as a 'campaign of plunder and destruction'.[15] After indulging in such excesses throughout the township, the soldiers boarded trains to the city to air their dissatisfaction.

The city next fell victim to the soldiers. In what was described as 'unprecedented scenes' shops were robbed, windows smashed and motor vehicles commandeered by mobs of soldiers. Particular attention was paid to shops owned by Italians and Germans. The mayhem petered out about midnight, but only after a shot from the military picket at Central Railway station put a sobering and bloody stop to the madness. One lighthorseman was killed, reported as being shot through the cheek and bayoneted in his left side, shoulder and neck. Five other soldiers and a policeman were injured in the fray.[16]

Although reports of the episode concentrated on the destructive aspect, there was also an element of order to the soldiers' behaviour. The march was clearly intended as a protest demonstration and, as each train arrived from Liverpool, the men were formed into columns of four and marched from the station by appointed leaders (or possibly the senior NCOs in the group). The column was headed by standard-bearers carrying the green and purple colours of the 2nd Battalion and a Union Jack. The core of the marchers moved in an orderly fashion; when trouble flared the leaders or sensible heads within the ranks addressed the men, appealing to their sense of fair play. This formation was loosely held during the whole of the march through the city. The unruly behaviour was caused by men on the periphery of the march and by various breakaway groups that dropped off as the march progressed.[17]

Conditions at Liverpool and Casula had certainly warranted some form of protest, but the nature of the protest that occurred was certainly regrettable and brought little sympathy to the volunteers. A number of letters by returned servicemen to the *Sydney Morning Herald* expressed disgust at the troops' behaviour and advanced the argument that their actions let down the troops at the front. It was implied that the men at the front endured far worse conditions and would not have participated in such an action.[18] A subsequent report on the conditions of Liverpool Camp clearly vindicated the men's grievances, if not their actions, and provided a lengthy list of recommendations to improve conditions and administration.[19]

State and unit pride were also wounded by the affair. The editor of the *Sydney Morning Herald* believed the honour of the state had been 'cruelly besmirched' by an event he branded as nothing short of 'rank mutiny'.[20] The editor of the *Daily Telegraph* used the affair to convey his disgust at the Labor party and trade unions, whose influence he clearly saw manifested:

> This outbreak, dangerous and disquieting as it is, is simply another and an extreme instance of the organised contempt for the law . . . It is a natural result of the pusillanimity with which the Government has allowed every body of men with real or imaginary grievances to down tools and defy the law by going on strike . . . When a man in civilian employ can go on strike whenever he chooses, with a good chance of getting what he strikes for . . . it is hardly likely that soldiers will be deterred from kicking up their heels and joining in the wild scramble that ignores the puny barriers of law.[21]

Serving members of the 2nd Battalion, whose colours had headed the march, and the 6th Light Horse, to whom the dead soldier belonged, were chagrined by the episode. The disappointment of the Light Horse was conveyed in a letter to the *Sydney Morning Herald* by the unit's chaplain. Another who wrote was an unidentified corporal of the 15th Reinforcements of the 1st Battalion. This was one of the groups that comprised half of 'the Waratahs'—the South Coast recruitment march volunteers. He was keen to distance his Battalion from the stigma of participation in the disturbance:

> In justice to the 15th Reinforcements of the 1st Battalion shortly going to the front . . . this battalion voluntarily and manfully took their stand on the side of law and order, working day and night at picket work to quell yesterday's rioting, and in advising soldiers to respect the King's uniform. They gained the thanks of their commanding officer, the adjutant, and the officers who shortly leave for the front with them . . . no contumely should attach to this battalion, which to a man, remained true to their King and officers, and hope to carry their colours, green and black, to the succour of their comrades at the front, untarnished, and with credit to Australia.[22]

In speaking of the Battalion 'to a man' the writer, as his opening sentence suggests, was probably only referring to the 15th Reinforcements. That members of the other 1st Battalion reinforcement groups were involved in this affair is likely, although it appears none was among the identified ringleaders. Of thirty-two soldiers court-martialled as a result of the strike, only one, Cecil Madden, was a 1st Battalion man and he was found not guilty of any of the charges laid.[23] The number of men who were to reinforce the Battalion who might, potentially, have participated in the disturbance was large. The 15th through to the 18th reinforcement groups were all in the camp at the time, totaling over six hundred men. The equivalent of almost half a battalion of 1st Battalion reinforcements witnessed this demonstration, and an undetermined proportion of them participated in and carried to war the experience of striking for soldiers' rights.

Since it was reported widely in the newspapers, news of the strike and earlier disturbances was conveyed to the men overseas. They, like the returned soldiers in Sydney at the time, exhibited little understanding or sympathy for the strikers' motives. Their attitude reflected a shift in the process of separation from home and a sharpening of their soldier identity. Referring to earlier reports of misbehaviour among the troops in Australia, Sergeant J. Ridley, of the Battalion's 11th Reinforcements, expressed the indignation felt by many of the soldiers overseas:

> I hear from reports and newspapers that the troops at home are playing up badly. It makes me feel disgusted to think that the uniform, the army, the country, the King, and finally the British Empire, is being disgraced by our own men. The honours and laurels won by such men as Wellington, Gladstone, Drake, Nelson, Roberts, French, and the heroes of the Dardanelles. Are they nothing to these men? Do they realise what they have enlisted for? They cannot for by their actions I would call them traitors, not patriots, for when their nation is down and in the fight for her life they heap coals of fire on her head by horseplay and riots.[24]

The men overseas applied their own standards of interpretation to the events, standards acquired under quite different circumstances. Military service overseas was much more rigid in containing the movements of the troops. The soldiers in camp in Egypt and in the line in France probably regarded the troops in Australia as enjoying more freedom than they themselves were allowed. By the time the AIF had reached France the majority of the reinforcement groups in Liverpool at the time of the strike were *en route* overseas and beginning to be sent on to the front. Their arrival was being monitored. Captain D. V. Mulholland, of the 1st Brigade's machine-gun company, made plain his thoughts:

> Cold-footed people are far better at home than here. The reinforcements arriving possess quite a number of those birds. Those Liverpool rioters have arrived and they are reaping their just reward. In a month's time if they are still alive they'll be very different people . . .[25]

The indiscipline that confronted officers of the 1st Battalion and other units in Australia was transported, largely unchecked, to Egypt. The confined space of the transports rendered the application of strict discipline and rigid training difficult. Such methods risked becoming oppressive and the men were spared its burdens. Drill was understandably limited, with the men restricted to rudimentary exercise and lectures. They spent much of their time reading, sleeping and gambling at cards so that at times the voyage assumed the appearance of a 'holiday trip'.[26] Another avenue of relief and expression was presented through the publication of a single-page broadsheet called the *Kangaroo*. The publication was produced on a printing press that had been presented to some of the men and was set up in one of the cabins. The first issue was in circulation on the second day of the voyage, and it was produced daily until journey's end. The *Kangaroo* was subtitled 'The representative newspaper of the Australian Imperial Expeditionary Force (1st Battalion)', a title that attached an essence of democracy to the Battalion's soldier identity. The paper relied on gossip, personal comment and a combination of humour, patriotism and sentimentality for its content.[27] In this respect its style was similar to other troopship literature. It has been suggested that such publications provided a useful safety valve by allowing the airing of 'minor grievances and irritations which always occur in any closed community'.[28] Such grievances were much in evidence in the *Kangaroo*. A distinct view of the Australian citizen soldier emerged in these journals. The 'digger' stereotype that would pass into the Anzac legend was the same as that depicted in some of the earliest outbound troopship publications. In this respect, according to David Kent, these publications formed an important part in the transformation of the volunteers from citizen to soldier and in their acquisition of 'a sense of identity as Australian soldiers'.[29] If his assertion is correct, then it is apparent that the volunteers had extended the image of themselves depicted in the daily press to include a larrikin element and suggests that behaviour manifested in this guise was acceptable and something to be pursued. By consciously embracing a divergent attitude to that advanced through formal military discipline the men were defining themselves as civilians first and soldiers second. Comments in the *Kangaroo* support this view: 'As for being soldiers, etc, none of us claim to be Kitcheners in embryo, and few of us the real, dyed-in-the-wool soldier; but for the nonce we have forgotten our civilian professions, and are learning the art of warfare as speedily as we can'.[30]

The relatively relaxed conditions of the voyage circumscribed the exercise of authority by the officers toward the men. This absence of authority fed the independent image that the men had of themselves, which was being perpetuated through the troopship literature. When authority was invoked it was often viewed as an unwarranted imposition and proved irksome to the men. For instance, when Alexandria harbour was reached on 5 December the men's disappointment was acute when they found they were to remain on board until the 8th. Breaking camp in Sydney had been the norm, and for some the temptation of going ashore was too great. The impediment of being anchored in the harbour was but a small hurdle for determined spirits who, with the help of native boat-men, disembarked by way of ropes and port-holes after dark and stole ashore. Private Reg Donkin noted that fifty-six men (5 per cent of the battalion's strength) were locked up as a result, and that on one night six men too drunk to climb aboard were left stranded on a buoy.[31] Nor were acts of indiscipline confined to these circumstances, William Swindells deplored as 'awful' the fact that the guard-room was always full.[32] The 1st Battalion had amassed 200 offences of indiscipline during the course of the voyage. An array of offences, including insubordination toward officers, were committed. On a later voyage, Herb Bartley of the 6th Reinforcements was the only original member of the Orderly Staff (that had left Sydney) who had not been discharged of his duties, some of his colleagues having been removed due to displays of insolent behaviour toward their superior officers.[33]

The main forms of punishment for offences were detention, extra fatigues and forfeiture of pay.[34] Such punishment, imposed within the confined environment of a troopship where individual liberties were already restricted, was largely inconsequential and hardly a deterrent to future acts of indiscipline. Furthermore, men were quickly apprised of the anomalies between the severity of British discipline compared to Australian discipline. The twenty days confinement awarded to one Australian volunteer for falling asleep while on guard duty aboard a transport compared most favourably to the ten years (a sentence granted on appeal over the death penalty) that was imposed upon a British prisoner who had been brought on board.[35] Such discrepancy in treatment sharpened the distinction with which Australian volunteers viewed themselves within the context of the British army. Australian soldiers' misdemeanours appeared to be independent of British transgressions and answerable to (more lenient) Australian authority, not British military law.

The cramped conditions also exacerbated existing divisions within the Australian force, notably those between the officers and men. While the men ate at crowded mess tables, the officers enjoyed the company of the ship's captain and mess and, when nurses were aboard, dances.[36] Undoubtedly some of the men imagined the officers to be leading a charmed life of leisure while they were drilled by the NCOs. William Swindells complained of the officers, though not his own captain and lieutenant, getting drunk and making an exhibition of themselves.[37] Officers were not always seen in this light and it was clear from one soldier's comment that their efforts in looking to the men's welfare and comfort were sometimes appreciated: 'The passengers and officers right through the voyage so far, have been exceptionally liberal to us all'.[38] Despite such 'charity' on the part of some officers it was apparent that a swell of resentment did exist against them and this was reflected in the high number of disciplinary infractions on the voyage.

The poor disciplinary record of the 1st Battalion did not improve with the men's arrival in Egypt. Although the journey from Suez to Alexandria and sub-sequent train trip to Cairo enraptured the men, the native population did not. An observation by Corporal P. Q. J. Collins was indicative of how many within the Battalion viewed or came to view Egypt and its native population: 'This is a bugger of a place you can smell the natives they are worse than the goats'.[39]

Suzanne Brugger has described the Australian presence in Egypt as representing a 'latter-day plague'.[40] Brugger suggested that the Australians, imbued with an air of racial superiority—evident in their adherence to the White Australia policy—unquestioningly applied their pre-existing prejudices towards Aborigines and minority racial groups in Australia to the native popu-lation in Egypt.[41] The positioning of the camps and restrictions placed on the movements of the troops ensured that Australian contact was limited to one section of Egyptian society, the donkey-boys, hawkers, various traders and prostitutes. It was also unfortunate that the Australian arrival coincided with a transitional period in Egypt's history. The restraints of medieval Islamic custom were beginning to break down in the face of modern technology and a large drift of the population from the countryside to the city had occurred. As a consequence, vagabondage (particularly among children) and crime rates rose in Cairo. Unable and unwilling to embrace the culture and excluded by the barrier of language and their own superficial assessments of Egyptian hygiene and honesty, Australian soldiers responded with frequent displays of violent behaviour. Brugger conceded that brutal treatment, such as the kicking and beating of natives, was not something introduced by the Australians but rather an 'over-enthusiastic adoption of local practice'.[42] The diaries of some of the men certainly sustain Brugger's concession. Of his first day ashore Pri-vate Donkin recorded how unlicensed fish and fruit vendors were set upon 'by the black police who spared no energy in propelling the boot at them. Also his cane made a great impression on them.'[43] Another chronicled a similar, if not the same, scene:

> two highly gilded officials went ahead to keep the crowd back. One of these would occasionally take a running jump at some unsuspecting pedestrian and kick him viol-ently in the middle of the back. On another occasion a native and donkey cart failed to get out of the road quickly enough, so the policeman seized the cart and pushed the whole affair over leaving both the native and donkey struggling on the footpath.[44]

William Swindells also wrote of the local method of law enforcement: 'The police in this country are a fine lot of men nearly all native army men they make no bones about cuffing the natives about'.[45]

There is little doubt that many men of the 1st Battalion behaved in a boorish manner and that violence toward the natives was seen as being acceptable. Not all, however, were insensitive to the misfortune of the Egyptians. H. L. Montague, formerly the Deputy Town Clerk of Kogarah, wrote to his local newspaper and provided a sympathetic and detailed account of Egypt and of the Egyptian plight. He noted, 'They can, to a certain extent, be compared to the aboriginals of Australia. As we possess and occupy Australia, similarly the French, Greeks, and practically every nationality occupies Egypt, leaving the poor old Egyptian to exist the best way he can'.[46] Nevertheless, the maltreatment of the native population by Australian soldiers contributed to the already high incidence of indiscipline and provided a further point on which officers, charged with controlling such behaviour, would clash with the men.

Discipline and control of the soldiers became a broader issue with the arrival of the Battalion at its encampment. The Battalion was now, unlike in Sydney, part of a larger military group, one truly national in its content. The men of New South Wales joined with those from the other states to give a visible reality to an Australian army. The troops of the various states were segregated by the nature of their state-based formations within the division. However, apart from shouted greetings that met the arrival of new reinforcements from the home state, the troops do not appear to have exhibited any inclination to view themselves as New South Welshman above being Australian.[47] From the outset, their enlistment in Sydney had been reported and viewed in a national context, and the accounts of the 1st Battalion do not support the notion of a state-based identity.[48]

The proximity of the camps to Cairo undermined, as they had in Sydney, the discipline of the force. The social life of camp was not altogether different from what the men had known in Sydney. Although it was not as homely, given the absence of family and friends, there still existed a degree of social normality with occasional visits from Cairo's French residents.[49] Discipline within the 1st Battalion remained poor. During the period 1 February to 4 April 1915, offences within the Battalion totalled 457, a figure that equated with an offence by nearly every second soldier in the unit. Insolence to officers was a major contributor.[50] The battalions of 1st Brigade appear to have been among the worst behaved in the AIF. Of 147 soldiers marked for return to Australia for disciplinary reasons in February 1915, 66 were from the 1st Brigade (18 of whom belonged to 1st Battalion).[51] It was clear, just as it had been in Australia, that the officers and NCOs of the Battalion were too inexperienced and lacked the necessary respect from their men to be able to impose their will. A last-minute binge by many of the men prior to their departure to the Dardanelles underscored the depths to which indiscipline had plunged. It was the luckless native population that bore the full brunt of the men's revelry. The events of that night were to be immortalised in AIF lore as the 'Battle of the Wazzir' and it is not intended to describe them in detail here. Men of the 1st Battalion undoubtedly had a hand in the mayhem of that night. Corporal F. A. C. George, who complained of being previously 'boned' for piquet duty in the town, delighted in his duties of clearing the streets: 'The way those "Nigs" bolted when they sighted an officer was as good as a keystone [cops movie]'.[52] Swindells recorded two men of his company as having been shot, one in the hand and one in the leg, during the riot, but little was done by the Battalion officers to investigate the involvement of their men in the affair.[53] In this respect, any calculation on the part of the rioters that their pending departure would be ignored by their officers and save them from punishment was correct.

Resistance to orders and perceived injustices by officers were not confined to individual reaction and resentment. Sometimes it overflowed into organised collective action. An incident described by Archie Barwick reveals how the lack of respect toward an officer and a grievance over poor rations translated into a sit-down strike throughout the Battalion:

> we had had quite enough of him [Battalion commanding officer, Lieutenant-Colonel Dobbin] and his promises so we lay stretched out like camels in the hot sand, by and by along comes the Brigadier and he listened with great consideration to our complaint . . . we had much better food from then on.[54]

That not all officers were insensitive to the men's comfort and were, sometimes, willing to circumvent their superiors is evidenced in an incident recorded by William Swindells: 'Marched out on the desert, the Major told the Captain we were too hard worked and intended to give us a spell but had to do this without the Colonel knowing'.[55] Consequently the Battalion was marched over a hill into a hollow and the men allowed to take their kit off and rest until 4 pm, when they marched back to camp with the colonel, presumably, none the wiser. The major was most likely Major Kindon, who was to prove an outstanding leader by example on Gallipoli and was respected by many of the men.

On 8 March there occurred another incident in which the men of A Company revealed the extent to which their sense of justice (a 'fair go') had yet to be quelled by military service. This company had, a few days beforehand, been singled out as having done particularly good work. This immensely pleased platoon commander Lieutenant H. E. Williams, who had recently told his men that he believed they would be a 'great fighting company'.[56]

The incident, not mentioned in either the Battalion or Brigade diaries, was described in detail by William Swindells:

> Up as usual for breakfast A coy all in a bad temper as we had been promised a holiday. When the bugle sounded for the dress parade the men decided that they would not go on. Sergeants came along and tried to get the men on parade but it was useless they demanded the holiday. Then the Sergeant-Major came down the lines and told the men to fall in stating the OC. would see the Colonel which he did but it was no use the Colonel said we had to go on parade and he would see what could be done later. The men would not take his promise as it had been broken so often and decided to stay in the lines, by this time officers were rushing about trying to get the men to form up but it was no use. Colonel, Adjutant, Major, Captain etc. appealed but all in vain, finally the Staff Major came down the lines and hearing one man say 'stick to it boys' he placed him under arrest [and one other] . . . while this proceeding had been going on No. 1 Platoon of A Coy fell in also about 8 men of No. 10 section they were loudly hooted by the men standing out as it showed signs of a break. Then one of the officers of No. 4 platoon appealed to the men on behalf of the OC. who is an officer we all like, and being told it would get him into trouble the men consented to fall in, immediately this was done the two men who stood out were arrested and marched to the guard tent to be tried as ringleaders of the mutiny. All this caused about 1 hrs delay and upset the Colonel, I think he was more upset b/c A Coy is the crack coy both in drill and shooting . . .[57]

Following this disruption the men were marched out to participate in a Brigade inspection. When the adjutant, Captain W. Davidson, who was blamed for the loss of the promised holiday, was thrown from his horse, his misfortune drew loud laughter from the men. To cap off what had been an extraordinary morning one of the men, apparently drunk, drew his bayonet and charged one of the officers. No harm came to the officer, and the man was immediately arrested and frogmarched to detention.[58]

The refusal of the men to go on parade had been fuelled by their resentment at having had a promised holiday denied by a senior officer. Swindells does not mention any dissatisfaction being expressed by any other companies so one assumes that this strike was confined to A Company.

That such actions took place raises serious questions about the quality of leadership within the Battalion and of its efficiency. Of the training period in Egypt, Bean declared in the *Official History* that the battalions of the 1st Brigade had assumed the qualities of their commanders. He described the 1st Battalion as having come 'under the influence of a number of spirited officers' and named Major Kindon (second in command) and Major Swannell (D Company) as examples. Significantly, he made no mention of the Battalion's commander, Lieutenant-Colonel Dobbin. Furthermore, he suggested a special spirit pervaded the Battalion in that the 'mere name of the "First" Australian

Infantry Battalion meant something to the men who bore it'.[59] This suggestion is supported by the comment of one soldier who wrote: 'We like to pride ourselves that the 1st Battalion is also first in smartness etc.'.[60] However, there is little sense of this feeling, generally, in the diaries and letters studied during the training phase of the Battalion's service. On the contrary, given the strikes and high number of disciplinary offences, the experience of the Battalion suggests the opposite. One week before embarking for the Dardenelles, Reg Donkin was still deploring the number of malingerers in the Battalion. According to Donkin these men were mostly old Imperial soldiers and Boer War men, who despised the 'Ragtime Army' of which they were now a part. 'All this would vanish', he declared, 'if we "could get at them" [the enemy]'.[61] Ken McConnel, too, shared Donkin's view of where the blame lay for the troubles in Cairo: 'the truth was that nearly all the men who caused the trouble were men who were not born in Australia and were of all sorts of nationalities'.[62] The fact that the majority of the Battalion were Australian-born and the high number of disciplinary offences within the Battalion indicate that the summations of Donkin and McConnel were probably incorrect. Nevertheless, the opinions of these men do reflect the growing sense of national pride and identification in their soldier and national identities. They clearly wanted to separate and distance themselves from unworthy behaviour within their Battalion and AIF. The most identifiable minority group upon whom this unbecoming behaviour could be blamed were the British-born within the force. There is no reason to suppose that British-born soldiers within the Battalion did not share the same pride in Australia as their native-born comrades. Scottish-born, Lance-Corporal D. F. McLeod wrote home during the Gallipoli campaign and urged: 'Get the boys to come and take part in the making of Australia's name—I wouldn't be out of it for worlds'.[63] McLeod, described as a braw Scot by one of his comrades, appears to have been a well-travelled sea-dog who revelled in new frontiers. His pet theme, according to Private Robert Grant, was 'Vancouver and district and the glories of America'.[64] His pride in Australia may have been a reflection of his interest in new worlds. Alternatively, or as well, his enthusiasm may have been part of a Richard Jebb-like vision of British imperialism, of a nascent Australia uniting in an alliance or partnership with Great Britain, the central metropolitan power of the Empire.[65]

Donkin's comments on the lack of discipline were especially interesting, since his remarks had been preceded two weeks beforehand by his criticism of comments made by Bean. The official war correspondent had attempted to make (with little success) the very point—that it was a hard-core element (many of whom wore the South African ribbon) which was responsible for much of the indiscipline. Comments attributed to Bean published in Australian newspapers drew the wrath of the troops.[66] In a piece of verse titled *To Our Critic*, Trooper F. E. Westbrook of 4th Battery, Australian Field Artillery, encapsulated the feeling toward Bean as well as a general disdain the man in the ranks held for officers:

> Do yer think yer Gawd Almighty,
> Cos yer wears a captain's Stars.
> Thinks us blokes is dirt beneath yer.
> Men of low degree & bars . . .
>
> . . . Let me ask you Mr Critic
> Try and face things with a smile,
> Don't be finding all the crook-uns,
> Studying them blokes all the while.
>
> Then write home nice and Proper,
> 'Bout the boys thats all true blue,
> And they'll love yer better mister,
> This is my advice to you.

Captain Davidson, the Battalion's adjutant, thought the poem 'rather good' and sent a copy home as well as a copy of Bean's cable in which the war correspondent attempted to defuse the controversy.[67] Bean was profoundly shocked and upset by the vehemence of the troops' response. Resentment continued and did not begin to dissipate until the commencement of the Gallipoli campaign and open acknowledgment from the men as to Bean's personal bravery among them.[68] The response of the troops to Bean's comments revealed how sensitive the men had become to their Australianness. This sense of national identity overshadowed the men's identification with their smaller military groups. Irrespective of the truth that lurked behind Bean's comments, his opinion was seen to impugn the men's positive view of themselves as soldiers.

Reinforcements were just as prone as the originals, if not more so, to misbehaviour, as the 'strike' at Liverpool clearly demonstrated. The port of Fremantle was also the scene for a number of disturbances by troops *en route* overseas. The 1st Battalion's 6th Reinforcements were among the participants in one such incident on 24 July 1915. They had arrived the previous evening and, although the ship's crew were allowed ashore, the soldiers were kept aboard. Extra guards and pickets were placed around the ship to prevent men smuggling themselves aboard the many motor launches cruising the harbour. A route march was arranged the following day through the town and to its parks. The men were ordered not to leave the park and dinner was supplied to them there. Hundreds slipped away into the town, and by nightfall one hundred men were still missing. Most were rounded up by the Battalion's guards and military police and returned to the ship 'dead drunk'.[69] On a later voyage the stay in Fremantle fuelled frictions between officers and men of the 10th Reinforcements, 1st Brigade, when officers were allowed to disembark while leave was denied to the men. According to Private Rostron, when tugs arrived to coal the ship the men refused to let them load until leave was granted. Men climbed over the sides into the tugs and from there were put ashore by small boats.[70] Private Locane's account of the same incident, however, revealed a sense of solidarity and co-operation on the part of the coal lumpers:

> Eventually the men who were loading coal on our boat refused to work unless we got leave, saying for an excuse we were in the way and prevented them working. Anyhow without waiting for them to get their answer someone took it into their head to walk off, he was immediately followed by the whole crowd who were anxious to see WA.[71]

Further trouble occurred a week later when one of the men was put in detention, later converted to a fine of five shillings, for disobeying an officer. By itself the incident is worthy of little comment, but the same night eight days of fatigues were meted out to the company as punishment for the men refusing to listen to the officers. The reason for their dissatisfaction stemmed from the officers again gaining leave.[72] Such incidents were hardly conducive to the fostering of goodwill in the ranks, who clearly saw such treatment as invidious and proof of the politics of privilege.

Paternalism and deference

The general indiscipline of the 1st Battalion and behaviour of the men toward their officers forms a critical ambivalence in the Anzac legend. On one hand, it supports the celebrated anti-authoritarian individualism of Australian soldiers. On the other, it contradicts the harmonious relations that characterise the soldiers and officers of the Anzac legend. As we have seen, the anti-authoritarian behaviour of the soldiers—whether derived from a natural or national inclination or arising from genuine grievances—had the potential to, and did at times, compromise the efficiency of the force. Given this fact, it is unreasonable to believe that relations between officers and men could be as harmonious as the legend ambiguously suggests.

The assumed easy-going relationship between Australian officers and their men is encapsulated in the anecdote cited at the beginning of the chapter. The use of first names as a method of address within the modern-day Australian workplace between workers and their bosses is part of the national idiom and highly symbolic of Australian egalitarianism. Australian soldiers, too, believed themselves to be equal, man to man, to their superiors. However, the diaries and letters of the 1st Battalion soldiers do not suggest that the relationships were as intimate as the anecdote implies.[73] Soldiers writing about their officers generally referred to them by their designated rank, sometimes by their nickname, and often by the more formal title of 'mister'. The formality of the last form of address is evident in a number of diaries and letters of 1st Battalion men. Archie Barwick provides one example of this deference as well as the frictions that existed within the lower echelons of command: 'Capt Price came on the bounce again this evening he has got a nice set on us. I know what it is all over "the tucker" for Mr Champion and myself kicked up a row over it the other day'.[74] Lance-Corporal D. H. G. Golding displayed similar deference in writing to his convalescing company officer:

> Since seeing you last, Sir, I have been made Lance-Corporal, why, I don't know. It wasn't for being of exemplary character I guess . . . Well, Mr. McConnell [sic] I close my letter hoping you have a good time when you are convalescent. I don't mind telling you I wish I could get a 'blighty' myself'.[75]

Golding was an English-born labourer and, at twenty-three years of age—two years older than McConnel—was clearly conscious of the social division between himself and his officer.[76] His admission of wanting a 'blighty' (a wound serious enough to send a soldier back to England) intimates a level of compassion within that relationship or, at least, a belief on the part of Golding that he had McConnel's confidence. Perhaps this was a reflection of McConnel's man-management skills for during the voyage to Egypt, Golding had displayed a marked disrespect of authority and, subsequently, a violent opposition to incarceration. His name appeared several times in the Battalion's offences book.[77] Nevertheless, his deference is hardly indicative of the informality generally ascribed to Australian officer–man relationships. That informality was clearly evident among intimate associates, as one would expect, and another letter received by McConnel from a brother officer is in marked contrast:

> I cannot say any more at present, old bird, except that Somerset is writing at last. Somerset wishes you to remember that cakes are to him the greatest use and that you must see that he is not left to pine away and die. Well, toorooloo, old chap, and good luck.
>
> Yours to a cinder
> P. Howell-Price

> Thanks for the eatables, old boy, but go easy as you may swamp the place. You really do take the Bun. Thanks, old boy.[78]

Officers and men were clearly not of the same stamp. They viewed one another differently and this affected their behaviour and attitudes towards one another. The writings, and presumably the speech, of officers like Howell-Price reflected the idiosyncratic vernacular of the English upper and middle classes that had become popular by the turn of the century. The mimicked language of these officers marked a certain social status or proclivity and, as was the case in wider British society, reinforced the notion of a social hierarchy within the Battalion.[79] The response to the war and to the regiment by men enamoured of the standards of brotherhood codified in the language and litera-ture of the time, and taught in the public and private schools throughout the British Empire, was an example of the power and success of social engineering in the late-Victorian and Edwardian period. The young men occupying the ranks of the junior officers of both the British armies and AIF drew heavily on the public-school ethos as a means of conducting and interpreting their duty.[80] Gary Sheffield has suggested that this ethos was so efficiently 'disseminated into public consciousness that no one disputed the right of eighteen year old lads to lead grown men into battle'.[81] Conduct of relationships on a first-name basis between officers and men was possible, particularly among former inti-mates where one had advanced in rank or, in less likely circumstances, where a friendship had developed as was the case with Private Harold Mercer and his officer, Lieutenant R. G. (Bob) Humphries.[82] The deference shown by Golding and Barwick to their officers confirms the existence of the public-school ethos to which Sheffield referred, but the continued high rate of insub-ordination in France suggests that it was a respect given conditionally by men in the 1st Battalion.

It has been argued that the appalling conditions of the front line endured by the men prompted a form of enlightenment among combat officers: feelings of compassion and understanding, which bridged the class barriers of pre-war Britain, were engendered by the shared miseries and dangers among men who, previously, had rarely associated with one another.[83] How far this applied to the Australian situation is difficult to gauge. There is certainly some evidence suggesting that officers felt a closeness to their commands, though how much this reflected a genuine philanthropy on their part as opposed to enjoying the status of command is unclear. Howell-Price's enig-matic attachment to his command was evident a few days before the Battalion's disastrous attack on Bayonet Trench. Writing again to the still con-valescing McConnel, he declared his happiness with the manner in which his 'boys' were bearing up under the appalling conditions. He then described emphatically the anxiety which gripped him over his planned leave: 'But know this, Son, that my company is to me as my brother and though rough and often rude I feel the losses as none but myself knows . . . and I am so self-ish and proud of them that I do not like handing them over to the care of any-one, not even for ten days'.[84] If Howell-Price's attachment to his troops was matched by a genuine and abiding concern for the welfare of the troops, it was not something that necessarily came automatically to all Australian officers. General Birdwood, having witnessed an Australian battalion left sitting about with the men unattended, many of whom were suffering from 'trench feet' after a stint in the front line, was compelled to issue a memo reminding officers of the need to address the welfare of the men, particularly at company and platoon level.[85]

An apparent divide between officers and NCOs was certainly evident in another letter by Philip Howell-Price to his wounded comrade Ken McConnel, in which he outlined the problems he faced, both personally and as company commander:

> My other two officers are two Sgts. promoted, Steel and McIntyre. They are not bril-liant and not up to the standard of my previous officers. Their responsibility does not seem to impress their childish minds, nor do they show any special knowledge of any sort whatever. We are well out of Pozières and safe as you must know, by now. Our Coy is much changed but there are still some fine fellows of the old lot left me. I am the only officer unfortunately and will be pleased to see anyone belonging before to the Company. I am very lonely and cannot be too lively now—Geoff Street has gone —George Wootten too and now Blackmore and yourself. The game is not good enough and the sooner I get strafed the better for me, I say. These sudden changes are now too frequent even for me, and I've nearly seen enough. It is most peculiar the manner in which the formations are changed continually and yet one never gets any more time for Camp training which is undoubtedly the foundations of discipline.[86]

This letter by Howell-Price reveals not only his paternalistic character but, importantly, a number of facets about the 1st Battalion's morale. The qualities of some men elevated to commissioned rank, at least according to Howell-Price, were not worthy of the officers that had preceded them. This point was reiterated officially in a Brigade report that noted: '40 new officers have been promoted from the ranks to fill the vacancies caused by casualties. The stan-dard has been steadily lowered and though the new men are very good men few are of what used to be known as the officers type.'[87]

Rising from the ranks: the myth of AIF officer selection

In the AIF, a distinct 'officer-type' was unashamedly pursued and there prob-ably existed more similarities than differences between Australian and British officers. This process of selection bias was evident in the appointments of the officers of the 1st Brigade at the war's outset. Brigadier-General H. N. MacLaurin, a 35-year-old barrister and commander of the 26th regiment of militia, was appointed to command the 1st Brigade. It was, according to Bean, a somewhat experimental decision based principally on an estimation of the untried officer's character. In this instance MacLaurin's credentials appeared impeccable: a keen militiaman since his university days and son of Sir Henry Normand MacLaurin, a prominent medical practitioner and one-time Chancellor of the University of Sydney. He appeared an obvious choice. His second in command was also a fellow member of the legal profession, Lieutenant-Colonel C. M. Macnaghten, and the first task of these men was to appoint commanders for three of the four battalions. Command of the 1st Battalion had already been assigned to Lieutenant-Colonel Leonard Dobbin. Like his colleagues, Dobbin, who was on the military's unattached list when war broke out, was also a member of the legal profession who had commanded in the militia.[88] Given the shared occupational backgrounds of these early appointments, it was little wonder that a notion emanated of 'a coterie of the Australian Club in Sydney' being responsible for the selection of officers in the 1st Brigade.[89] Dobbin, in fact, claimed to have selected most of his junior officers and NCOs from his pre-war militia unit, the Australian Rifle Regiment.[90]

Dobbin was not alone in exercising a preference for selecting men with a common connection, and it was clear that a system of preferment was in vogue at the outset of the Battalion's formation and continued throughout the war. Following a major reorganisation in February 1916, when half of the 1st Battalion were assigned to form a new or 'sister' battalion (the 53rd), a shortfall in officers was compensated for by drawing men from the 2nd Light Horse Brigade. Ken McConnel, educated at the University of Sydney and Harrow in England where he was a member of the school's officer training corps, was one of these men.[91] Despite his own admission that he knew nothing about infantry drill and tactics, he was granted a commission in the 1st Battalion after a short interview with the Battalion's colonel that entailed 'a few questions as to service and education.'[92] Similarly, after the heavy losses sustained in 1916, a number of men were selected from the 1st Field Ambulance to boost the 1st Battalion's pool of officers. Nearly one-third (30.43 per cent) of the Battalion's lieutenants were transferred into the Battalion from other units. This compared to only 12.5 per cent of sergeants transferred into the Battalion. In regard to reinforcement officers, a policy appears to have been adopted that awarded commissions in units other than that to which the reinforcement group belonged. Lieutenants Graham and Vine-Hall and second lieutenants Kelleway, Prior and Edgely were all transferred from the 2nd Battalion, and five second lieutenants of the 1st Battalion reinforcements were sent to the

2nd Battalion.[93] This may have allowed the authority of the officers to be given a fresh start free from any prejudices and frictions that may have existed in the reinforcement group. The battalions, too, would be spared such undesirable tension.

The directive applicable throughout the AIF that all reinforcements, except those selected from the officer schools, must enter the ranks as privates clearly did not carry with it an obligation for those men to work their way through the ranks. Men of perceived ability (particularly social equivalents) were not going to be left to languish in the ranks and were advanced rapidly. T. J. Richards, one of the Field Ambulance men transferred to the Battalion, had been a corporal prior to his promotion to second lieutenant.[94] Ken McConnel had only been a lance-corporal prior to his elevation, as had been Lieutenants McKell and Parkes who were promoted soon after the Lone Pine fight on Gallipoli.[95] Herbert Chedgey, another former Sydney University man and co-author of *First Battalion*, was transferred to the Battalion via officer training school, from a cyclist battalion where he had been a lance-corporal. AIF policy allowed for the advancement of NCOs by more than one step at a time in special cases based on merit, provided authority was given by the Divisional CO. Although this system was meant to reward meritorious service, it could easily be abused by the prejudices of a local commander. Promotions above the rank of sergeant had first to be authorised by Brigade CO.[96] Having gained this, it was unlikely that recommendations would be denied by Division when vacancies existed.

Other soldiers, like Noel McShane, who were deemed to be officer material were drawn from the non-combative sections of the Battalion. Such selections were not well received, as McShane noted: 'When we (Transport men) got our commission there was considerable discontentment amongst the senior NCOs'.[97] The selection of men from outside the ranks of the 1st Battalion and from the unit's non-combative arms can be interpreted as a sign that those with command selection authority did not consider the men with the requisite skills to reside within the ranks of the Battalion. When, in February 1916, AIF battalions were asked to supply names of NCOs and men who could be recommended for commissions in the new battalions being formed, the 1st Battalion submitted no names. Only two names were submitted from the entire 1st Brigade, compared to eighteen and fourteen from the 2nd and 3rd Brigades.[98] The lack of recommendations may have reflected a shrewd retention of good men or, on the contrary, it may have represented a lack of confidence in the men due to the poor disciplinary record of the Brigade—the worst in the Division. If a lack of confidence existed, it casts doubt over the stereotypical notion that initiative and leadership skills were possessed by most Australian soldiers. One would have thought the officers required could have been selected from the hundreds that formed the other ranks of the Battalion.

The requirement that all men revert to the ranks on being taken on strength by the Battalion was also a source of disappointment throughout the war for men who had enjoyed the responsibility and authority of being an NCO within the reinforcement groups. Private J. Ridley echoed this sentiment when he wrote despondently:

> I have had bad luck lately, losing my rank which means so much to me . . . it is a very hard blow . . . to be a private and serve under people who in many cases know very little of military work, and meanwhile my knowledge lies sleeping.[99]

The obverse of Ridley's disappointment was displayed when he was promoted to corporal: 'The only trouble is that our appointments have caused a lot of bad feeling among the old hands of the company who consider we should not get any position because we have not seen action'.[1] Such ill-feeling was not conducive to the advancement of good relations within the lower echelons of the Battalion's command structure. Nor was the selection of inexperienced men such as McConnel and Richards without its pitfalls. It ran the risk of openly holding up their limitations to ridicule by the very men whom they were charged to control. Both men provided accounts of incidents in which their own lack of training led to a degree of personal humiliation in front of the men. After a week of practice in the desert doing 'skeleton drill' (practising commands and drill without the men), McConnel recalled his first real experience in command:

> I shall never forget our first parade with D Company. We had battalion drill and of course all or most of the things we had learned at skeleton drill went right out of our heads, and we made some awful bungles. After we were dismissed Price [Howell-Price] got his officers together and gave us a proper slating.[2]

Lack of knowledge about relevant commands also embarrassed Richards on successive days. He describes the bewilderment that occurred during an inspection of rifles, which required a two-part command, 'Fix', on which the right-hand soldier stepped forward as a guide, and 'Bayonets', on which the platoon proceeded to fix their bayonets to their rifles:

> I was not aware of this and gave the order 'fix bayonets'. The men came forward all right and got the whole party ready for another command which I did not know of. A pathetic look overspread their faces, then in desperation they fixed bayonets and the guide went back to his place and I went on examining the bayonets. Oh! but what a blunder on my part.

The following day, after forming the company into column of platoons, he did not know the command necessary to set the unit in motion and was rescued by the sergeants, who moved the men off. He felt his inadequacies keenly, noting: 'It's a mean imposition keeping Dingle [another field-ambulance man] and myself here without schooling'.[3] The platoon sergeants proved the saviours of many inexperienced junior officers, as another officer commented about his appointment to the commissioned ranks: 'Sergeant McCowan practically ran the platoon for me until I found my feet, for there is a vast difference between giving and taking orders, particularly in the front line'.[4]

Who a soldier knew, as well as their occupational background, was clearly an advantage to men seeking commissioned rank. Ken McConnel used his influence within the brigade to gain his friend, Aubrey Biggs, a commission in the 2nd Battalion.[5] Philip Howell-Price was able to write home to his father and inform him that the colonel had written to have Howell-Price's brother transferred into the Battalion so that he could give him a commission.[6] Ben Champion's accession to commissioned rank followed soon after the return to the Battalion of Captain Jacobs, Champion's old militia commander.[7] Though one cannot conclusively prove a preferred bias in Champion's case, its presence seems likely given other cases. When Lieutenant R. B. Finlayson joined the 1st Battalion in the line in France he was able to report with some satisfaction: 'Many old Sydney pals are in this Batt. as officers . . . The Banks are well represented'.[8] Les Dinning, a practising Christian of the same denomination as the Battalion's Methodist padre, the Reverend Colonel Green, was asked by the reverend whether he would consider applying for a commission. The padre had declared that he would be only too happy to assist in recommending Dinning, who thought a 'letter from him (Green) would mean a good deal'.[9] The importance of having someone in authority looking after a soldier's interest was suggested by Archie Barwick's lament when his company commander was sent to a school of instruction in England: 'I am sorry he has gone for he was pushing Len [Barwick's brother] and I along, now I expect we will be forgotten'.[10] Barwick considered that this officer, Captain MacKenzie, had 'done all in his power to get both Len and I chucked out of the Battalion just before leaving for France' but that had all changed following Barwick having done the Captain 'a good turn on the night of the great charge at Pozières'.[11] Murray Knight, a former naval cadet, was another who was keen to gain a commission and one whose friends had clearly benefited through their connections:

> Oll and Vic are getting on in the game. They are well in with the heads of their Brigade, through Oll of course . . . I wish I had his opportunities. If I could get someone in Sydney to put in a good word for me . . . I might have a chance of a commission.[12]

Whether as a result of merit or patronage, a soldier's opportunity of gaining a commission lay squarely in the hands of the Battalion's commander. Patronage appears to have played a prominent role in the selection of 1st Battalion officers. However, it was not unknown for soldiers to be promoted in the field following an outstanding performance. A 2nd Battalion soldier, Private O'Keefe, is one example. He was commissioned after displaying initiative and bravery in the face of the enemy. He had taken charge of his platoon after his lieutenant fell victim to shell-shock and all his NCOs were wounded.[13] However, men presenting themselves for commissions, although some were obvious candidates, were not always accepted, as one soldier revealed:

> Vic Fowler was wonderful during the Pozières engagement—for some reason or other he was turned down for a commission just before going into action. Whether he offended a senior officer or not, no-one knows, but if anyone deserved it he did.[14]

A soldier's 'quick temper and ready tongue' could, as Lieutenant A. W. Edwards said of one of his men, militate against promotion.[15]

The difference in the status of officers and the attendant privileges of rank was recognised by the soldiers of lower rank. Officers were paid more money, were entitled to more leave, and were entitled to their own mess. Front-line service naturally limited the opportunity to indulge in the latter. The formation of a mess, however, was highly symbolic of the divisions in rank and was sometimes, as Lieutenant Sydney Traill noted, 'not appreciated'.[16] Though Traill did not elaborate on what it was that made a mess not appreciated (it may have been the bother involved in setting one up), the establishment of a mess could and did sometimes prove a point of contention, as Archie Barwick recorded:

> What do you think, our Major refused to let us run our Sergt's mess the other day, rotten I reckon and only for us shifting there would have been a fine row for the Committee were going to go further with it to Bde if necessary for we are entitled to a 'Mess' and unless he has a very fine excuse he will get into hot water and serve him right . . .[17]

The establishment of officers' and sergeants' messes, apart from being a further reflection of the gradations of rank within the army, also had a positive value in that they provided a venue for officers and sergeants to acquaint themselves with each other. It also facilitated the introduction of new officers and sergeants into their new-found fraternity. Newly promoted Ben Champion recorded one of his first experiences as an officer: 'I stepped out in fear and trembling to go to the Officer's Mess', but on being greeted by former members of his old militia unit and chatting over old times, his anxieties were calmed and he 'went to bed tired and happy'.[18] Above all, the mess provided a welcome comfort to officers and sergeants from the rigours of the front line. It provided a haven where they could associate with men who understood and who had shared the nature of each other's experiences. Yet there can be no doubt that the existence of messes—as well as, in the case of officers, the provision of batmen (personal servants)—carried with them an impression of comfort and elitism that was not available to the common soldier or volunteer.[19]

Men making the transition from NCO to officer were aware of the need for and expectation of new behavioural standards, a point evident in T. J. Richards' comments about his promotion:

> This book is being commenced under remarkably different circumstances to the other dozen or so diaries . . . As an officer of His Majesty's army I will not take the liberty of writing in the same unrestrained manner, maybe I will not be able, or rather, have the occasion to do so as my position is now changed . . . my present company will probably see things from an entirely different standpoint from the rankers, but so far, in this respect I have not noticed any great differences. Officers have their petty grievances and troubles as does the privates, and many of them are working under the same imaginary 'drops'.[20]

For a volunteer to gain admittance into the officer fraternity, a first step to advancement was to gain a position of responsibility in the reinforcement groups, and this was the advice proffered by Lieutenant C. A. Sweetnam to a cousin.[21] Although men like Murray Knight were desperate to advance in the 'game', not all were imbued with the same desire or possessed with enough confidence to apply. Les Dinning had confessed to his father that he had often persuaded himself that he would not be competent enough to hold a com-mission.[22] Others did not seek or want the responsibility. Frederick Buchan, who had held the rank of lance-corporal for six months, reverted to the ranks at his own request.[23] Herb Bartley was another who, early in his service, was happy with his lot as a private: 'I was offered the positions of Pay Corporal, or Corporal, but I never took either on. The plain old Private will do me for a while yet'.[24]

Given the paternalistic and ambitious nature of many of the men who became officers, it is unlikely that their relationship with their men could ever become friendly. In fact there exist instances of total breakdown. Two examples from the Gallipoli campaign illustrate the depth of resentment that soldiers were capable of manifesting toward their officers. Private John Gammage, whose disdain for officers had degenerated into absolute disgust as the cam-paign progressed, recorded his vivid impression of the fighting at Lone Pine, which by virtue of the criticisms he raised was at considerable variance with the official descriptions; it also included a startling revelation, though one that needs to be treated cautiously:

on reaching Jacko's first trench I jumped onto a wounded Turk . . . The moans of our poor fellows and also Turks as we tramped on the wounded body's [sic] was awful . . . At 3am. I was with about 40 men who were sent over the parapet between our lines and the Turks and given instructions not to rush their trench but to wait until daylight. But when daylight came we were like mice in a trap, not even able to raise our heads to fire. Jacko shot many of my mates and let bombs after the rest of us. We were shouted out to from the rotten drunken officer who sent us out not on any account to try and fire but keep low in a small hollow until dark and then try and get back, needless to say he never came with us . . . 11am. a few of us got back . . . we heard that the drunken cad who sent many good men to their death was shot by our own men. I nearly had a foal when I heard it, a pity he never got one hours before . . . I got the SM. [sergeant-major] the man who tried to make my life a misery; he is a rotten cur—curled up in safety while his own comrades were dying in hundreds all around him fighting to save his and a few more of his sorts, miserable cowardly carcase. I threatened to carve him up with my bayonet if he did not come out and do as other men were doing. I had just ten thousand very close shaves today. The officer we all thought would squib it was the only one to be seen, most of them waited for a communication trench to be dug but we got on better without such curs.[25]

John Gammage noted after one of these attacks that the Australians had been 'the heaviest loser by far but what a target they gave us this morning [the 9th] not one of them reached our trench alive'.[26] He could not resist another swipe at his officers, whom he described as being conspicuous by their absence, leaving the NCOs to carry on without them. Gammage was wounded in the leg four days later and evacuated, to the envy of his comrades, men he believed to be the best God had 'put breath in'.[27]

Gammage's disparaging remarks about the performance of the officers appear to have some substance when viewed against the Battalion's and Brigade's casualties. According to the *Official History*, the 1st Battalion entered the fight with 21 officers and 799 others, of whom 7 officers and 333 others became casualties. The proportion of casualties amongst the officers was therefore 33 per cent compared to nearly 42 per cent among the men. That in itself is perhaps not startling, but the figures are surprising given the losses in the other battalions of the Brigade. The 2nd, 3rd and 4th Battalions lost 95, 91 and 75 per cent of their officers and 73, 66 and 63 per cent of their men respectively.[28] The lower casualties of the 1st Battalion can be attributed in part to its being a support to the main assault. However, the low casualty rate among the officers is surprising. At the landing the Battalion had suffered a similar number of total casualties and the officers had suffered in higher proportion to the other ranks. Of course, at Lone Pine the officers may just have been luckier; or maybe the heavy loss among the officers of the other battalions was known and the 1st Battalion officers were detailed to less

dangerous positions to act as a nucleus for the Brigade, though such a cir-
cumstance is highly unlikely and not revealed in either the Battalion or 1st
Brigade diaries. Against this it should be noted that some of the Battalion's
officers displayed outstanding courage at Lone Pine. Captains Sasse and
Shout fought with conspicuous gallantry. Shout, who died as a result of
wounds received, was awarded a Victoria Cross for charging and bombing
the enemy from strong positions. Sasse was awarded a DSO for leading
several bayonet charges—the close fighting at Lone Pine being one of the few
occasions in the war that allowed for the bayonet skills practised so often in
training.

One who shared some of Gammage's antipathy was Reg Donkin, who
had been wounded during the landing and returned to the fighting in a
melancholy mood:

> What is this wholesale carnage that deprives man from pursuing his peaceful way.
> The world is mad. Can't the powers settle their squabbles without our blood, for the
> price? . . . I wish I had Alma's photo. What castles in the air I have built? Will I lie on
> Gallipoli and these dreams be shattered?[29]

With the conclusion of the main fighting at Lone Pine, Reg Donkin's war was
to take a decided turn for the worse. After a row with an officer, Captain
Sasse, Donkin—as a result of what he believed to be the captain's spite—was
ordered back to the company. This turn of events did not please him: he
described himself as being 'back amongst the rottenest crowd of Officers and
NCOs there are to be found. They are nearly always half-drunk on our rum,
especially the Quartermaster.'[30] This damning indictment (whatever its truth)
may have been a result not only of his own misfortune but also of what he felt
for his home town. News of the death and wounding of his mates from
Maitland left him feeling 'rotten', and he knew of only three Maitland boys
left, including himself. 'Poor Maitland', he declared.[31] Donkin's civilian ties
clearly impinged upon his perception of war. The following day Donkin volunteered to join the machine-gun section, a cause for some celebration as it
meant an escape from Captain Sasse. The next day was soured by news of the
death of another of his 'old "G" Co.' mates, and brought the plaintive cry
'How long, Oh, Lord, how long will we have to suffer thus'. With enemy shell
fragments 'tearing perilously' close to him as he wrote, Donkin closed his
diary entry for 13 August with 'This job is one of the most costly ones the war
has seen'. Next day he was dead, killed outright when a shell smashed his
gun, and his castles in the air, to pieces.[32]

The bitterness toward his officers that Donkin carried to his grave might
have had its genesis in an incident that occurred two months prior to his
death. On 18 June, Donkin had been charged on two counts, talking in the

ranks after the men had been called to attention and laughing after being reproved by an officer (probably in connection with the first crime).[33] The default of a day's pay, when locked into the trenches on Gallipoli, was hardly a deterrent. Nor was Donkin alone in his insolence. Statistics of crimes committed in B Company for the period 11 April to 2 August 1915 show that one-third (23 of 69) were recorded for insolence or refusing and failing to comply with orders.[34] If the experience of B Company was mirrored in the other companies then the equivalent of one-quarter of the Battalion were charged with some offence during that period. That is hardly a sign of efficiency or of respectful behaviour of the men toward their superiors. Occurring in the cramped confines of the transport ships and Gallipoli, these figures intimate that significant tension existed between the officers and men.

The move from a training environment to one of active operations saw a change in the nature of crimes committed. The officers' attention and greater care toward military detail and procedure in the firing line were evident in the increase of charges relating to neglect of duty and disobedience of orders. The emphasis on detail may have been seen by the men as reflecting the officiousness of the Battalion's officers. The men's defiance came in the form of insolence, insubordination and a general slackness in their responses. Certainly slackness, though not necessarily deliberately hostile in its nature, was in evidence, as Lieutenant R. G. Casey had observed a month after the landing: 'The 1st Battalion were to have sent a party to collect this gear [Turkish ammunition] at 7 pm. They arrived at 10.30 pm. It is wonderful how unpunctual and unbusinesslike some Battalions are.'[35] Unless Casey's tone was one of heavy irony, his comment suggests that such slackness was not only tolerated but also viewed as a strangely admirable quality!

Tony Ashworth has suggested that a soldier's perception of his military experience is shaped by the nature of the officer–man relationship in the unit in which he served. The descriptions by Donkin and Gammage suggest that this relationship, during the Gallipoli campaign, was a poor one in the 1st Battalion.[36] Following the Gallipoli campaign, and with the expansion of the AIF, an opportunity afforded itself to dispense with officers who had proved inadequate as fighting commanders. The 1st Battalion's commander was one such casualty, evacuated from Gallipoli on several occasions due to illness; his casualty and service form was kindly noted 'unable to be absorbed'.[37]

Relations were also strained in France. In the two-month period (1 April to 5 June 1916) immediately following the Battalion's arrival in France, 177 offences are recorded. Absence without leave constituted almost half of these but incidents of disobedience and insolence, which represent direct clashes in the officer–man relationship, accounted for nearly one-fifth of offences (18.64

per cent).[38] Archie Barwick, who had generally spoken well of the Battalion's original officers, was far less accommodating in his descriptions of his officers in France:

> we have a rotten lot of officers in my opinion at the present time and they are here under false pretences drawing the country's good money, no wonder this war is costing so much when we carry so many drones on our backs, they are a lovely crowd.[39]

Not all soldiers described their officers in such derogatory terms. Norman Langford was one who gave his unqualified support to the Anzac legend's treatment of the officer–man relationship: 'Never have I ever in my life seen such comradeship, understanding and devotion between officers and other ranks as existed amongst the "Diggers".' Some caution is needed, however, in accepting Langford's account as a true indication of the state of relations between officers and men within the Battalion. It is drawn from a retrospective narrative and Langford was prominent in the encouragement of post-war accounts of the Battalion's deeds in the RSL journal, *Reveille*.[40]

Officers did have the power to counter resentment toward them through their leadership in battle and could earn respect through their combat performance or by showing concern over the men's welfare in and out of the line, as is shown by one soldier's observation: 'When Stacy, our CO, came round— he was not popular, but everybody admits he is a fine soldier, and stands cool as a cucumber, without flinching . . . when ironmongery is flying; and he comes round regularly to see how things are going'.[41] Stacy's action was an egalitarian gesture, 'a concrete demonstration of a commander's belief that the community of fighting men is more important than the formal structure of rank'.[42] Such action, highly symbolic as it was, cannot be construed to suggest that the officer–man relationship was conducted on an equal footing. Nor was it true that the two groups shared the same values. When it came to serious breaches of discipline the officers held the upper hand, especially in France where the AIF was locked into a stricter military environment than had previously been the case, and men could do little to resist the enforcement of military law. Within the confines of the Battalion itself, however, the men were still able to exert a measure of control over that relationship by a variety of behaviours, in particular, the withdrawal of their labour and non-participation in routine tasks. When second Lieutenant Ken McConnel sought volunteers for a raiding party, his appeal met with a poor response due to the men having been 'slanged by their company commander after a hard nights barbed wiring'.[43] Another ploy, when detailed to long hours doing fatigue work, was simply to employ the 'government stroke'.[44] Such methods frustrated the officers, some of whom found the bullying tactics employed against the men a necessary but humiliating experience.[45]

Frictions between officers and men could sometimes reach chronic levels. Mid-May 1917 was one of these periods and, according to Archie Barwick, ill-feeling was much in evidence as a result of the zealous attention to detail being displayed by Captain 'Tubby' Pearce and the Battalion's RSM: 'I reckon and I should not be surprised to see a mutiny here any day. For old Tubby Pearce and the RSM are simply detested by both officers and men, matters are approaching a climax I should think and something is bound to happen for there is such a thing as going too far.'[46] Something did happen, though exactly what cannot be ascertained, for Harold Mercer on his return to the Battalion recorded: 'was given quite a nice reception by the boys . . . They have heard of the business which resulted in Captain Pearce's downfall, and seem to appreciate it.'[47]

Generally speaking, Australian officers were both able and willing to enforce military regulations and punishments on their men. Sometimes this incorporated a spirit of vindictiveness that reflected a mutual loathing, a feeling more generally associated with the other ranks toward their officers, as one 1st Battalion officer's comments reveal: 'There's a man in this company, a half-caste who [I'll] break yet. There's a natural antipathy between us, and if I don't get him 10 years quod [sic], [he'll] put a bullet through me. I'm getting in first, its always best'.[48] This adversarial attitude, recorded early in 1918, indicates that the officer–man relationships within the 1st Battalion continued their rocky path toward the war's conclusion, and suggests the necessity, at least from an officer's perspective, of establishing and exerting the power inherent in the army's hierarchical structure. Moreover, if such a mean spirit were displayed widely, it suggests that the 1st Battalion mutiny in September 1918 (see Chapter 5) may have been inspired by more than just the physical and mental exhaustion of the men.

The regular occurrence of court-martials, recorded in the Battalion's routine orders, and the prosecution of over one hundred Australian soldiers who were subsequently awarded death sentences during 1916–17—even though it was known that the Australian government would not confirm capital sentences—are proof of the officers' reliance on the disciplinary system.[49] This was a period in which the 1st Battalion was at its most dispirited level and its readiness for further battle after Pozières, as at Bullecourt, was far from optimal. It is during such periods that Stouffer, in his study of American soldiers of the Second World War, found the officer–man relationship, as expressed through favourable comments about a soldier's officers, to be the most strained.[50] It must also be recognised, however, that soldiers writing letters and diaries who were generally satisfied with the *status quo* would not necessarily be drawn to comment on the qualities of their officers. Particularly bad or good officers were likely to be most mentioned. On both counts, one must be wary of attributing too much of their behaviour as being widely representative. Nonetheless, certain plausible generalisations can be advanced.

Class, if not 'everything' as Sergeant Larkin had suggested, was certainly pivotal to the establishment of a distinct officer caste in the 1st Battalion. Officer–man relations were not as even-handed and amicable as suggested in the 'Alf' anecdote. Whatever the antipathies between the two groups, the great redeemer for both officers and other ranks was their performance in battle. Soldiers who could prove themselves through the test of fire earned for themselves great praise from their comrades. If one accepts that acts of indiscipline were a proof of the individuality of Australian soldiers, one needs to ask whether that individuality was replicated where it mattered most, on the battlefield.

3

GALLIPOLI

The landing at Gallipoli on 25 April 1915 was the catalyst for the positive impressions of Australian soldiers and the fledgling nation they represented. According to the legend it proved that Australia's soldiers were the equal to, if not better than, those of other nations. It is a theme that still finds public expression, as the following editorial excerpt reveals: 'The Anzacs demonstrated that Australians are the measure of any other people in the world and that lesson is as pertinent in these days . . . as it was 80 years ago'.[1] Gallipoli set the scene from which the 'digger' stereotype would triumphantly emerge. Through the landing at Anzac Cove, the legend—in the most general terms—advances the qualities of *initiative,* displayed by an irrepressible dash across unexpected rugged terrain; and *resourcefulness,* exemplified through the use of jam-tin bombs to supplement a lack of grenades or the use of time-delay triggers on rifles to cover the withdrawal from Anzac (although both were used at Cape Helles by British troops).

The stereotyping of and admiration for Australian soldiers was quickly established.[2] The first to extol their achievements and ability was the English war correspondent Ellis Ashmead-Bartlett. His despatch of the fighting involving Australian soldiers at Gallipoli set the pattern for much that followed. Apart from the dash and *élan* that he suggested they displayed in battle, Ashmead-Bartlett described a contentment on the part of the Australians, illustrated in the cheerful behaviour of the men least likely to be— the wounded and dying. This was paramount to the fulfilment of the nation's expectation of its soldiers: 'They were happy because they knew they had been tested for the first time, and had not been found wanting'.[3] Any thought that Australian soldiers would be found wanting dissipated after that moment. That Bartlett had observed only the barest outline of the fighting from afar on board the battleship *London* was of little consequence.[4] His positive description swept aside any doubts and anxiety that had been held in Australia about the performance of the nation's army. The reliability of Bartlett's 'eye-witness' account was little doubted. The authenticity of Bartlett's despatch was only corroborated by the publication of Sir Ian Hamilton's report, in which he described the Australian attack: 'Like lightning they leapt ashore, and each man as he did so went straight as his bayonet at the enemy. So vigorous was the onslaught that the Turks made no attempt to withstand it, and fled from ridge to ridge pursued by Australian infantry.'[5]

Ashmead-Bartlett was the first of many British correspondents to be excited by the Australians. The awful modernity of the 1914–18 conflict, which reduced the pageantry of war to a wasteland dominated by industrial might, did not dampen enthusiasm for robust and colourful reporting. Romantic notions and images of war had not dissipated during the late-Victorian and Edwardian period despite the occurrence of bloody conflicts such as the Zulu and Boer wars. The First World War effectively destroyed such notions in European literature in the post-war years, but during the war they still lingered. After the shock of the opening months of the war, and given the increasingly unromantic nature of trench warfare that presented itself in Europe, the Australians (and other Dominion troops) offered salvation to disillusioned writers. Warriors from the other side of the world, from a land that still held many mysteries and dangers, and with their seemingly casual dress and manner which challenged existing military conventions, were a boon to the pens of war correspondents.

John Masefield's description of the Anzacs (and Royal Naval Division) is well known and contains a grace that was seductive to readers: 'For physical beauty and nobility of bearing they surpassed any men I have ever seen; they walked and looked like the kings of old poems' that reminded him of the Shakespearian line: 'Baited like eagles having lately bathed'.[6] Predatory and godlike, the Australians were worthy of the reverence normally reserved for royalty. Similarly, the physique of three Australians, 'not one of whom was less than six feet four inches tall', encountered by Compton MacKenzie were more synonymous with the soldiers and gods of fables.[7] Descriptions such as MacKenzie's have contributed to the identification of athleticism and prowess as typical traits of a tall, bronzed Anzac type. A study of the attestation papers of 1st Battalion soldiers reveals the unlikelihood of MacKenzie's description, since less than 2 per cent of the unit's soldiers exceeded the six foot mark.[8] The poetic language and Trojan backdrop that characterise Masefield's description created a further sense of the epic. The reputation of the Anzacs was further enhanced when Reverend W. H. Fitchett, author of the immensely popular *Deeds That Won the British Empire,* compared the Australian troops, confronted by an 'almost perpendicular cliff' at Gallipoli, with the British soldiers at Waterloo: 'Wellington's lads would not have had the initiative and daring to climb that cliff. That was the "Australian touch".'9 Fitchett's intent was to celebrate not only the qualities of Australia's new heroes but also the manhood of the British Empire. The Australians were a proof of the excellence of British stock in the antipodes. Inadvertently, his description had introduced a further element—the superiority of the Australian soldier over his British counterpart. At an early date then, the alleged qualities of independence and resourcefulness that Australians were considered to possess were equally seen to have been deficient in British troops (particularly the English). This was an aspect of the Anzac legend that would foment over time into a strong anti-British sentiment.

Australian editors joined the celebratory chorus of their British cousins. Independence in action by Australian soldiers was quickly advanced as contributing to the presumed success of operations even though detailed knowledge of the fighting was absent. The early effusive and chauvinistic nationalism had a pragmatic patriotism about it. It was a call for unity in a time of perceived crisis, and the Gallipoli landing acted as a rallying point for greater commitment to the war effort. Had the truth of the confusion and bungling at the landing been conveyed to the public, confidence in the nation's involvement might have been seriously undermined. Contemporary political imperatives of that time should no longer inhibit our pursuit of the truth of the Australian experience. Yet such obfuscation continues to intrude on descriptions of the campaign. A most recent example of the interplay between Australian proficiency and English deficiency (and British *modus operandi*) is provided by Australian historian, Jonathan King. In eulogising the lives of ten Anzacs, King states:

> These are the last of those bronzed gladiators who sprang onto the world stage at Australia's debut, forging a legend that laid the foundations of our identity. All 10 I spoke to fought bravely at Gallipoli, were badly wounded but still got up to fight again when called to the bloody battles in France. They are the ones who refused to say die when landed by British allies at the wrong beach on an impossible suicide mission. Despite that narrow exposed beach and perpendicular cliffs, they repeatedly charged the Turkish guns pointing straight at them from high above. They even succeeded in capturing Turkish forts like Lone Pine, in battles British troops refused to fight.10

The suggestion that British troops 'refused to fight' is unsubstantiated nonsense. That claim, along with the article's rhetoric and the assertion that the Australians were embarked on a 'suicide mission', shows that the Australian public continues to be subjected to serious historical distortions about the performance of Australian and British troops in the Gallipoli campaign.

Geoffrey Moorhouse has posited that the 'popular antipathy' of Australians and New Zealanders toward 'Pommie bastards' and 'bloody Poms' has its genesis in the Gallipoli campaign. Moreover, he asserts: 'Unfortunately, a mythology of craven behaviour at Gallipoli by inferior British troops has never been seriously challenged in Australia and New Zealand, where it is generally assumed to be an accurate account of what happened in 1915'.[11] Moorhouse's observation taps into a significant undertone of the Anzac legend —a strong anti-British sentiment. Another to have detected this sentiment is British historian Robert Rhodes James, who claims Australian journalistic and historical writings are tainted by 'a kind of nationalistic paranoia' in regard to differentiations between Australian and British involvement.[12] King's article is testimony to this.

In regard to the veracity of assumptions about the poor standard of British troops and the high standard of Australian soldiers, Moorhouse is correct— they have not been challenged. King's article, and the attitude of one soldier quoted within, suggests that there is some basis for believing that such bitterness existed and still exists. A 100-year-old Gallipoli veteran, Ted Matthews, is quoted as saying: 'Churchill and his British General, Hamilton, mucked the whole thing up . . . If they had have had an Australian in charge we might of [sic] won Gallipoli.'[13] Matthews' view was revisited in another article in which he claimed:

> When some British soldiers landed at another beach, Cape Helles I think it was, they thought they were going on a picnic. They had lunch on the beach, went for a swim and played soccer before setting off for the cliffs. But the Turks massacred them before they got off the beach. We lasted eight months on a much worse beach.[14]

The testimony of old soldiers is critical to the portrayal and acceptance of the 'digger' stereotype that has been passed down through successive generations.[15] Veterans are accorded special, if not reverential, treatment in our society, particularly in the weeks in which Anzac Day and Remembrance Day fall. Their views on their experience are sought to embellish coverage of those days of remembrance. The alleged deeds of these men, irrespective of how mundane or unheroic their actual war service may have been, are celebrated. Their participation in war is enough to endow them as worthy of the Australian warrior of the legend. They are heroes by association.

The acceptance of the questionable performance of the British is a theme that has become ingrained in Australia's popular memory of the war. When such prejudice appears in the guise of an old digger's personal testimony, it introduces a new audience to the apparent truthfulness—through the words of a revered Gallipoli veteran—of what occurred at Gallipoli. Matthews' view may only be that of one old soldier but when it is published uncritically in a major daily newspaper, as it was, historical accuracy is ill served and the competence of the British further maligned.

Individualism defined

How well, then, did the experience of the 1st Battalion fit the legend? Did these New South Welshman epitomise the rugged resourceful individual of the Anzac legend? As the quality of individualism is central to the argument of this and the following chapters, it is important to establish some definition of it. What is meant by a soldier's individuality or individualism? How do we define it, and was it peculiar to Australian soldiers? Individualism is a term not readily defined in military textbooks or narratives, although it is used often to describe the behaviour of Australian soldiers. It is generally seen as a positive quality and one to be encouraged in the fighting soldier. A 1915 handbook based on official manuals gives the following definition under intelligence and initiative, which encapsulates what individualism is understood to be:

> Military Training teaches the soldier to use his own judgement, to think, make up his mind and act quickly, and when necessary to act on his own initiative. It teaches him to retain presence of mind and to act with determination under the stress of danger. It teaches him to be thoroughly self-reliant and resourceful in emergencies. The day is past when the soldier was more or less an automaton, with his mind entirely subordinated to the will of his officer. Obedience is still, of course, absolutely essential for success in battle. But obedience to orders now calls for the exercise of intelligence and judgement on the part of the soldiers if they are carried out properly.[16]

This expectation of the individual soldier marked a significant shift from previous military doctrine. Furthermore, this desire to empower the individual in battle was not limited to specific soldier groups. In theory it was something that would be reflected in all British soldiers: regulars, territorials and dominion troops. Yet, as we have seen, if Australian indiscipline was a measure of Australian individuality, it was a potentially ruinous quality if allowed to run unchecked—although the legend suggests that the two were not synonymous, through its depiction of the Australian soldier as a natural fighter.

Undefined, individualism remains another of the many intangible qualities that are applied to Australian soldiers. As a social theory that favours free action by individuals, individualism clearly needs some redefinition to fit a military context. Absolute individualism, of course, leads to anarchy. Such potential chaos would clearly render military formations and their function in organised warfare irrelevant. Although chaos was a state that was often reached during the course of battle, it was not something to be encouraged at the outset. Organised warfare requires planning and leadership on the battle-field. It is when these two important factors are compromised that military authorities look to the qualities of their individual soldiers. Individualism in a military context, then, might be described as an ability of the individual soldier to overcome and achieve objectives when confronted by unforeseen circum-stances, in the absence of officers, or when battlefield leadership has been compromised through casualties or other crises.

An important distinction to be made, and one that at times is somewhat contentious, is between individualism and courage on the battlefield. Although the two are not opposites and can exist in tandem, they can also exist separ-ately. On the first day of the Somme offensive, a private of the 8th Battalion East Surreys advanced alone to the farthest objective (over a mile beyond the German front-line trench) before reporting to the nearest commanding officer. He did this after the entire platoon to which he belonged had become a collec-tive casualty. His action fulfils the criteria of individualism. He showed great courage and, given the dire circumstances, great initiative. It was definitely an example of individualism, despite the private's divisional commander citing his achievement as a demonstration of the value of training in that he had continued on to a set objective.[17] Courage, on the other hand, is not necessarily synonymous with individualism. When the 1st Battalion's Private Leonard Keyzor was awarded a Victoria Cross for his actions at Lone Pine, he was cer-tainly displaying conspicuous bravery and devotion to duty—he had held a precarious position during the fighting of 7–8 August and, despite being wounded twice, refused to leave until the situation was stabilised[18]—yet he was not necessarily displaying individualism. We expect courage in soldiers, even though we know that psychological and physical exhaustion can impov-erish a soldier's will to fight to such a degree that courage cannot always be displayed or sustained. To advance toward or face an advancing enemy takes courage, but it is also a standard expectation of a soldier's duty. We do not hold the same expectation of soldiers to be capable of overcoming problems and achieving objectives by themselves. If all soldiers were capable of this there would be no necessity for leaders. Yet the AIF, in particular, and the military in general, held and still hold the value of combat leadership to be essential to the success of an army. Leadership was crucial to the success of Australia's First World War soldiers. Iven Mackay, in his role as commander of the 1st Brigade in 1918, stated: 'Many people such as politicians and news-paper correspondents think that the Australian soldier is born with tactical knowledge and can organise and win battles without officers. He is just as helpless as anybody else would be without officers'.[19] Although Mackay was writing in 1918, his comments were as pertinent, if not more so, to the Aus-tralian soldier of 1915.

The 1st Battalion: 'fit for war'?

Without a benchmark for comparison, the AIF was from the outset its own interpreter; it tried to project a confident face. On 16 February 1915, after two months of training in Egypt and a little over two months before the landing, the Brigadier of 1st Brigade addressed the men and declared them 'fit for war'.[20] This address clearly impressed those that heard it, and it was mentioned by a number of the men as well as being recorded by the 1st Battalion historians.[21] The circumstances and timing of the Brigadier's address added to the power of his words. It was delivered to a parade of the Brigade following the completion of three days' manoeuvres in the desert to complete the men's training.[22] The completion of training and the Brigadier's verbal stamp of approval, in the absence of any previous tradition, carried similar connotations to a passing-out parade.

The Brigadier's words endorsed the men's growing belief in their ability. Already comparisons of competence were being made between the Australians and the English. Noting, misguidedly, that the Turks were inferior in marksmanship, Reg Donkin commented: 'they can't shoot like Australians and nor can the Tommies of old England, so Gen. Birdwood says'.[23] A rapid improvement must have occurred in Australian marksmanship, for three weeks earlier Les Dinning had written to his father, stating: 'If the shooting of the Turks and Germans is no better than that of an average company of Australian Infantry at 900 yards, I think most of us will have a good chance of coming out safely'.[24] Birdwood's role in the creation of Australian morale was important. It is not uncommon for generals to talk their troops up over others, and Birdwood's propensity to do this endeared him to the Australians of the 1st Division. That Birdwood himself was an Englishman gave added substance to his words; he definitely helped imbue the men with a self-confidence and perhaps disingenuously planted the seeds of disdain toward the English soldier that would grow and persist through the war.

Irrespective of the morale-boosting endeavours of its generals, the 1st Battalion and other Australian troops had been inadequately prepared for the Gallipoli campaign. Training had been deficient in a number of areas. Standards in marksmanship had been compromised by a limit imposed during training in Egypt of seventy-five rounds per rifle. Furthermore, field training concentrated on manoeuvres suited for open battlefields with unobstructed fields of fire.[25] In defence of the army's training method it must be said that the desert terrain was hardly conducive to any alternative. In this regard the Turks were better prepared for the initial engagements in the Dardanelles, having trained on the terrain with special consideration given to sniping and throwing hand grenades.[26] Even if training had been tailored to meet the upcoming campaign, it was, in itself, no guarantee to a soldier's success in battle. Only after the experience of combat can a soldier truly assess himself as a fighting man. The soldier's ability to stand or run in the face of battle is the nub on which the fortunes of war so often turn. No amount of training can guarantee a man's response when he moves from the practice and theories of the training ground to face the reality of the battlefield. Hero or coward, according to Elmar Dinter in his study of morale in battle, was the unspoken question of every soldier.[27] It was a question that weighed upon the minds of the Australians as they trained in Egypt and in the final weeks before their baptism of fire. Not only were their own doubts and fears uppermost in the minds of some, but there was also the thought of fulfilling the expectations of those in Australia. As one 1st Battalion soldier commented: 'we are all elated at the thought of "getting at 'em" and proving to all that we can and will do what is expected of us at home'.[28] Officers, too, were desirous of upholding national (and family) honour, as Major Davidson revealed in a letter home: 'I know you would not care to hear of Dad getting a white feather, the Colonel asked me today if he wanted a Coy Commander, would I take it and of course I at once said yes'.[29]

A man's private battle with his own nerves had to be overcome if he were to perform on the battlefield. On the eve of the Gallipoli landing many soldiers began to attune their minds to the immediate future. Private Grant observed that the gaiety on board the transport ship was quickly transplanted by a general mood of solemnity and quiet. It was a change Grant considered 'remarkable' and, he thought, was given added significance by the sight of discarded ammunition packets floating past.[30] Private Alan Mitchell's description, on the other hand, contrasted with Grant's; he described the men's behaviour as that of a lot of schoolboys who spent the day playing pranks on one another. While allowing for a few minutes of pensiveness, Mitchell considered the future something abstract that did not suit introspection and serious thinking. Nevertheless, when the time came, he assured his father, he would 'endeavour to always act the man'.[31]

The resolve of the men was to be tested in the most trying of circumstances. The testimonies of two 1st Battalion men reveal that some of the Australians were still coming to terms with the psychological battle in the moments prior to climbing into the landing boats. Robert Grant's description conveyed not only a vivid scene of the carnage of battle, but also a sense of his own vulnerability:

> The destroyer *Scourge* came alongside. Her funnel was riddled with bullet holes and her decks were slippery with the blood of the wounded she brought to our ship. I watched them slung aboard. Never did I hate a ship more or want to leave it less than I did the *Minnewaska*.[32]

Grant was not alone in his fear and lack of enthusiasm for the fight ahead, as Henry Lanser recorded: 'Senior Sergeant McLaughlin of old F Company planted himself on the *Minnewaska* the day we were to land, he got an attack of cold feet and I am sorry to say many more did too but they did land'. In the same letter, Lanser suggested that another of the sergeants, Douglas Eckford, had shot himself in the big toe and that another comrade, 'big Mitchell', had been spotted digging in (deeply) in a gully 500 yards from the firing line.[33]

Irrespective of the personal demons a soldier had to confront before battle, his endeavours were also subject to influences beyond his private sphere. Good leadership and a sound battleplan were two crucial factors that could assist a soldier in fulfilling the role assigned to him in battle. During the Gallipoli campaign the absence of those two factors would compromise the efficiency and effectiveness of the 1st Battalion on more than one occasion, and the experience gained in battle there, particularly in the first few days, would prove pivotal to the men's definition of themselves as soldiers. When the time of reckoning arrived, thirty officers, of whom only two could claim any previous active service, were to lead 942 other ranks into battle.[34] Most had never before fired a shot in anger. The Battalion, by any military assessment, was an inexperienced one that, on balance, could not realistically be expected to perform with distinction in its first battle.

25–29 April 1915: a landing and a legend established

In any appreciation of a unit's performance in battle, it is essential to understand its assigned role. The actual tasks and achievements of specific Australian battalions have been blurred through general descriptions of Australian soldiers in battle. The role of the 1st Battalion was not the same as the units that formed the initial landing force. The varying terrain of the battlefield and of the battle itself, while often similar, were not the same. The performance of the 1st Battalion cannot, for example, be assessed alongside that of the 7th Battalion, which formed part of the second wave and suffered terribly in their seaward approach to the position known as Fisherman's Hut.[35] Their experiences were sufficiently distinct and peculiar. What, then, was the experience of the 1st Battalion at Gallipoli and particularly at the landing? Was its performance noteworthy and deserving of the high praise generally attributed to the Australians?

On 25 April 1915, a date fixed after rough seas had forced a postponement of two days, the 1st Battalion formed part of the third attacking wave in support of the 3rd 'All Australian' Brigade, which was to land at dawn. The 3rd Brigade was to push inland and consolidate a beach-head to allow the landing of the remainder of the force to carry out the main advance. Thereafter, evidence for the existence of a detailed plan, or at least one understood by the men, is lacking, as the 1st Battalion history records:

> We knew very little of the actual plans for the attack. In fact, the whole thing seemed to be rather up in the air, and so it proved. We understood that the 3rd Brigade was to land from warships at 4 am., and endeavour to rush the enemy positions and hold on until the rest of the Division got ashore—and that was about all.[36]

Brigade operation orders, issued on 20 April, were quite specific about what the men were to carry and how they were to conduct themselves during the landing phase of the operation. They did not, however, address any details about objectives for the battalions.[37] The historian of the 3rd Battalion stated:

> The instructions which had been issued to all ranks in the division the night before the Landing were explicit. In them was nothing that could possibly be misunderstood. In effect, they were the orders given to the 3rd Brigade—'push on at all costs'.[38]

Orders that required soldiers to 'push on at all costs' made the assumed initiative of the Australians in scaling the scrubby knolls and ridges at Gallipoli a matter of course. In pushing inland the Australians were simply obeying their orders and not employing any great initiative in doing so. The general nature of the order was, of course, to prove disastrous. The headlong pursuit of the enemy that the orders implied ultimately resulted in many small parties advancing unsupported and being overrun as Turkish supports reinforced their positions.[39]

The day prior to the landing the Commander-in-Chief, Sir Ian Hamilton, had issued a General Order to all troops and told them that the eyes of the world were upon them and that he knew they would succeed with the help of God and the Navy.[40] For the Australians, as representatives of a nation that had yet to make the 'blood-sacrifice' that characterised the emergence of so many European nations, Hamilton's worldly rhetoric had special poignancy: would the Australians' deeds measure up to the military traditions of the established nations?[41]

In the dark of the morning of the 25th, with the General's confidence and the belief that they were about to enter the world's stage, the men were sent below decks to breakfast. There, with the sounds of battle from the shore clearly audible, they settled down to what would be for some the last hot meal for days and for others, like condemned men, the final meal before fate overtook them.

The battle had been in progress for nearly two hours before the 1st Brigade was called to reinforce the 2nd and 3rd Brigades.[42] At about 7 am the 1st Battalion prepared to disembark from its transport. Unlike the covering force that landed at dawn, the 1st Battalion landed in comparative safety. The lead companies of the Battalion clambered down onto the decks of a destroyer, which then dashed to within fifty yards of the shore and lowered its boats for the men to make the final leg of the journey, each boat under the guidance of a Royal Navy midshipman. The men, in groups of thirty to forty per tow, were set down in waist-deep water. They had already heard the firing from afar and had witnessed the broken bodies of the wounded being returned to the ships. Now they waded ashore and were greeted by the full sound of battle and the aroma of trampled wildflowers.[43] With the main fighting taking place beyond MacLagan's Ridge, the Battalion was relatively untroubled in its approach to shore, although some casualties were inevitable. Private Reg Killick witnessed nine men from his landing boat killed outright.[44] Once ashore, the companies were formed in an orderly manner and awaited their orders. Those orders, when received, were vague. According to Brigadier-General H. Gordon Bennett, then a major and second-in-command of 6th Battalion, the instruction given to each company was: 'move over that hill and reinforce the firing line'.[45] The exact whereabouts of the firing line (a position subject to many shifts in the first few hours and the following days) could only be guessed at by the units collecting on the beach as they tried to adjust to the surroundings. Private V. E. Jones thought the battlefield, with its shady ravines, holly and wildflowers 'would be a nice place for a picnic' and added somewhat surrealistically: 'I received my first wound while laying in a lovely bed of daisies'.[46]

Having formed on the beach, the Battalion was sent toward the firing on the right flank. Some casualties were sustained in the advance to the first ridge without significant loss of formation, but in the rush to the second ridge, under heavy rifle fire and with casualties mounting, the various companies and platoons quickly lost touch. How easily men could become separated is shown in the following incident. When Private Grant's company (B) moved off, he found himself left behind with three others. Major Swannell's D Company was the last of the Battalion to arrive on the beach and he ordered Grant's party to join him. The Major sent Grant and his companion, Private Hall, forward to identify a group of men that could be seen ascending a hill. Grant moved off and identified the men but when he signalled back he found Swannell had already moved on. Grant and Hall then took shelter and discussed their next move. Grant decided to join an ammunition party and commenced carrying ammunition to a depot established midway between the beach and firing line, while Hall decided to wait and join the next party moving up to the firing line.[47]

The 1st Battalion history found it difficult to give a coherent story of the Battalion's actions in the opening days of the campaign because its companies were so mixed and split. It placed the companies, albeit indefinitely, in the following positions—A Company was in advance of the Pimple in the vicinity of Lone Pine with B Company on its right; C Company lay between Wire Gully and the Chess Board; and Swannell's D Company held a line on the left just above the Fisherman's Hut and extending to Pope's Hill.[48] Writing to his father, Private V. E. Jones of Captain McGuire's B Company described the advance from the beach:

> We had to advance over two hills and we had shrapnel and snipers at us all the time. As we were badly needed we had to go at the double. I will never forget that run as long as I live. When we reached them, there was only 6 of my company with our 3 officers and we had to wait till the others came up. I wasn't sorry for the spell either. When they came up we made a final dash to the firing line. I was sadly disappointed when I got there, for there was not a Turk visible and we were under a hail of fire from shrapnel and machine guns. It was very annoying laying down with shrapnel and bullets cutting the ground all around and not being able to respond. Some of our chaps blazed away on chance of getting something but as we were told to save ammunition I only fired one shot.[49]

One of the most perplexing aspects of the battle, as Jones suggested, was the invisibility of the enemy. The men scrambled to take advantage of every possible cover from the murderous fire of their unseen host. Frederick Muir remembered the situation as being 'a case of every man for himself'.[50] With the Battalion's disintegration, its use as an effective fighting instrument diminished. By the afternoon effectiveness was lost; most were lying low, attempting to preserve themselves until dark so that they could safely entrench. An unnamed officer, whose account was quoted at length in the Battalion history, recollected feeling 'considerably disgusted' by the confusion and recalled the men as seemingly 'suffering from a paralysing inertia'.[51] Tony Ashworth in his study of trench warfare interpreted inertia as symbolising 'a willingness to give up the choice of aggression'.[52] As such, it stands in direct contrast to the warrior image of the stereotypical 'digger'.

The account of Captain H. G. Carter, commander of the original E Company but second in command of B Company at the landing, confirmed the existence of confusion and terror within the 1st Battalion ranks. Carter assumed command of the Company within five minutes when his commanding officer, Captain McGuire, 'stopped one in the stomach'.[53] His account concurs with others as to the utter confusion of the Battalion and he had to rally, on two occasions, men retiring in disorder. The final break of the advanced position came about 4.30 pm when the line in front of the Bloody Angle gave way and the men came running back shouting what they no doubt considered sound advice to their colleagues: 'Get to buggery. The Turks are coming on—thousands of them.'[54] To Carter the moral effect of the shrapnel

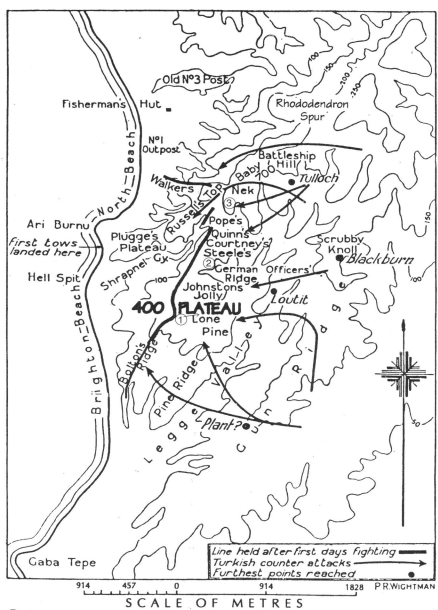

① The Daisy Patch
② MacLaurins Hill
③ The Chessboard

Australian strategic positions on the first day of fighting, mostly clustered around
the dominant position Australia failed to capture (*Winter*, 25 April 1915, p. 157).

on the men was the worst aspect and he, a combat officer, found himself lying on his stomach hardly daring to move until nightfall, when he was able to report to Brigade Headquarters on the beach. Carter's paralysis was symptomatic of the general state of the Battalion's front line by that stage in the afternoon. Brigade HQ was completely out of touch with the front line and not even in signal contact. The beach had become crowded with the wounded and hundreds of men lost and disorientated by the day's events. Carter returned to the firing line and tried to instil some semblance of order to the scattered and intermixed troops within his immediate vicinity.[55] Some 300 stragglers of the Battalion, representing at the very least 30 per cent of its line strength, had collected on the beach by the evening of the 26th and they were held in reserve just below the junction of Shrapnel Gully and Monash Valley from where they were used as supports for the firing line.[56]

How innocently this straggling could occur is apparent in the experience of Les Dinning and John Reid. Reid, who had been wounded in the head, was carried to safety by his best mate Dinning (who had himself been slightly wounded in the arm the previous day). Reid wrote later: 'As I said goodbye to Les and left him to return to the fighting I felt as if I were deserting him'.[57] Dinning, in leaving the line to carry his mate to safety, had in fact compromised the efficiency of the Battalion. The clearance of the wounded was a job for designated stretcher-bearers, undermanned and overworked as they were. Dinning's actions, however, were hardly surprising. There were few men among these early citizen soldiers sufficiently imbued with military discipline to abandon their best friend. Dinning did return to the fight. His action was probably repeated many times over on that day. The large numbers of stragglers, however, suggest that many of the men did not share Dinning's devotion to duty. Irrespective of the obvious harm such actions had on maintaining the strength of the front line, Dinning's action was acclaimed publicly through the publication of his friend's letter. The article, basically a letter by Reid to Dinning's father, is headed 'Saved by his Chum' and begins 'Pte. Jack Reid, writing to a Sydney friend, tells of the heroism of his chum'.[58]

Those who had survived the dangers of the first day and had remained in the front line experienced a trying night. Lying with a dead and a dying man on either side of him, Private Muir pondered on how long it would be until his turn came. Entrenching was not rendered any easier by the actions of the men who had discarded their entrenching tools during the advance. Overcoats, too, had been cast off in similar fashion and their loss was rued when steady rain fell through the night. To discomfort was added the sounds of what one contributor to the Battalion's history described as a 'medley run riot':

Bugles (really Turkish) blowing the 'Cease fire'; messages, reports, rumours, inform-ation that the troops in front were Indians. Then the news that such information was false, alarms and false alarms of attacks, sudden panics, and so on kept the rifles going all through the night, firing into the darkness at nothing and keeping our pluck up.[59]

The failure of the Australians to expand the beach-head left them in a con-fined position that precluded opportunities for manoeuvre. At its deepest point the Anzac position extended no more than a thousand yards from the beach and was only a mile and a half in length. Into this area were crammed some 20,000 soldiers. The most stultifying aspect was that the Turks held the higher ground. This, as well as the lack of artillery support and numerical inferiority of the attackers after the first day, offered little chance for the Australians to break out of the position. It was equally true that if the Aus-tralians stood their ground the Turks could not break in. Modern rifles and machine-guns manned by entrenched and resolute defenders would beat down most frontal assaults.

One of the ironies of the first days of battle was that many of the wounded who were returned to Australia and feted as 'Heroes of the Dardanelles' had had little opportunity to engage the enemy. Indeed, some of them had not even fired a shot at the enemy. These men had not gained any substantial experi-ence of battle, yet in the eyes of the public they were heroes and veterans. They could not claim to have demonstrated the qualities of the stereotype, but they provided the first tangible proof of Australia's contribution to the Empire's war effort.[60] Privately they expressed indignation at the hand they had been dealt. Wrote one soldier to his brother:

> I only lasted in the firing line for about four hours . . . I think it is very hard for most of the chaps to train for nine months, and then get potted out the first day: but I sup-pose we will get our revenge, although a lot of us will have to come back to Australia without another chance at the enemy.[61]

The disorganised state of fighting of the first day continued into the next. At midday, 26 April, General Bridges visited the front line and began to re-organise and straighten the line. Captain Carter recorded: 'General Bridges himself came along and ordered us out of our trenches to join in the advance'.[62] Two platoons of the 4th Battalion were ordered forward as part of this movement, as well as a portion of the 1st Battalion. The movement ordered required a change in front and advance by the right flank. The men moved off smartly over the open ground but heavy shrapnel, machine-gun and rifle fire soon drove them back. The men were rallied and began to dig in on a steep-sided valley. At night Carter's line was able to fall back to the main defensive line.[63] Carter despaired at the fact 'there was no-one in charge of us and nobody knew what to do'.[64] Such was the disintegration of the Battalion that an outline map sketched by a staff officer, Major Glasfurd of the 1st Division, placed it as only one of a number of 'bits' of battalions making up the centre of the Australian line on the 27th.[65]

The Battalion was withdrawn from the line on Thursday, 29 April, and assembled at the northern end of Brighton Beach, a little south of Hell Spit. It was the first opportunity for many of the men to rejoin the Battalion since becoming separated on the first day. Roll-call was taken and the survivors were confronted with the grim extent of the casualties. Captain Carter listed B Company's casualties as: '9 killed 65 wounded (incl 4 officers) and 28 missing'. Carter himself was exhibiting symptoms of nervousness as he stood on the beach. The noise of the naval guns got on his nerves and he noticed himself continually fidgeting.[66] The Brigade commander, Colonel MacLaurin, was dead, as were a number of other senior officers. Over 50 per cent of the Battalion's officers were casualties, many the victims of deadly accurate sniper fire. Major Bill Swannell, an international rugby footballer and well liked throughout the Battalion, was among the dead. According to one soldier,

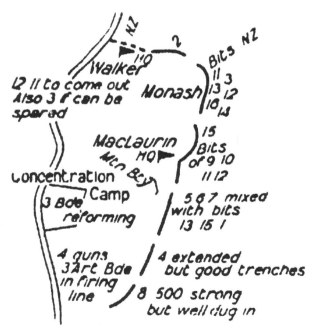

Dispositions of mixed units, copied by Bean from Major Glasfurd's notebook, 27 April 1915.

Swannell had his 'head half blown off' as he called for his men to undertake a bayonet charge.[67] The matter-of-fact manner of that description contrasts with Bean's heroic sketch: 'Swannell had felt sure he would be killed, and had said so on the *Minnewaska* before he landed, for he realised that he would play this game as he had played Rugby football—with his whole heart. Now, while kneeling in order to show his men how to take better aim at a Turk, he was shot dead.'[68] Bean's description portrayed a clean and idealistic death that highlights the disjuncture between actuality and myth.

In light of the Battalion's experience, what judgement can be made of its performance? The actions described offer some scope for criticism of the historical construction of Australian performance at the landing. The high percentage of men who drifted back to the beach was not a sign of efficiency in battle, although it would not be unexpected of untried troops. A contributing factor in this was without doubt the absence of officers in many parts of the field. Reg Donkin referred to this problem: 'All day I never saw any of our own officers—all out of action, dead or wounded and the sergeants also—It was impossible to keep sections together or even companies'.[69] The blind nature of the fight also compromised performance, with the troops fighting without clear objectives. This had a demoralising effect. While the officers of the smaller formations attempted to lead from the front, most did so with no clear directives from above. The *Official History* is glowing in its portrayal of the Battalion's second-in-command, Major Kindon, yet strangely silent on the performance of its commander, Lieutenant-Colonel Dobbin. In his description of the first week's fighting, in particular that on '400 Plateau', Bean mentioned Dobbin in only one sentence: 'Thither also the headquarters of the battalion under Colonel Dobbin eventually found their way'.[70] The use of the word 'eventually', in this instance, appears to be an example of polite reproach by the official historian. Certainly Dobbin does not appear to have imposed his presence on the field. The entry in the Battalion diary for the period states: 'The whole Bn was thrown into the firing line and worked independently of Bn hdqrs'.[71] Despite the confusion, there were great acts of valour. Apart from the many unrecognised acts, nine officers, six NCOs and two privates were mentioned in Army Corps orders for conspicuous gallantry and valuable services during the period 25 April to 5 May. The most revealing of these, in regard to the Battalion's performance, was the award of a Distinguished Conduct Medal to Lance-Corporal T. Kennedy 'for displaying the greatest coolness and pluck in running round under heavy fire and *collecting stragglers, whom he formed and led into the firing line. This he did time after time with excellent results.*'[72] Many of the men had faltered, but in the end the Battalion, despite its fragmentation, had stuck; it was that fact which provided a base for the men to build a reputation.

The 1st Battalion had not shown itself to be an outstanding unit at the landing. It had straggled badly and had not been well led. Courageously led at times, certainly, but not efficiently so. Similarly, some of its men had displayed exceptional courage, and in accordance with the Division's pre-battle instructions, had attempted to 'push on at all costs'; some, not all. One of the Battalion's signalmen wrote candidly about the Battalion's performance:

> Owing to lack of discipline and confidence in our officers very few of our unit remained together. This was the same throughout the whole of the Division. It was days before we got the Battalion in anything like order.[73]

A private's account of the second day's fighting confirmed the leadership vacuum with which the Australian NCOs had to contend: 'The various battalions were now hopelessly mixed and the loss of officers was being badly felt. Sergeants would send messages down the line asking for instructions.'[74] On that day the sergeants' actions were hardly indicative of a desire to 'push on at all costs' as had been the order of the previous day. Their circumspection was not surprising and certainly more sensible. The position at Anzac had changed. The Turkish counter-attack had contained the landing, and the mindset of the senior Anzac leaders had shifted from attack to defence.[75] The sergeants' actions reveal that cohesive action and displays of initiative and resourcefulness were unlikely without officers to direct the men. When the perimeters within which troops must work cannot be set (through the necessary orders) then the role of the individual in combat is severely limited. Overall, it could not be said that the 1st Battalion's experience supported the Anzac legend's portrayal of Australian soldiers being resourceful and displaying initiative. On the contrary, their inexperience in conjunction with the poor planning and rough terrain had quickly rendered them ineffective as an offensive force.

Self-reflection of performance

When the situation at Anzac stabilised, it allowed the soldiers time to reflect on the momentous events of the first few days. They began to assess their performance. Private Jones doubted if any troops had 'ever viewed such a baptism of fire' and thought the men would now think nothing of ordinary fire.[76] Jones' phraseology was indicative of the language of the time and, apart from it being a common reference to a soldier's first battle, carried the wider connotation of this battle being a national rite of admission to something larger, something only vaguely defined. William Swindells, in a statement which reflected the desire to measure up to British regulars which had been instilled into the men during training in Egypt, believed that 'no regular regiment in the World could have done more or bore up under such trying circumstances better than our chaps and I am sure it will live in history forever'.[77] John Reid held a similar conviction, though he reserved his highest praise for the troops that had preceded the 1st Battalion: 'How the 3rd Brigade charged up here and drove the Turks back surprised us as we followed on, and its accomplishments must stand as a great military feat'.[78] How *great* a feat was a subject of some distortion, as one soldier's diary reveals: 'The operation of landing the army in the face of modern weapons in spite of wire entanglements in parts 50 yards wide and under the sea as well as on the land, land mines, and deep pits with spikes at the bottom, has thus been accomplished'.[79] Major William Davidson, an ex-Seaforth Highlander and man of twenty-three years' service in the military forces of his adopted country, also highly praised the Australians. After hearing of the response in Australia to the landing, he wrote: 'The people of Australia I hear had a great day when they heard of the success of our boys, they may well be proud of her representation, no troops in the world could have fought better than they did'.[80] As a senior officer, Davidson had probably been privy to Australia's response via cabled information to Headquarters and the official war correspondents. Whether he confined such comment to his letters or communicated similar information to the troops is unknown. For other ranks, the wait was at least two weeks before mail was received after the first news reports of the landing.

Some of the first letters home describing the fighting suggest that the men's response was free from any influence, at least from kith and kin, as their descriptions were often prefaced by phrases that assumed their readers had heard of the landing and were clearly written before any letters or newspapers had been received that detailed the commencement of the fighting. For example, John Reid wrote to his friend's father: 'Knowing that you will be anxious to learn how we fared as soon as you hear that the Australians were in action at the Dardanelles I have taken the liberty to write to you.'[81] Two weeks after the Landing, Frederick Muir wrote: 'I see from your later letter that you had then heard of our landing: we are anxiously waiting to see the Australian papers with the detail of our doing.'[82] This time lapse is crucial to understanding the process of affirmation regarding the men's view of themselves as soldiers. By the time of the Turkish counter-attack of 19 May, they had established in their own minds, quite independently of the lavish praise generated in and refracted back from Australia, a positive view of their abilities and one not necessarily supported by the Battalion's performance. In addition, the soldiers' comments reinforced the laudatory exclamations of the press and gave added resonance to the high praise bestowed upon the Australian soldier. Furthermore, the press reports were read avidly by the soldiers (generals, too) and Ashmead-Bartlett's celebratory despatch, in particular, fed the self-acclamation that had already been expressed by the men. General Birdwood was among those keen to gain a copy of Bartlett's despatch: 'I heard that a good account of our landing had appeared in the papers by Ashmead-Bartlett . . . you must keep it as they tell me he writes well'.[83] A 1st Battalion officer who had read the report declared: 'Bartlett's account of the landing is true to a word'.[84] The men of the 1st Battalion believed they had performed heroically.

If the soldiers of the 1st Battalion had harboured any doubts about inadequacies in their performance, it was not long before they were appeased by the alleged poor performance of the Royal Naval Brigade. The 1st Brigade was relieved by two battalions of the Royal Marine Light Infantry (RMLI) on 29 April and returned to the lines on 1 May. The performance of the Marines during the intervening period was to have a profound effect on the Australians' interpretation of English ability. The Marines were a regular British regiment with a long tradition and the Australians were surprised to find their relief to be raw young recruits, little resembling what they expected of British regulars.[85] A portion of these troops were driven from their trenches on the first night in Wire Gully and this fact, irrespective of the many extenuating circumstances surrounding it, was seized upon as a point of pride and honour, tinged with a sense of national superiority. Writing about a year later, Archie Barwick was scathing in his recollection of the event:

> now we thought at that time that the English soldiers were unbeatable, but we soon had that silly idea knocked out of our heads, for they were no sooner in one trench taken by the 4th Brigade than they lost it, and the 15th Batt had to retake it and help them hold it.[86]

Not all were imbued with Barwick's disdain. E. M. Luders noted that the Naval Brigade and the Marines had been subjected to 'several heavy counterattacks and they had all they could do to hold on to their position'.[87] Frederick Muir was another who wrote home about the landing and subsequent events but without malice about the failure of the Marines. His account, too, confirmed that the Marines had had a difficult position to hold: 'Lying close to our trenches were several Marines and New Zealanders, who had been killed while trying to entrench themselves, and who could not be brought in owing to the heavy fire'. Muir's interest in the Marines was more narcissistic. He gloried in their praise of the Australians being 'mad' (a compliment to their storming of the heights—a feat the Marines suggested was worthy of medals the size of soup plates). As well, he noted their eagerness to swap their pith helmets for the slouch hat of the Australians and commented: 'they flattered themselves they looked like Australians'.[88]

Although the diaries and letters of the soldiers reveal little immediate antipathy toward the Marines (Barwick's diaries were written after the campaign), it is plausible that the Marines' performance was quickly and openly derided. Bean was quick to pass comment in his diary: 'our Australian troops are good and the Naval people feeble . . . these poor RMLI and Naval Brigade lads seem unfitted to hard fighting'.[89] General Birdwood, too, held a low opinion of the Naval Division troops, although his view may have been shaped more by the health of the Marines. When they were transferred elsewhere he confided to his wife that he was 'not at all sorry . . . as they were nearly useless'.[90] If such sentiments emanated from Headquarters and staff, it is likely they held sway in the ranks. Steel and Hart have emphatically opposed the Australian view of the Marines. Their account of the Marines' actions at Gallipoli exemplifies how degrees of emphasis shape historical accounts. They make only oblique reference to the Marines' withdrawal (an incident critical to the shaping of Australian perceptions) and mention that the first Victoria Cross awarded at Anzac was won by Lance-Corporal Walter Parker of the Portsmouth Battalion.[91] Of the Marines' performance, they state:

> The sharp criticism of these troops, many of whom had already been in the line for four days and defeated a concerted Turkish attack, which has frequently been directed against them, is unfounded and in fact, despite moments in the line on MacLaurin's Hill when their inexperience showed, the RND's [Royal Naval Division] time at Anzac was not discreditable.[92]

Even if the naval battalions were inferior to Australian units they were not necessarily a reflection of the quality of all English troops. Their inferior quality, real or imagined, provided a convenient deflection for criticisms of Australian performance. It also provided the cornerstone on which Australian troops' feeling of superiority over English troops would continue to build. The 2nd Australian Brigade's advance against Krithia spur, a week later, where they advanced further than any of the previous attackers, also provided a measurable proof for adherents of Australian superiority.[93]

Other 1st Battalion actions

The lack of any tangible evidence of marked resourcefulness and initiative in the actions of the 1st Battalion during the landing was also true of their three other major actions on Gallipoli—the Turkish attack of 19 May, the raid on German Officer's Trench, and Lone Pine. The failure of the Turkish attack on 19 May is commonly cited as marking a change in the attitude of Australian soldiers to their enemy, whom they saw as gallant and, above all, human and little different from themselves.[94] After four days an armistice was arranged for the burial of the dead and removal of any wounded lucky enough to be still alive. The armistice allowed some of the men to fraternise briefly with the enemy. The gruesome sights of the massed Turkish dead may have had a sobering effect on many but for Reg Donkin, to stand impotent within twenty yards of the enemy was a matter of great vexation: 'God! How I wished I could kill the whole lot and not damage our lads.'[95] It revealed other things too. An entrenched defender clearly had an advantage over an enemy attacking frontally over open ground. Also, a battle in which the Battalion stood crowded in their trenches, firing on the enemy as if 'shooting rabbits, coming out of a warren',[96] is hardly proof of resourcefulness or initiative. On 19 May, the Battalion had fought courageously. However, nothing in the nature of the fight supported or allowed for displays of initiative or resourcefulness. The Turks had offered easy targets and had been shot down accordingly. The courage of the men to stand in the face of the onslaught, even though firing from the protection of their trenches, is not doubted. Some men sat above or astride the parapets so that they could take better aim, exposing themselves recklessly to greater risk of harm. Such individual acts of valour (or stupidity) were not proof of individualism as we have defined it.

The tactical advantage of the defender was further highlighted in the 1st Battalion raid on German Officer's Trench, on 5 June 1915. This was one of the few major raids conducted at the Anzac position. The absence of an expansive, flat no man's land precluded the use of raiding as a viable or worthwhile tactic. The purpose of this raid was to silence a machine-gun that had prevented patrolling in front of Courtney's Post and which threatened to compromise an upcoming attack. The attack was undertaken to eradicate the machine-gun that would have played upon a New Zealand attack against the Turk's position at Quinn's. That attack was part of a larger demonstration to support a third offensive at Cape Helles.[97]

The raid was arranged following the failure of an earlier attack on the evening of 4 June and was meant to have taken place before moonrise. It actually took place after moonrise, a fact attributed to the moon not being visible from Divisional HQ which was located on the beach, below the position to be assaulted. Five men were killed and twenty-eight wounded in this ill-planned escapade, and the destruction of the machine-gun (which in all likelihood would have been replaced), though reported, remained in doubt. The plan showed little imagination on the part of the Australian commanders and required little initiative of its soldiers. It was a straightforward charge across open ground. After the rush of the first line, the second line started forward but was ordered back as the first was already returning. Sergeant Higbid, who had been wounded as the Australians fell back, was able to find some positives in the engagement. The supposed success of the mission was one, and as another he added: 'Isn't it wonderful 36 men were hit and only three killed'.[98] The Turkish defenders, had they known the Australian casualty figures, would probably have drawn comfort from the 72 per cent strike rate they had scored with their rifles and machine-guns.

Despite Higbid's optimism, ill-conceived missions of this nature served only to undermine the men's confidence in their leaders. This was evident from a postscript to the raid the following night. On that night the Battalion's most recognised scout, Sergeant Harry Freame, took two others on a patrol to verify the destruction of the machine-gun. This done, Freame's party began their return to the lines, where tragedy visited the scout's offsiders. A shot from their own lines struck Thomas Elart in the face and the bullet passed through him and hit his companion, Walter Morris, who was following behind. Elart died from the wounds while Morris, who lost an eye, survived. Following the heavy loss the previous day, this incident was recorded with bitterness by one soldier: '[two] of our men shot by our own blooming fools, our officers to blame, one of which should be shot for manslaughter he is not fit to be in charge of Cadets in Australia'.[99]

Despite the patrol's failure, it was still advanced as an example of Australian courage and dedication. Bean chose to feature Freame's mission in a despatch to Australia. The story had obvious appeal to his journalistic eye and the tale, as told by him, was clearly designed to appeal to people's patriotism. It had a scout of mixed origins who had fought in a number of small wars and resembled a Mexican bandit in appearance. Above all, it was a story of moral redemption. Thomas Elart, whose real name was Thomas Hart, had previously served as a sailor on board HMAS *Australia* but had deserted prior to the war. The war provided an opportunity for him to redeem himself and wipe out the shame he felt for his previous behaviour. This he detailed in a letter to his divisional commander prior to going out with Freame. Bean summed up the 'boy's' death with patriotic flourish: 'Elart had achieved his honour—and Australia's'.[1] Bean's elevation of Elart's death masked the waste of lives as well as the bitterness felt within the ranks toward the officers who planned the disaster. In its place Bean advanced an idealised view of sacrifice to provide the nation with higher meaning and comfort as compensation for the death of its soldiers.

There was another story in Bean's despatch for those who looked closely enough. If we accept that Bean's account is accurate and free of invention then we are presented also with an account of men (possibly) going back on their word and leaving a job to others—in this case, according to Bean, to two of the Battalion's youngest members. Bean wrote:

> So he [Freame] set out to choose two men. A good many had made him offers after previous excursions. 'Look, Harry,' they said, 'the next time you're going out, let me know—I'd like to come with you.' He went to hunt up some of these, but they were not forthcoming. Then he thought of two youngsters—two New South Wales boys— two of the youngest in the battalion.[2]

That men would be reluctant to volunteer themselves for a scouting mission, which could only be expected to be hazardous given the casualties sustained the previous night, was hardly surprising and perhaps indicated that a sense of self-preservation had developed among them. The raid on German Officer's Trench and the disastrous end to Freame's scouting mission challenge the notion of any exceptional prowess on the part of the 1st Battalion generally. Portraits of Freame himself, however, have contributed to impressions of the individuality and resourcefulness of the Australians in general. His exploits, including an unsubstantiated account of an escape from behind the Turkish lines, were featured in a post-war series of the AIF's outstanding personalities.[3]

As with the landing and 19 May, Lone Pine offers few examples upon which a general claim of Australian resourcefulness and initiative can be based. A thorough discussion of the fighting at Lone Pine is beyond the purview of this study; suffice to say that Lone Pine resembled a charnel house in which men were slaughtered and maimed in droves. The living, at times, were dependent on rations taken from the haversacks of the dead.[4] After three days' solid fighting the Australians had virtually secured the trenches at Lone Pine and repulsed a number of desperate counter-attacks. A number of new reinforcements were rushed into the fight. The experiences of these men were traumatic and their inexperience was directly responsible for the death of some. The battle assumed the proportions of the worst nightmare come true for many of the new men among the Battalion's supports. The Battalion's 5th Reinforcements had arrived the previous day and the 6th Reinforcements arrived early in the morning of the day of the attack. There was to be no ac-climatisation period for these men and they were to gain as bloody a baptism as the originals on the day of the landing. It was with 'horror and fright' that J. B. Bell responded to the news that he was to be sent straight into what he thought was 'a fairly severe fight'. He had thought the men would be rested at the beach till daylight. Bell was 'frightened to death at first' but got through three days without sleep, experiencing what he described as 'a jittery time'.[5] The sight of so many wounded and his inability to assess Turkish reaction to the fighting had almost driven him 'Battle mad' and he had been possessed by a compelling desire to leave the trench and charge. Fortunately cooler heads prevented him.[6] Captain H. G. Carter described a similarly inspired incident that illustrates exactly what Bell's fate might have been: 'one poor chap tried to look over but got one thro' the head—dropped like a log—a new reinforcement chap too—they do not realise what they are in for'.[7]

The guilt associated with the fate of some of those men was evident in the recollections of the 1st Division's Chief of Staff, Colonel C. B. B. White:

> no recollection is more bitter than the complaints of the men themselves that they had not had sufficient training to give them a fair chance. That complaint was made to me bitterly before the battle of Lone Pine, and, in such few hours that remained to us efforts were made to remedy the deficiency. But time was not available, and the need of the men was great, and ever, in consequence, rests upon our consciences a deep sense of the responsibility incurred.[8]

Natural abilities were no substitute for appropriate training. Nor did slaughter-houses, as the trenches at Lone Pine were, provide scope for manoeuvre and the expression of such abilities.

As a military achievement the fight at Lone Pine stands as a testament to the courage of the men who fought there. It was a mind-numbing and horrific experience. As one Australian soldier who looked upon the carnage noted: 'The major is standing next to me and he says "Well we have won". Great God—won—what means a victory and all those bodies within arms reach— then may I never witness a defeat'.[9] Again, as with the engagement of 19 May, the action did not allow for general displays of individualism. Perhaps the most enduring image in the public memory of Lone Pine is of Australian soldiers ripping up the pine logs that roofed the Turkish trenches. A diorama of this incident has been on constant display at the Australian War Memorial. The log covering had not been expected and it might be argued that this action of the Australians, in ripping it up, was a display of initiative. It certainly embraces our definition as it was an act that was not prefaced in the attack orders. It was the men in the first waves of the attack who had to confront and dismantle the obstacle, not the supporting wave. The 1st Battalion was quickly pushed into the fight but ten minutes had elapsed before they set off. Doubtless, some of the 1st Battalion would have engaged in this work but they certainly did not instigate it. The experience of the 1st Battalion in both battles and raids at Gallipoli was hardly supportive of the stereotypical qualities of the legend. This was of little concern to commentators at the time whose national and imperial values were best served by advancing positive descriptions about Australian soldiers. Those views have, over time, coalesced and contributed to the formation of a 'digger' stereotype that continues to be projected.

After Lone Pine many of the Battalion's soldiers, having experienced and witnessed the grisly sights of the battlefield, lost any enthusiasm they might have had for war. Les Dinning, in a letter to his step-mother, described his dread at the thought of charging across a gully known as the 'Valley of Despair'. He hoped that any attempt was some time off and that they were only holding the trenches.[10] To an auntie he had declared: 'every man jack here will tell you that he has had enough of it, that five months hell is enough for anyone, and that there are enough spare men in Australia to take our places'.[11] It is questionable whether men imbued with such feelings would display much initiative in their soldiering, except, perhaps, in the instinctive urge for self-preservation which could assert itself in two ways in the front line. A soldier could be careful to take no risks, which of course compromised any notions of enterprise that his commanders hoped to cultivate. On the other hand, during intense fighting such as that of 19 May and Lone Pine, it could translate itself into the brutal and simple philosophy of 'Kill or be killed'.

Lone Pine was the last major fight of the Battalion on Gallipoli. It was one of a series of diversionary attacks at Anzac to prevent Turkish reserves being sent to the Suvla area, where a surprise landing was being conducted by British troops on 7 August 1915. The failure of the new offensive at Suvla sounded the death knell for the continuance of the campaign. Like the Helles and Anzac landings, the British landing at Suvla had been contained and the deadlock remained. Perhaps the greatest legacy of the campaign emanated from the Lone Pine fight and the perceptions of the British failure at Suvla. The failure of the Marines had already provided the Australians with one example that made the alleged Suvla ineptitude all the more believable. The lack of blame in the diaries and letters of the 1st Battalion reflected the fact that the men were really only aware of events in their immediate vicinity. Thus the performance of the Marines drew comment whereas the landing at Suvla, occurring some miles to the north, was little mentioned. However, with the publicity surrounding the Dardanelles Commission, which coincided with the expansion of the AIF and its training prior to arriving in France, it was not long before an Australian version of events was in place. Archie Barwick, who was a private at the time of the withdrawal from Anzac, lends support to Moorhouse's hypothesis of Australian antipathy. An entry in his diary conveys an intense feeling of pride and sheets home the ultimate failure of the campaign squarely to the English troops:

> How it hurt to leave all our mates who were lying buried there at the mercy of the Turks. You can imagine for yourself but the bitterest part about it was the Suvla Bay failure, they had a child's task compared to the Australians and New Zealanders but they missed their opportunity, while our weak Brigade was holding up and battling with a whole Division of Turks at Lone Pine they were fooling about on the beach at Suvla instead of finishing on for all they were worth. The 1st Division and New Z

held practically the whole of the Turkish Army up for nearly 2 days and nights so as to allow the English troops who landed at Suvla to seize the ridges running to 971 and Anafarta. They failed miserably as we all know and our losses were in vain.[12]

Barwick was admittedly always passionate in his description of events and his words convey a strong sense of martyrdom. His interpretation is mirrored and perpetuated in Weir's film, *Gallipoli*, the 'fooling about' replaced with the more conventional story of the British drinking cups of tea.

Aside from comparisons with the English troops and the assertion of Australian superiority, the Anzac stereotype was reinforced through the appearance of the Australians at Gallipoli. Within weeks of the beginning of the campaign the 1st Battalion had begun to look like seasoned campaigners: gaunt, tanned and clad in uniforms torn and cut to adapt to the summer heat. They contrasted dramatically with the spit and polish generally associated with British soldiers, even though the clothing of those at Cape Helles had been similarly reduced and adapted. Ben Champion, a young Australian-born reinforcement whose father had finally consented to his enlistment after the Gallipoli landing, was struck by the difference in his own appearance in regulation uniform and that of the 'old hands' who looked like 'bushrangers'.[13] Impressionable new arrivals, whose only knowledge of the Gallipoli campaign had been gleaned from the papers and wounded soldiers, brought with them an ignorance of the actual facts of the landing that only served to reinforce the burgeoning Anzac legend. The originals resembled the bushmen whose qualities the legend espoused, and that contrast of image may have contributed further to a belief in Australian independence. Furthermore, the reinforcements were more receptive to the general impressions of Australian soldiers as, on arrival at Gallipoli, they had not yet been integrated with their battalions.

The 1st Battalion soldiers identified more strongly with the 1st Division than the Battalion at this stage of the war. The absence of a battalion identity is apparent in accounts of the reinforcements. In a letter home, Billy Goode, spoke only of 'the Battalion we are reinforcing'.[14] This lack of identification with the 1st Battalion was partly because in the early part of the war the reinforcement training officers, though nominally part of the Battalion, had not yet had any direct contact with its fighting arm. They could not instil a Battalion ethic into the recruits as no tradition had yet evolved. This also meant that the performance and tradition of British regular regiments were advanced as role models. There was, too, an awareness on the part of the reinforcements that they were not yet a *bona fide* part of the Battalion. They had not yet had the experience of battle that admitted them to that select fraternity. That feeling of separateness was conveyed by John Bell in a letter home: 'You say in the first letter that the *Battalion* had just gone to the front, you should have said the reinforcement company I belonged to, for the 1st Battalion had been fighting for three months'.[15]

Susceptibility to good impressions of the Australians may also have been heightened by the increased percentage of Australian-born in the ranks of the reinforcements.[16] Champion found the men's apparent distinctive Australianness a compelling fact: 'Grouped together, they had a sameness which I never realised before. There was a definite Australian character, which is hard to explain but which was present in every one of them.'[17]

Evacuation and the consolidation of the 'digger'

By September, through a combination of poor diet, dreadful living conditions and nervous and physical strain, the health of the Australians had deteriorated. Casualties and sickness had stripped them of their earlier healthy appearance. General Birdwood had described the men's pitiful condition to his wife in terms that suggest they were incapable of even the most basic soldierly activities (let alone displaying the initiative and resourcefulness of the stereotype): 'So many of them have got so weak that they really are useless except to stand behind a wall and shoot'.[18] To combat the fatigue and sickness a system of reliefs were arranged to give the battalions a spell from the battlefield. The island of Imbros was selected as a rest place and the 1st Battalion left Gallipoli for a week's spell on 29 June. The strength of the Battalion, which had already received six reinforcement lots (approximately 850 men) to that time, was a little over half its full strength and stood at 19 officers and 536 other ranks. Three hundred of the Battalion, however, were left on Gallipoli as a working party to assist with digging tunnels. The Battalion was rested again from 9 September to 29 October on the island of Lemnos. This was a welcome and much-needed break as the condition of the Battalion was poor.

Due to a combination of censorship and desire to support the war in a positive manner, sections of the press continued to romanticise the stereotype. Writing of the difficulties of the Gallipoli position, a contributor to the *Round Table* paralleled the experience with the hardships of the bush:

> In peace time, during drought and bush-fire and flood, she [Australia] has too often faced and beaten difficulty and disaster to believe them invincible now that they come on her beneath the form of war. And for all these causes, if she be allowed, she will hold on till victory or death to the little plot of earth which she has purchased with her life-blood.[19]

The article was written just prior to the public admission of the evacuation. A footnote, acknowledging the evacuation, qualified the Australian disappointment, suggesting the relief at the relatively bloodless escape had deflected any bitterness that might have emanated against the British. According to the author, the holding of Anzac had given Australia 'tradition' as well as a 'fuller feeling of Imperial fellowship'.[20] Australian soldiers were little concerned with such grand notions while they inhabited their fly-blown 'selection'. Daily survival and comfort dominated their thoughts. However, the promotion of a tradition did come to the fore following the evacuation.

The evacuation of the Anzac position was ordered by the British Government on 7 December and, beginning the next day, was effected in stages until the last troops filed from their trenches to the beach in the early hours of 20 December. Although the men were glad to put the snow and frost that had been experienced in November behind them, the abandonment of the ANZAC positions, nevertheless, evoked a range of emotions within the Battalion. On the eve of the evacuation Lieutenant N. E. McShane wrote home with some trepidation: 'I hope you in Australia are not ashamed of us; we have done our bit and no blame can fall on us'.[21] Nor was the last day the day to play hero. Captain H. G. Carter completed his inspection of the forward positions and noted his own reticence toward his duty: 'I did not care about looking over the top for too long as it would have been hard luck to be potted just then'.[22] Following the evacuation, John Bell, who was thankful to still be alive after Lone Pine, confided to his wife and sought some consolation for the withdrawal: 'It broke me up when we had to leave the Peninsula, after burying so many good, brave, lads, but we all knew that it was the best thing to do under the circumstances. Don't you think we did well to get away without having one man killed?'[23] That remarkable aspect of the escape has further enhanced the reputation of the Australian soldier. The evacuation of Anzac was painstakingly planned with exact timetables to facilitate its execution. But it is significant that British troops, at Suvla and Helles, also stole away unscathed. The evacuations of Suvla and Anzac were carried out conjunctively. The evacuation at Helles was completed on 8 January 1916; with the Turkish knowledge of the Anzac and Suvla evacuations, it was potentially a more precarious exercise.

The evacuation at Anzac stands as a bookend to the glorious beginning espoused in the legend. Sir Charles Rosenthal, a prominent AIF officer, described it as 'an achievement almost as meritorious as the landing'.[24] More recently, Kit Denton's interpretation of the withdrawal reflects accurately the contemporary traditionalist view:

> Of all the things the months brought to that peninsula of pain and death, none was as remarkable as the leaving of it, defeated in purpose, battered in body, a retreating army leaving its dead on the battlefield yet with a strange new strength and unity

and, in the manner of its departure, even a certain dignity. What they had done in that place, the way they did it and the way they left it were to build for them a reputation for great deeds . . . There was, after Gallipoli, a reputation to maintain, a certain standing in the eyes of the world. They had established themselves as tough men, as men who could endure; they could fight and go on fighting no matter what; and even if they were beaten, it was never for lack of courage or stamina or spirit. They were something special. They became the core of the Anzac legend, the heart centre of the soldiers from Down Under in Australia and New Zealand—often reckless and undisciplined, except in action; not much given to passing military courtesies, except where their officers had proved themselves; ready to fight anyone, except their mates.[25]

Denton's view taps into the qualities of the stereotypical Australian soldier. It relies on generalities. It does not adequately reflect the experience of the 1st Battalion. It fails to address the uncertainty they felt about their defeat or the disgust they expressed about their own officers and NCOs. It fails to acknowledge the debilitating effect that casualties and broken health had on performance. Nor does it acknowledge the men's reluctance—albeit perhaps temporary—to engage in further fighting.

The separate and distinct nature of the Gallipoli campaign and the unique situation at Anzac has provided a convenient and seemingly uncomplicated window to view the performance of Australian soldiers. Australian soldiers were in the majority at Anzac. Although this was the case at Anzac, Australia was only one of a number of nations represented in the campaign. It should be remembered that Australian casualties (26,094) represented only 12 per cent (approxiamately) of the total British casualties (205,000). The French, too, who provided a force of comparable strength to the Australians, suffered similarly with 27,004 casualties. However, the absence of any sizeable contingents from other nations (the New Zealanders being an exception) allowed the stereotype to grow unchallenged. Australian performance was viewed singularly with little criticism. Apart from the individual qualities that the legend advanced, which in truth were not general qualities, the quality of endurance is also promoted. Endurance is a term applied to the experience of survivors. Its application ignores the attrition within the battalions. Nearly two thousand men represented the 1st Battalion during the eight-month campaign, a figure double the full strength of a battalion. The high level of casualties and turnover of personnel that this figure represents had clear implications for the efficient conduct of, and confidence in, the performance of the Battalion. It undermined both.

General descriptions of Australian soldiers intimate a continuity in experience. This was not the case. Many of the men who had represented the Battalion at the landing, where the legend was forged, were not in the ranks during the charge at Lone Pine. Late reinforcements, such as Ben Champion and most of those who arrived after the Lone Pine fight, participated in no major action. Their experience was not the same as the originals or early reinforcements. Performance and experience of individual soldiers were not typical, they varied. The 1st Battalion's experience, by regimental designation, does carry a sense of continuity. Its name appears on the battlefield maps from 1915 to 1918. In reality, that experience was a collation of those of the many individuals who formed the Battalion. Furthermore, the 1st Battalion's experience of modern warfare under the unique conditions imposed at Anzac had proved that the opportunities for displays of individualism in battle, on any appreciable scale, were limited. However, the Gallipoli experience had provided the Battalion with a tangible experience to measure future combat against. Despite having participated in a grand military fiasco, the Australians were nonetheless confident in their own ability.

4

'MECHANICAL SLAUGHTER' ON THE WESTERN FRONT, 1916–1917

The Australian soldier emerged from the Gallipoli campaign with a reputation as a battle-hardened veteran, a stubborn, individualistic and resourceful fighter who did, indeed, epitomise the 'digger' stereotype:

> These clean-shaven, sun-tanned, dust-covered boys, who had come out of the hell-fire of the Dardanelles and the great drought of Egyptian sands, looked wonderfully fresh in France. Youth, keen as steel, with a flash in the eyes, with an utter careless-ness of any peril ahead, came riding down the street.[1]

Despite this positive perception of the Australian soldier there existed a belief that the Australians had not yet been fully tested, a belief encapsulated in Douglas Haig's comment to the Australian staff during the fighting at Pozières: 'You're not fighting Bashi-Bazouks now—this is serious, scientific war, and you're up against the most scientific and most military nation in Europe'.[2]

The type of modern warfare being waged in France was expected to be the supreme test for the Australians. The battles for Pozières and Bullecourt, in particular, had specific significance in the general evolution of the reputation of Australia's First World War soldiers. At Pozières the 1st Battalion would be exposed to a very different mode of warfare, of which it had no previous experi-ence and only the vaguest comprehension. Its performance, however, would be gauged against the same general qualities of the stereotype that had been applied at Gallipoli. The severity of the mode of warfare in France shocked all newcomers, to whom it became quickly apparent that the preponderance of artillery and machine-guns circumscribed the individuality of the infantry-man in combat.

The fighting in France and particularly that at Pozières has assumed immense symbolic importance, not only in the broad history of the AIF, but also in the post-war commemoration of the 1st Battalion through the annual Pozières service held at St Columba, Woollahra.[3] Pozières assumes a some-what incongruous duality within the Anzac legend, representing both the destruction and the endurance of Australian soldiers. The region of the Somme, of which Pozières is a part, has come to be seen as a distinctly British battlefield. The Americans would claim the shredded woods of the Argonne as theirs, as would the Belgians the waterlogged fields of the Yser. France had Verdun and a host of other battlefields where French blood had spilled to overflowing.[4] The village of Pozières, while not quite the ossuary of Verdun, was nonetheless the area that came to symbolise to Australians their endur-ance and unflinching sacrifice under the yoke of British incompetence on the Western Front. The inscription on the raised stone memorial slab of the Australian 2nd Division, set at the site of the old windmill on Pozières Ridge, gives expression to the significance of the battlefield within Anzac mythology:

> The ruin of Pozières Windmill which lies here was the centre of the struggle in this part of the Somme battlefield in July and August 1916. It was captured on August 4th by Australian troops who fell more thickly on this ridge than on any other battlefield of the war.[5]

Bullecourt also holds a special place in the legend. It represents Australian soldiers overcoming the odds to secure not only victory but a distinct Aus-tralian victory. In doing so it has perpetuated perceptions of Australian supe-riority. The battle also has special significance to the cultivation of *esprit de corps* within the 1st Battalion. At Bullecourt the Battalion fought courageously in a manner that might well be argued as befitting the legend. Other battles in which the Battalion fought or participated will also be discussed. Smaller actions such as Mouquet Farm and Bayonet Trench form vital links between the major actions of the 1st Battalion at Pozières (1916) and Bullecourt (1917). They provide a sharp focus on the Battalion that reveals an alternative experi-ence to that usually associated with Australian soldiers. Each action, large or small, represented a stage in the Battalion's growth with distinct meanings for the Battalion.

The experience of Australian battalions was not the same, and not all bat-talions participated in actions that the legend celebrates. This was particularly so in 1918 when the AIF participated in a number of successes. The 1st Battalion could not lay claim to any of the successes achieved at Villers-

Bretonneux, Hamel or Mont St Quentin. All were highlights in the Australians' performance in 1918 that contributed significantly to the positive perception of Australian soldiers. Through the aggregation of Australian successes the legend has projected a continuity in positive Australian performances. Those successes, however, were achieved by a variety of units. It is through the collation of positive examples that the legend is reinforced. It is possible, given the greater timespan involved, that descriptions of the AIF's fighting in France, rather than Gallipoli, have been more prone to this method. Subsequently, critical appraisal of the performance of Australian soldiers in battle represents a black hole in the nation's First World War historiography.

France: a new theatre

In the period between the evacuation of Gallipoli and the Battalion's arrival in France it was apparent that the Battalion had assumed immense symbolic importance to some of the men. Private D. Horton recalled that the Battalion was an 'unknown quantity' following its reorganisation.[6] Nevertheless, he claimed that a feeling of *esprit de corps,* built upon the traditions of the Peninsula, permeated the Battalion, and that the men had vowed within their hearts 'that the new name in France would rival the old in Gallipoli'.[7] Where the original members had looked to British regiments to compare themselves, reinforcements now looked to the original Anzacs. Norman Langford, who had been a 2nd Battalion reinforcement but was assigned to 1st Battalion, reflected this movement: 'Here now I was with men who had already had their baptism of fire and I listened to their stories of the Peninsular, what hardships it entailed and felt proud to be amongst them—they who had placed Australia on the map'.[8] This shift in the process of identification from an imperial perspective to a national one was a major contribution to the good morale of the Australians as well as to their belief in themselves as soldiers equal to any within the Empire. It was a belief that would grow further in their—and the national—consciousness as the Anzac legend took hold. But could and would the Battalion be able to match the reputation of Australian soldiers that the public and the AIF's leaders were cultivating following the Gallipoli campaign?

Australian battalions arriving in France could hardly be accorded veteran status. The majority of their members had not seen action and it remains unexplained how the presence of the Gallipoli veterans practically assisted their inexperienced comrades in the battles in France. The high casualties and sickness at Gallipoli had ensured a high turnover of men that kept the Battalion in a state of flux. Furthermore, the decision early in 1916 to increase the infantry component of the AIF from two to five divisions (the 4th Division to be formed in Australia) resulted in further dislocation to the Battalion and diminution in its veteran component. Half of each of the original battalions were used as a nucleus for the formation of new battalions. The sister battalion to the 1st was the 53rd Bn, 5th Division. It shared the same rectangular colour patch, black over green, but wore it vertically rather than horizontally. With the approach of the first anniversary of Anzac Day, Bean was keen to find out how many originals were left in the ranks. On Anzac eve he spent time in the line with the 1st and 2nd Battalions and was told by the men that only about 25 per cent of them were original Anzacs.[9]

Gallipoli had also provided some obvious tactical lessons about the infantry charge. The failure of this method had not been lost on the soldiers, as the reminiscences of a 1st Brigade officer reveal:

> I believe attacking in a single line is no way to win a battle. Units become mixed up, men are separated from their commanding NCOs and officers and I personally never felt happy when I mixed with men I didn't know and never trained with . . . the line attack failed at the landing, failed at Lone Pine, failed when the light horse men charged at Quinn's Post and the Turks failed when they used it in the 19 May attack. In France it was abandoned in favour of advancing in self-contained groups where everyone knew each other and knew the NCOs and officers.[10]

The officer's comments emphasise the need for leadership among fighting units. While it was true, too, that the single-line attack was abandoned for lines in depth and small group formations, the change was gradual rather than automatic, as the Somme and subsequent offensives proved. A measure of the resistance it had first to overcome is evident in the notes of a British staff officer early in the war (issued January 1915):

> The German infantry . . . are apt to adopt rather close formations . . . the French use small groups. Ourselves long lines. The French criticise our infantry as being too thin, I am not so sure, there does not seem much wrong with it, but I rather lean to the French formation, as it seems to adapt itself to the ground, at the same time the thin line is historic and I would be loathe to advocate any change to it.[11]

It was partly due to this sense of the historic that the word 'charge' is so often encountered in the soldiers' descriptions of the battles at both Gallipoli and in France and Belgium. The infantry charge and the British penchant for the bayonet had coloured many of the descriptions of battle that the soldiers of the First World War had been exposed to in their youth. When it came their turn to describe battles, the term maintained its resonance. This was only part of the reason. The fact was, in France until mid-1917, the attacks of Australian and British infantry continued to be governed by that same, unimaginative tactic.[12]

While Gallipoli had provided the 1st Battalion's 'baptism of fire', the men's knowledge of the fighting in France was framed with little conception of the actual nature of the battles there. John Bell, who was recovering in hospital from rheumatism and debility (most likely a recurrence of the shell-shock he had suffered on Gallipoli), wrote to his wife that he had had enough of the trench fighting at Anzac and hoped that he would participate in 'at least one big fight in the open'.[13] France offered that hope, forlorn as it was, but Bell would be spared the upcoming trials as he, along with many others, was returned to Australia. Any notions of open warfare, if they were still held within the Battalion, were quickly dispelled. During the Battalion's second tour in the trenches (10 June to 3 July 1916) at Fleurbaix (considered a quiet sector), sufficient of European war technology was on display for the men to adjust their assessment of the tactical situation before them. Ben Champion observed: 'From seeing the artillery fire that can be brought down on each opposing trench I am of the opinion that these lines are held by Artillery fire alone, and that the men of the front line are only there for ornament, as each side can level the opposite line anytime they like'.[14] Following one particular bombardment, Archie Barwick, commented on the emasculating effects on the individual: 'When you are in a bombardment it makes you realize how small and puny a man's strength is when he is face to face with these power-ful and terrible weapons of man's brain'.[15] He pondered on what the experi-ence of the French at Verdun might be like. At Verdun the Germans had launched a massive and sustained attack in a bid to bleed France white. He concluded that it must have been 'ten times worse'.[16] The soldiers had been quick to realise their vulnerability.

It was, in fact, the experience of the French that underpinned the strategy of Haig's offensive along the Somme into which the Australians would be committed. The date 1 July 1916 (the first day of the Somme) and the images it evokes dominate Britain's modern memory of the First World War. It has come to be seen as representative of the nature of fighting during the war, emphasising the incompetent leadership and the waste of lives. Australia has shared that memory. Although the AIF was not committed to the battle until three weeks after its commencement, it suffered comparable casualties. Aus-tralia would not, indeed could not, be spared from the slaughter. Haig's commitment to a continued offensive after the general failure of the first day was never in doubt. The foundation of his rationale has been succinctly expressed by Peter Charlton: 'Day 1 of the Somme was Day 132 of Verdun'.[17] Haig was effectively bound by the unanimous resolution of the Inter-Allied Military Conference held at Chantilly on 6 to 8 December 1915. At that confer-ence it had been agreed that only simultaneous action by the Coalition armies could bring decisive results.[18] As Haig was hostage to a war of Coalition so too were the Australians, as members of the Empire, hostage to the fate of the British armies.

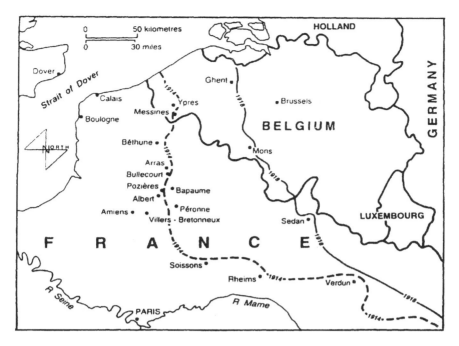

The Western Front, 1914–18, showing movement of the Allied line (Dennis et al., *The Oxford Companion to Australian Military History*, p. 653).

The Battalion commenced its move southward to join in the Somme battle on 9 July 1916. It was with a sense of anticipation that the men readied themselves for the march to the battlefield. Morale within the Battalion was particularly good at this time. Ben Champion considered it 'a pleasure to belong to a body of men such as the 1st Battalion—each one knows the other, and there is a wonderful spirit permeating the whole unit'.[19] According to Second Lieutenant McConnel the men of his company were 'as keen as mustard', with many making the journey despite poor feet lest they miss out on the forthcoming 'scrap'.[20] In this buoyant mood the Battalion swung through Albert under the fallen Madonna and onto the cobbled Roman road which ran east to Cambrai through Pozières. As they marched they sang, according to one soldier, 'wishful of impressing the Tommies with our martial ardour'.[21] Their enthusiasm was tempered somewhat as they neared the front line and became aware of a countryside in ruins with the stench of the dead hanging in the air.[22] The supposed efficient and well-disciplined character of the Battalion was not reflected in its march from the billets at Warloy to the position in the line.[23] The Battalion came under fire and the column became broken and strung out. The rear sections lost touch and required men to be posted along the line of march to guide the way. After the ordeal of the march the men, 'loaded like mules, dog tired and frightened' were set to digging out their new line.[24] Battlefield conditions soon made a mockery of parade ground precision.

The modern battle

Before any description and assessment of the 1st Battalion's performance in France can be discussed, it is first necessary to develop some understanding of the nature of the modern battle and of the role of the infantry in it. It is appropriate that a description given by the AIF's eventual commander-in-chief, General Monash, be quoted at length to establish a context for the discussion of this chapter. A civilian engineer and militia officer before the war, Monash rose progressively through the command levels and was praised for his meticulous and innovative planning. He wrote:

> Modern war is in many ways unlike the wars of previous days, but in nothing so much as in the employment of . . . 'set-piece' operations . . . [which are] the direct result of the great extension, which this war has introduced, of mechanical warfare . . . 'set-piece' because the stage is elaborately set, parts are written for all the performers, and carefully rehearsed by many of them. The whole performance is controlled by a time-table, and, so long as all goes according to plan, there is no likelihood of unexpected happenings, or of interesting developments. The Artillery barrage advances from line to line, in regular leaps, at regulated intervals of time, determined beforehand, and incapable of alteration once the battle has begun . . . [although] one or two halts of ten or fifteen minutes are often introduced into the time-table to allow the infantry line, or any part of it which may be hung up for any reason, to catch up. Following the barrage, comes line upon line of infantry in skirmishing order, together with the line of Tanks when such are used. The foremost lines advance to capture and hold the ground, the lines in rear to 'mop-up' and deal with the enemy either showing fight or hiding underground, the rearmost lines collect prisoners or our own wounded, or carry supplies, tools and ammunition. In a well-planned battle of this nature, fully organized, powerfully covered by Artillery and Machine Gun barrages, given resolute Infantry and that the enemy's guns are kept successfully silenced by our own counterbattery Artillery, nothing happens, nothing can happen, except the regular progress of the advance according to the plan arranged. The whole battle sweeps relentlessly and methodically across the ground until it reaches the line laid down as the final objective. It will be obvious, therefore, that the more nearly such a battle proceeds according to plan, the more free it is from any incidents awakening any human interest . . . The story of what did take place on the day of the battle would be a mere paraphrase of the battle orders prescribing all that was to take place. . . . In a deliberately prepared battle it is not too much to say that the role of the Infantry is not, as a rule, the paramount one, provided that all goes well and that there is no breakdown in any part of the battle plan. That does not, however, imply that the

Infantry task makes no demand upon courage and resolution. On the contrary, these are the essentials upon which the success of the Infantry role and therefore the whole battle depends.[25]

Monash's description encapsulates the method of battle as it was composed during the Australians' involvement between 1916 and 1918. There were, of course, variations in the method over those years as new and improved technology became available. Nevertheless, the intended role of the infantry did not differ markedly in that time. The infantry's prime role was to occupy and hold the line. It was in this capacity that the infantry suffered the majority of its casualties rather than through close combat with the enemy—it was the defensive barrages and counter-bombardments that decimated the infantry ranks on most occasions.

Given the static nature of warfare at Gallipoli and on the Western Front, it seems hardly credible that there existed much scope in battle for the natural qualities and individuality that were ascribed to the Australians by war correspondents. Peter Liddle has argued that the failure to achieve a breakthrough on the Western Front was due to the 'inexorable determinants' in land warfare to that time.[26] Artillery and the machine-gun were among the most dominant of these determinants. It has also been suggested that assessment of the tactical problems of the war 'in terms of technological determinism . . . is over simplistic'.[27] While accepting that there does exist a greater complexity in the conduct of tactical operations, it is difficult to dismiss the oppressive effect that modern technology imposed upon the common soldier during the First World War. Increased artillery firepower had heralded a new form of war and, as Trevor Wilson noted of the Mons campaign (1914), 'heavy industry was threatening to render obsolete the skills and valour and endurance of individual fighting men'.[28] The modernity that confronted the soldiers must have forced a radical re-evaluation of their pre-war conceptions of warfare. Like those of us struggling to adjust to the current explosion in computer technology, soldiers of the First World War must also have struggled to comprehend the technology that confronted them. At times modern weaponry seemed to pass the bounds of reality and assume fictional dimensions. This was evident in the comments of a 1st Battalion soldier who, in writing of the German gun that was able to shell Paris from a range of 96 miles, noted: 'it must be a fearful Jules [Verne] affair'.[29]

In the ideal modern battle described by Monash, the qualities of initiative and resourcefulness are not prerequisites for success. Courage and resolution, according to Monash, were the cornerstone of the infantry's success. The modern battle, however, was notorious for going terribly wrong. When it did, it was the infantry who suffered. In such cases the infantry was thrown back on its own resources to fight its way onto or toward its objectives. Numerous examples of infantry successfully attacking pill-boxes left undamaged by artillery fire can be found in Australian and British unit histories. Tactics of fire and movement were practised and utilised to overcome such strongholds. Whether such incidents exemplify qualities of 'initiative and resourcefulness' over 'courage and resolution' (or both) is contestable.

One incident that was advanced as a proof of Australian individuality on the Western Front was a counter-attack led by Albert Jacka at Pozières Windmill. It checked a German advance and also led to the release of about forty Australian prisoners who were being led away, the captured men themselves taking up the fight for freedom when presented with the opportunity. Bean described the attack by Jacka and seven or eight comrades as 'the most dramatic and effective act of individual audacity in the history of the AIF'.[30] It might well have been. As critical as such attacks could be to the local success of units, there are few examples of them being so broadly effective as to warrant acclamation on a grand-tactical or strategical scale. Moreover, if in assessing the effectiveness and character of Australian soldiers, we laud the actions of Albert Jacka, we should be equally prepared to question the motivation and willingness of the Australians who surrendered in the first instance. Jacka's action highlights the observation that has been made about Canadian soldiers and which could equally be applied to the AIF: 'Most soldiers, laden down with weapons, ammunition, and kit, were supporting players for the minority of desperate fighters . . . who determined success or failure'.[31]

By Monash's account—and this was reflected in the experience of the 1st Battalion—the modern battle generally denied the display of the stereotypical qualities of individualism expressed through initiative and resourcefulness.[32] In the cut and thrust of battle, men might resort to what might be described as resourceful actions, such as using the bodies of the dead as barricades and utilising captured enemy weapons. However, these things are hardly reflective of any greater resourceful capacity in Australian national character than in other nations. If acts of initiative and resourcefulness are to be ordained as proofs of national characteristics they need to be more *grandiose* than those described. The battles of 1916 and 1917 offer few examples in the experience of the 1st Battalion that could be interpreted in that Jacka-like light.

Pozières

The village of Pozières and Pozières Ridge were set as objectives for I Anzac Corps (to which the 1st Division and 1st Battalion belonged) as part of a general attack by General Gough's Reserve Army. The village had been originally designated for capture on the first day of the Somme offensive and again during the advance of 14 July.[33] The general failure of Haig's initial assault meant that the advance had been gradual in the face of dogged German resistance. The British had advanced no more than three thousand yards in three weeks. It was with the knowledge of those failures that the Australians readied themselves for battle.[34] Success at Pozières would not only be a success for British arms, it would also demonstrate to the Australian soldiers that they were superior soldiers to the British, particularly the English 'Tommy'. This was a belief that would grow rapidly in France. This notion of superiority had, in a physical sense, been given a tangible example with the Battalion's first stint in the line in France. They had relieved the 17th Lancashire Fusiliers 'Bantams', whose physical stature was noticeably smaller than the Australians. As a consequence the Australians had to lower the fire steps in the trench.[35]

The reasons for the failure of the British attack on 1 July were numerous. One explanation, of tragic consequence, was that Haig and his generals had insufficient confidence in the New Army divisions to conduct operations of any complexity. Any possibility of local initiative on the part of many of the division commanders was negated. Jon Cooksley, writing of the experience of the Barnsley 'Pals' battalions, described the consequence of this mistrust:

> The fact of the matter is that the Army had not trusted Kitchener's men in their first major encounter with the Germans and had planned accordingly. The resulting plans had been so rigid that battalions like the Pals were never given the opportunity to display their undoubted talents to the full. The stifling strategy with its ponderous timetables and plethora of supplies and equipment, had been the Pals' undoing.[36]

At Pozières, the same desire that had been displayed to protect the New Army divisions from complex operations was also evident in Haig's handling of the Australians. The day before the attack, Haig visited General Gough to 'make sure that the Australians had only been given a simple task'.[37] The Australians would benefit from this as well as some of the other lessons learned. In fact, a memorandum in the 1st Division War Diary intimates that its General Staff made direct enquiries to the British 7th and 19th Divisions about their recent successful operations. That experience was subsequently utilised in the 1st Division's operational planning.[38] Exact timetables would still govern the troops' employment but the two major factors that had compromised the British failures, the inadequacy of the preliminary bombardment and the distance the troops had to advance, were both improved. Pozières had been reconnoitred, troublesome fields of fire were identified, and the support bombardment was carefully planned.[39] To assist the approach of the 1st Division during the attack, trenches were dug that allowed the men to advance as close as eighty yards to the German line before the assault.[40] Importantly, the 1st Division's British commander, General 'Hooky' Walker, had argued for and won a delay in the operation, originally set for 19 July, to allow the necessary adjustments to the line and artillery planning that would give his men the best possible chance for success.[41]

The objective of the 1st Battalion at Pozières was a straightforward one. They were to capture part of the German position located in Pozières Trench just south of the village. A heavy barrage was to be laid on the enemy position, and the infantry were to follow and rush the German line as soon as the barrage lifted. In the week prior to the battle the Battalion had practised rapid movement to prepare for the charge that was to follow the bombardment. They would follow hard on the fringe of the barrage. The steady walk that had governed the advance of the majority of British units on 1 July had proved disastrous. It would not be repeated. At exactly 12.28 am, 23 July, the supporting barrage erupted in a 'sheet of flame . . . and long drawn deafening roar'.[42] The frightening intensity of the barrage and its moral and physical effect on the Australians were described by one 1st Battalion soldier:

> The tension affected the men in different ways. I couldn't stop urinating, and we were all anxious for the barrage to begin. When it did begin, it seemed as if the earth opened up with a crash. The ground shook and trembled, and the concussion made our ears ring. It was impossible to hear ourselves speak to a man lying alongside. It is strange how men creep together for protection. Soon, instead of four paces interval between the men, we came to lying alongside each other, and no motivating could make them move apart.[43]

The men had crowded together, as was the tendency of men under fire, and many had rushed beyond their objectives with the supporting waves of the 3rd Battalion. Second Lieutenant Ken McConnel described the difficulties he experienced in leading his men forward:

> It was the devil's own job to keep the lads going in the right direction, as they had never been over the ground before and kept trying to swing round towards the left. It was hardly possible to hear a man shouting at the top of his voice a yard or so away . . . I thought we should never reach that first line and when we did we found B coy had made a mistake at the fork road and had left 70 yards of trench untaken. However there were only a few Germans in it, and we finished them off . . . Just before we got to the Tram line, I saw that the men were bunching up on the left and leaving a big gap on the right, where there was no sign of Blackmore's men. I didn't know what the hell to do at first, but finally I got ahead and gesticulated wildly at them, shouting 'Come in first battalion' and then 'spread out to the right'. Anyway the beggars understood and we got to the line in fairly decent extension.[44]

Another problem before the attack had been the difficulty in explaining the nature of the operations to the NCOs and men due to the heavy shelling that continually interrupted efforts to keep the men together.[45] Fortunately, the disorganisation and chaotic nature of the advance did not affect its success. The artillery bombardment had proved devastatingly effective, and the 1st Battalion met with little resistance from the dazed defenders who had survived and not fled. Some instances of killing German prisoners were noted. John Hayes was a member of a party of five Australians who encountered the enemy: 'Had a little scrap and they said "Mercy Kamerade" so we stuck one who was giving a bit of cheek and took the rest to La Boiselle and returned to the boys'.[46] There is no evidence to suggest that such behaviour was ever accepted as doctrine in the 1st Battalion or that Australians killed prisoners more often than other soldiers of other nations.

After the initial attack, it was with some exaltation that the men settled down to consolidate their gains. Private Horton recalled:

> We in the fullness of our conceit . . . congratulated ourselves on the wonderful success . . . and we were not slow in saying that the magnitude of victory was out of all proportion to the number of casualties. We were young and had much to learn. The next 60 hours taught quite a lot about attacks and the aftermath thereof.[47]

Indeed, what followed was unrivalled in the Battalion's experience. The German counter-bombardment, once organised, was relentless. The succinctness of Sergeant Elvin's diary is a stark reminder of the men's experience until their relief:

> Heavy firing all morning—simply murder. Men falling everywhere . . . Ground covered by shell fire. No casualties going over. Hell itself in the wood. Expecting death every second. 23 men smothered in one trench. Dead and dying everywhere. Some simply blown to pieces. Shells falling like hail during a storm. Five left in trench.[48]

The horror of this bombardment and its unhinging effects on the infantry were further elaborated by Archie Barwick:

> All day long the ground rocked and swayed backwards and forwards from the concussion of this frightful bombardment . . . any amount of men were driven stark staring mad and more than one of them rushed out of the trench over towards the Germans, any amount of them could be seen crying and sobbing like children their nerves completely gone, how on earth we stood it God alone knows, we were nearly all in a state of silliness and half-dazed.[49]

Men functioning in such a state, one imagines, would be incapable of exhibiting anything beyond the most basic of soldierly duties. Indeed, Colonel Jess of the 7th Battalion sent a message to 2nd Brigade headquarters that stated his men were 'so dazed that they are incapable of working or fighting'.[50] Under such circumstances it is likely that feelings of self-preservation and fear would have become influential in the governance of mind and body. The Battalion's predicament was further strained by the fact that British heavy artillery was also firing into the Australians' position. A 1st Brigade report stated that this belief had been conveyed to headquarters on eight occasions during the course of operations.[51]

At one stage during the bombardment elements of the 3rd Battalion began to waver under the deluge of shells and Howell-Price's A Company (1st Bn) was pushed forward to the shattered remains of Pozières Wood to assist them. The churned-up ground over which they advanced was littered with Australian corpses, and the unavoidable act of stepping on them gave the men, as one soldier described, the 'creeps'.[52] The effect of the horrific sights on the men was further alluded to in one soldier's account of the Battalion's advance: 'We saw the 1st and 2nd battalions disappear in the darkness, driven, as we were, nearly mad by the cries and groans of our wounded'.[53] In this maelstrom, which cowed the bravest of men, some individuals shone through like beacons in a storm, providing guidance and showing the way. Sergeant R. I. C. MacGregor was one such person whose method was described by Ben Champion: 'he walked about in the open, unarmed, supervising, swearing, bullying, coaxing, whichever best served the purpose, and by his courage and contempt of shell fire, instilled into many wavering men something of his fatalism'.[54]

Sergeant MacGregor's actions were not the norm, but it was upon the courage and condemnation of men like him that the weaker elements in the ranks relied. He made men stay. In writing of Australian soldiers at Gallipoli, Bean recognised this behaviour: 'Doubtless the weaker were swept on by the stronger. In every army which enters into battle there is a part which is dependent for its resolution upon the nearest strong man.'[55] The difference was, according to Bean, that there were more of these stronger types in the Australian army. Moreover, he stated that it was their belief in Australian manhood and its inherent code, of sticking by one's mates, that sustained them.[56] There is no proof that this was the case. Yet it is that belief, more than anything else, that underpins the Anzac legend. When one considers the Australian casualties at Pozières and the little ground gained there (at most twelve hundred yards in the first four days),[57] the inescapable conclusion is that their experience was comparable to the British divisions that had fought their way to the vicinity of Pozières.[58] In fact, the results of the Australian attacks on the Somme were chequered. Following the capture of Pozières, nine assaults were made on the German positions; four of these failed, three were successful, and only small or partial gains were made in the other two.[59]

As shocking as the effects of battle were at Pozières, the official historian was still able to extract positives from it. Pozières was seen by Bean as a defining moment and the supreme test of Australian character. It was his opinion that the Australian soldier had passed that test, although its results still concerned him. In the preface to the third volume of the *Official History*, he wrote:

> In the present volume the writer has endeavoured truthfully to exhibit the Australian character as evinced under a strain that, at first gentle, suddenly increased at Pozières to terrible intensity, then eased, and in the early winter again suddenly racked the men to almost breaking point. So cruel, indeed, was the test that the human material was suspected by those who best knew it—though not by other onlookers—of having suffered permanent damage. When the volume ends, the stress shows signs of abating; and—though the fears of breakdown are not yet wholly dispelled—there are tokens that nerves and spirits may regain all their former resiliency.[60]

Bean was drawn to the psychological effects of battle and believed: 'The most interesting book that could be written about the War would be a thorough treatise upon wartime psychology'.[61] Australian soldiers suffering permanent neuroses did not fit his belief in the ability of the Australian character to overcome all difficulties, challenges and conditions. He accepted that temporary insanity visited men in battle but did not contemplate the possibility of long-term effects. In this he was exhibiting the ignorance of war neuroses that existed at the time, as well as the belief that insanity could be neutralised by the commitment of oneself to the higher ideals of national life.[62]

The men who had survived the ordeal unscathed and who manned the ragged trench line on the 1st Division's relief provided the core for the legend's assertion of Australian endurance at Pozières. Their experience also marked a rite of passage for the reinforcements, whose performance met with approval from the Battalion's old hands. John Hayes, who had fought at Gallipoli, noted: 'The moral effect was great on our people but they stuck it like the old boys'.[63] Those that had not, the dead and wounded who accounted for half the Battalion, were added to the jetsam and flotsam of the war that clogged the back areas of the armies. In the stories of Australian soldiers in battle their plight, once rendered *hors de combat*, has been little discussed. While escape from the front line via a wound was seen as a godsend by many, the reality for the wounded was often an arduous and tortured experience. Ken McConnel, for example, was wounded and spent six hours lying in a trench with another wounded man before he was collected by the stretcher-bearers. He was finally evacuated on a horse-wagon and endured a three-mile ride over corduroyed roads to Albert. The journey was not 'a happy one' and he engaged in a 'bawling match' with a fellow passenger, who was suffering from a broken leg and wrist, as the wagon jolted to its destination.[64]

The Battalion's casualties at Pozières are given as 13 officers and 473 other ranks (486 men) in the *Official History*. The *First Battalion* gives a higher casualty total of 532.[65] The Battalion's strength at the end of June, prior to the battle, was 27 officers and 990 other ranks (1017 men). Casualties sustained at Pozières therefore represented either 47.78 or 52.31 per cent of the Battalion's strength, depending upon which figures are used. If the latter are accepted the Battalion shares the dubious honour with a number of other units engaged on the Somme of having suffered over 50 per cent casualties. On 1 July, 32 British battalions suffered in excess of 500 casualties.[66] On the figures in the *Official History*, eight Australian battalions (not including the 1st Bn) suffered in excess of 500 casualties during the capture of Pozières and Pozières Heights. At Fromelles, six Australian battalions had suffered over 500 casualties.[67]

The massive Australian casualties underscored the vulnerability of the individual to the dangers of modern war. Its horrendous and relentless nature was described by a 1st Brigade soldier who survived the battle: 'War—it's nothing but mechanical slaughter'.[68] Mechanical slaughter, with the connotation of industrialisation that it so obviously carried, was an appropriate label for the war in France. The Australian arrival had coincided with an escalation in the industrial output of Great Britain. The British government, stung by revelations that British guns had run short of ammunition during the 1915 offensives, in what was dubbed the 'Shells Scandal', had established a separate ministry for munitions, headed by Lloyd George. The Germans responded in kind through the 'Hindenburg Programme' and by 1917 Germany's war production was in full swing.[69] The systematic process of mass production ensured the ground over which the infantry of friend and foe alike had to pass would be deluged. In the 1916–18 period artillery accounted for 85 per cent of German casualties as opposed to 49.29 per cent in 1914–15. Artillery accounted for 58 per cent of all British casualties during the war.[70] It is likely, given the increased preponderance of artillery fire in the second half of the war, that Australian and British casualties caused by artillery fire would have been similar to those of the Germans in 1916–18. As contributing tools of destruction, infantry weapons had diminished as the war progressed despite their diversity having increased.

The 1st Battalion filed out of the line at Pozières on 26 July. The reaction of the Australians to the Pozières bombardment and their eventual withdrawal from the line has been the subject of further mythologising. Bean wrote home exclaiming: 'What is a barrage against such troops! They went through it as you would go through a summer shower—too proud to bend their heads, many of them, because their mates were looking. I am telling you of things I have seen'.[71] The dust jacket of one history makes the claim: 'in Flanders the survivors of enormous slaughters walked slowly and reluctantly out of battle when ordered to withdraw'.[72] This generalisation, in all likelihood, owes itself to a description of the withdrawal of the 13th Brigade that appeared in the *Official History*: 'The way was absolutely open . . . and others were bending low and running hurriedly . . . Our men were walking as if in Pitt Street, erect, not hurrying, each man carrying himself as proudly and carelessly as a British officer does'.[73] Presumably these 'others' were retiring Australians and not the Canadians effecting the relief. The dishevelled and shell-shocked appearance of the 1st Battalion belied any proud, reluctant and carefree manner, as one soldier intimated: 'We saw 7th Brigade march in . . . They gave us a cheer, which I'm sure was out of sympathy for our appearance than for anything we had done'.[74] Another 1st Battalion soldier, more concerned with the relief itself rather than the identity of the relieving troops, noted: 'we were too excited to see who it was [that] relieved us . . . we were pleased to be getting away from such a slaughterhouse'.[75]

Although every second man in the Battalion was a casualty and despite the desperation of the men to leave Pozières, the authors of the Battalion history positively described the demeanour of the men immediately after the battle: 'All were in excellent spirits, and the men joked and sang as we marched on the weary way to Tara Hill'.[76] Sergeant E. J. Rule of the 14th Battalion passed survivors of the 1st and 2nd Brigades, on the second day of their march away from the line; his description differs markedly:

> They looked like men who had been in Hell. Almost without exception each man looked drawn and haggard, and so dazed that they appeared to be walking in a dream, and their eyes looked glassy and starey. Quite a few were silly, and these were the only noisy ones in the crowd . . . I have never seen men quite so shaken up as these . . .[77]

It is difficult to imagine the men described by Rule as exhibiting the 'excellent spirits' that the Battalion history described, even with the knowledge that they were marching out of harm's way. Rule's impression was not the officially expressed view. An official report of the 1st Battalion corroborates the 'singing' version given in *First Battalion*: 'In spite of having had practically no sleep or rest since the 22nd inst. The men were in good spirits and sung on the march'.[78] It is clearly, given Rule's observation, an incomplete account of the men's reaction to their experience at Pozières.

In terms of actual fighting the Battalion had 'done' little. Combat between the opposing infantry was rare, as Les Dinning revealed in a statement that underscored the impotence and passivity of the unit during the battle: 'It wasn't fighting, it was . . . murder. I hardly think there were more than 100 shots fired from the rifles of the whole First Battalion'.[79] The lack of confrontation between the opposing infantry was also commented on by an unidentified 1st Division officer, who wrote: 'They came out once about 400 strong . . . Not a man came within 200 yards of us; they simply turned and ran, and, what's more, never fired a shot. But their artillery was hell itself '.[80] In writing about the Pozières fighting, General Birdwood noted that neither the taking of the village nor of the second line of German trenches gave the Australians any 'really great trouble'.[81] Birdwood reiterated this sentiment in a letter to Lord Derby in which he described the taking of Pozières as not 'such a difficult job'.[82] The holding of the position was a separate task in itself and Birdwood fully recognised the duress it had placed upon the troops. He subsequently informed the 1st Division's commander of his pleasure at the 'really magnificent bit of work you have all put in'.[83]

Overall, the Battalion's performance revealed few, if any, examples of resourcefulness. Again, as had occurred in the first days at Gallipoli, the Battalion's inexperience was exposed. Its lines had become mixed in the advance but it was a point of little consequence. The initial success of the battle had been achieved through the overwhelming effect of the British and Australian artillery on the German trenches. While the Battalion had to survive the German bombardment, survival was due more to good fortune than to any individual enterprise. Soldiers had to battle their nerves to face the ordeal: some succeeded and some did not, needing men like Sergeant MacGregor to provide leadership and to stiffen their resolve in the crisis. While MacGregor may have conducted himself in the midst of the barrage as though he was walking 'through a summer shower' it is unlikely that such apparent calm visited many of the men, as the examples previously quoted suggest.

Others found an alternative way of dealing with the stress. Sleep was one method of escape, even if a sometimes involuntary one (through exhaustion). Les Dinning, who described his nerves as 'very shaky', was able to find a spot in a trench where he rested until the following morning.[84] Private Locane recorded that 'about 10 pm I fell asleep up against the parapet . . . and at 3 am the corporal in charge of our gun woke me up'.[85] During the Battalion's four-day tour at Mouquet Farm, Jack Hayes noted, 'I got shell shock and after a good sleep, well again'.[86] At Pozières it was estimated that 25 per cent of Australian casualties were a result of shell-shock compared to 40 per cent in British units. Garton has suggested the possible explanations for the higher incidence in British officers and men than Australian ranging from a higher morale or greater *esprit de corps* among the Australians to a greater reluctance of Australian medical officers to classify shell-shock cases.[87] A. G. Butler regarded the absence of a meaningful task to be a major contributor to the 'apotheosis' of shell-shock during the First Somme, 1916. He noted that once the offensive degenerated into

> [a] crude contest in attrition devoid of 'surprise' or tactical refinement. It became difficult for the soldier to regard his tasks as part of an intelligent plan. Lacking thus the firm 'shield of faith' the troops in the later stages of the offensive (in which the AIF took part) were thrown into the inferno morally disarmed save for the traditions of their race and army and the strength of their own character.[88]

The principal features of the 1st Battalion's front-line experience at Pozières were those of chaos, luck and exhaustion. It is difficult to find evidence within the actions of the 1st Battalion to support the claim that the I Anzac Corps (1st and 2nd Divisions), to which it belonged, had demonstrated 'fine fighting prowess'.[89] It should also be remembered that the 2nd Division's first attack at Pozières failed. It was eventually relieved, after a successful second attempt, by the 4th Division, which Peter Charlton described as 'demonstrably a better division than the 2nd'.[90]

As had occurred after the Gallipoli landing, the men of the Battalion again sought to affirm their reputation as soldiers. H. J. Cave wrote with some prescience that he was experiencing what were 'indeed historic and remarkable days' and noted: 'the "Immortal" Division was still in the forefront of all that's going on this side as regards Huns and work'. Cave was not, however, deluded about his experience. He had described Pozières as an 'Earthly Hell' and like many of the letter writers was keen to allay any fears held for his safety.[91] Nevertheless, the theme of immortality, though hardly appropriate to the fate of many of the Battalion's soldiers, was reinforced by another Battalion member in a retrospective account that recalled the Pozières experience: 'So must the hero who freed the Valkyrie have strode through the ring of living flames that surrounded her'.[92]

In a more immediate account, R. A. Cassidy believed the fighting at Pozières had been worse than Lone Pine and wrote home with characteristic humour: 'It was (somme) fight'.[93] Cassidy, wounded at Lone Pine and evacuated with shell-shock from Pozières, had sent a cable to his mother in the hope that it would reach her before the publication of the casualty lists. The dread with which relatives in Australia scanned the lists can only be imagined. Furthermore the military authorities sent telegrams to the next of kin, via local ministers of religion, to advise of all battle-related casualties ensuring mixed emotions of anxiety and relief, to relatives of men wounded in action. Cassidy's letters to his mother were undoubtedly written to ease her worst fears and, although he acknowledged the horror of war, his battle accounts were generally couched in typical *Boy's Own* rhetoric that masked the reality. From Gallipoli he had written of how on the first day, driven by revenge, they had gone 'wild and charged the hills with our comrades' blood hanging to us'.[94] Now he felt compelled to let his mother know that 'The Anzacs made a big score'.[95] People in Australia perusing the ever-increasing casualty lists were becoming acutely aware of the German tally in reply.[96] Nevertheless, despite the shattered illusions of the soldiers who now fully realised the extent of the horrors of modern warfare, the daily press was, in the midst of that carnage, still extolling the virtues of the nation's soldiers first heralded at Gallipoli. An article published in September carried the banner: 'The Men of Anzac: Great in War—Adepts in Sport'.[97]

After the Battalion's first stint at Pozières its commander, Lieutenant-Colonel Heane, who was described as the *'beau ideal'* of a commanding officer, addressed the men and highlighted their deeds as adding to the short but illustrious record of the Battalion. His words as remembered by one soldier were:

> Officers and men of the 1st Battalion as you all know I am a hard man and a hard man to please but as I look around (he looked round and the tears glistened in his eyes as he saw all that was left of his splendid Battalion) I feel proud to think I have held command of such men as you. Men . . . the Battalion had a wonderful name on Gallipoli but today you have done work equal to if not better than anything that was ever done on the Peninsular [sic].[98]

Pride in the Battalion was manifest. Reinforcements were quickly informed of what was expected of them. One group who arrived a few days after the battle and who incurred an officer's wrath were told that it was only discipline that made the Australians the finest soldiers in the world.[99] If the nation's soldiers looked to gauge their performance against those of other countries, it was equally true that Australian battalions compared themselves against each other. Such comparison reveals that Australian soldiers, too, could be perceived to have performed poorly. Archie Barwick used the performance of other battalions to highlight that of the 1st Battalion:

> I believe General Smythe gave the 3rd Battalion a good talking to over so many of their men leaving the trenches when the heavy shell fire was on, a lot of the 11th Battalion also squibbed it, our Colonel took nearly a company of them back to their position, those were the only two that showed the white feather.

Barwick had earlier claimed that the Australian 4th Division were a 'rotten lot they reckon they can't be trusted in the lines'.[1] Descriptions such as these found no expression in narratives after the war. They were muted in

FRED LEIST

1189. THE CRUSADERS 1915.

'The Crusaders' by F. Leist. Front cover of the War Memorial's publication
Australian Chivalry (1933).

Ben Champion, now a sergeant, had his own views as to why 'in a few minutes, a glorious unit had suffered losses which could never be made up'.[15] He declared that the mud was too stiff, rifle bolts had jammed as a result of the weather, the men's reserve strength and spirit were used up (from garrison duty and marching in mud), and as a final condemnation of the attack planning: 'A boy was given a man's job'.[16] It is unclear to whom Champion was referring. The Battalion was commanded by 42-year-old Lieutenant-Colonel Heane at the time, hardly a boy. The 'boy' may have been Howell-Price, commanding the lead company in the attack, though that seems unlikely given Champion's description of him as 'a most efficient officer'.[17] Champion may have meant too small a force was used—a boy-sized force to do a man-sized job. Generally though, the reasons outlined by Champion were similar to those of the Liverpool 'Pals' battalions two weeks previously on 18 October.[18] On this occasion the Australian experience had been almost identical.

Of particular interest is the comment by one of the 1st Battalion soldiers captured by the Germans. In a post-war statement regarding his capture, Private Liney was unable to name any of the officers involved in the attack: 'I do not know what officer was in charge of the whole operation nor do I know the names of any officer who took part in it'.[19] That he was unable to do so is surprising. It was in the smaller groups, such as platoon and section, that the officer–man relationship was supposedly most intimate. According to Liney, the section of bombers to which he belonged was headed by a corporal. It would seem that none of the officers under whom Liney served had possessed any memorable qualities of personality or leadership. The fact that Liney could not remember any of his officers' names, barring any effects of amnesia, suggests—at least in his case—a lack of intimacy with his officers. As such, his experience undermines notions of a closely developed relationship between officer and other ranker. This lack of intimacy, if it existed generally, did not necessarily preclude the success of an operation but, as the legend would have it, it was the combination of that intimacy with the Australians' natural abilities that contributed largely to the successes achieved.

Bayonet Trench marked the end of the Battalion's fighting for the year. Its failure was felt keenly. Archie Barwick summed up the prevailing attitude: 'it was the first time we ever had to acknowledge defeat and I can tell you it hurt some'.[20] During the Battalion's relief, the sight of the Guards marching by lifted the flagging spirits of the men, prompting reaffirmation of the Battalion's ability. In a statement of self-reassurance reminiscent of those which followed the landing at Gallipoli, one soldier stated: '[the Guards] could not have done any better in the line than we did, for all their spit and polish'.[21]

Another took comfort in the fact that 'whole battalions' had since failed to take the position.[22]

The year had been a costly one for the Battalion. Whatever hopes the men had carried to Europe for an end to the fighting, those hopes were now crushed by the reality of war on the Western Front. The leveling effect of modern technology and attrition in all armies was plainly evident. T. J. Richards, a former member of the Field Ambulance recently commissioned in the infantry, described the malaise that afflicted the Battalion's weary soldiers as the year neared its close:

> There seems to be an awful feeling of depression concerning the state of the war just now. Men who were confident we were winning easily are now shaking their heads asking 'Will we be in a final peace conference at all, or will Germany have it all their own way?' There is no doubt we have paid heavily for our successes on the Somme and now that the enemy have given us a display of their power in overcoming Roumania with such rapidity and apparent ease our chances look very gloomy indeed. The Australian people have shown clearly that they are sick of the whole business . . . Although the honours of war will go to the Allies there will be no spoils for the victors, in fact I can not see that there is going to be any victors at all, it is like a dogfight in which both contestants are weakened to despair, physical and financial ruin, too weak to continue battle and at the same time neither is strong enough to move ahead to grasp the spoils of victory. '*Stalemate*'.[23]

If a postscript were required for the dissatisfaction that the men of the 1st Battalion felt for the war, it came with the belated news of the experience of the 5th Division and their sister battalion (53rd) at Fromelles. The 5th Division's fate did not begin to become known to the men until October, a fact that highlights the blinkered view that most soldiers had of the war. The misinformation that the High Command had spread about this attack, described in a communiqué as 'an important raid', was exposed in a manner that only served to further misinform its recipients about the real nature of operations.[24] The way in which Lieutenant Richards was informed highlights this. Richards was privy to a conversation with two fellow officers, from the 4th and 11th Battalions. His recollection of the conversation revealed a bitterness toward the hapless Tommies, who again made convenient scapegoats, and provided an exaggerated account of the casualties and the nature of the operation. Nevertheless the tenor of his diary entry was genuine enough:

> the 5th Division were positively slaughtered at Flanders not only were they let down by the Tommys on either side but they failed to get orders and went to their death. Some 9000 Australian casualties were reported and nothing gained whereas the charge was a glorious success and would have broken the German line to hell had there been any support for the men . . . They say it is positively the worst mistake since the war started and these mistakes have been many and gigantic.[25]

Ben Champion became aware of the Fromelles disaster a little earlier. He mentions being informed of the losses of former 1st Battalion officers by an officer of the sister battalion, the 53rd.[26] The 5th Division had suffered, in fact, 5533 casualties on 19–20 July 1916. Bean described the bitter judgement of the Australians toward the British as 'particularly unfortunate, but almost inevitable' and considered them an extension of the distrust that had become deeply impressed following the Suvla landing in the Dardanelles campaign.[27] Peter Charlton has suggested that, as a result of the battles for Fromelles, Pozières and Mouquet Farm, relations were soured between the Australian troops and their British commanders.[28] This 'disillusion' and 'distrust', he argued, was widespread among regimental officers and soldiers.[29] There is little evidence of this distrust among the letter writers and diarists of the 1st Battalion immediately after Pozières. Distrust in the British High Command would begin to manifest itself more directly in 1917. However, the delayed knowledge of the Fromelles disaster, combined with the bitterness of their repulse at Bayonet Trench and the revulsion they had formulated toward the type of warfare which now oppressed them, all contributed to a general disillusionment within the Battalion at the end of 1916. The futility of the battering-ram tactics against massed artillery and machine-guns had been plainly recognised by the soldiers.

The prospect of another year of fighting in France left the men of the 1st Battalion dispirited. Morale was at a low ebb. While the trying winter of 1916–17—the most severe in forty years—contributed to the men's despondency, other factors also depressed them, especially the failure to introduce conscription since it denied an obvious source of relief.[30] Impressive as the much-acclaimed *esprit de corps* of Australian battalions might appear in the high diction of post-battle accounts, there is no tangible evidence to suggest it served as an inspiration in battle. It must be acknowledged, however, that any intrinsic value it may have had cannot be adequately measured. The days of rallying around regimental battleflags on blood-soaked sands were long past. Men in battle had little conception beyond the immediate sphere of the section or platoon to which they belonged; their actions were dictated by instinct and reaction to the chaos abutting their isolated world. High morale was quickly eroded by constant and excessive casualties. Following the Somme battles, the signs of recovery that Bean had described in the *Official History* were not so evident. Lieutenant Richards described the demeanour of the men in January 1917:

> [at church parade] I wondered why the Chaplain didn't sing a hymn or two, but I guessed when the whole Battalion nearly broke down singing the National Anthem. The fellows seem to have no spirit at all. Yesterday the 3rd Battalion band was playing

'Keep the Home Fires Burning' and although it is well known and very popular, there was no attempt to sing the words. I really cannot understand it at all. The men are so dead, like so many petrified corpses, and won't wake up, although their drilling and marching is quite good. This, however, seems to be mechanical.[31]

Like Charlie Chaplin in the 1936 film *Modern Times* the men had become the machine.

Bullecourt and the 'clockwork' battles of 1917

British morale was given an overall, unexpected boost early 1917 when it was discovered, albeit belatedly, that the Germans had commenced a withdrawal to their newly constructed Hindenburg line. The pursuit of the Germans was not particularly vigorous. Patrols advanced by degrees in the face of a German rearguard whose resistance was tempered to the timidity of its pursuers. The failure of the British armies to exploit the German withdrawal committed the soldiers to more walk-up confrontations against fixed defences. New tactics, however, were being evolved that gave the infantryman greater responsibility in combat and as a consequence more confidence. These changes in tactics were initiated by the General Staff. The attack formation suggested by Ivor Maxse following his Division's experience at Trones Wood was widely distributed.[32] The formation placed the advancing platoon in four sections, bayonet men and bombers in front with Lewis gunners and grenadiers behind. The system allowed for the Lewis guns to be fired from the hip and grenades to be fired over the heads of the bombers. It allowed greater flexibility and also displayed the High Command's desire to diversify the role of the infantry—in fact, to make them more individual by giving them greater control in combat. This led immediately to an increase in the morale of soldiers who had, so far, been accorded little capacity to act independently within the clockwork battles that characterised the fighting to that time.

Australian commanders relied on the doctrines of the British army for the adoption of combat tactics. Contrary to popular perceptions of the British General Staff being wooden-headed donkeys, the headquarters general staff were constantly reappraising the fighting and issuing instructions to the men in the field. In fact, it is unlikely that the common soldier had ever before been informed and trained with such attention to detail as the British and Dominion soldiers in 1917. Lectures and training on all aspects of trench and semi-open warfare were undertaken throughout the British armies.[33] Suggestions and advice on new methods of combat were being constantly forwarded to the front-line battalions. How much of this information reached the men in the line depended on how well it was disseminated and distributed by divisional staff. In this the 1st Australian Division was well served. The Divisional diary reveals that its senior general staff officer, Thomas Blamey, was issuing these tracts on a regular basis.[34]

The first major action in which the 1st Battalion was committed in 1917 was the second Australian assault at Bullecourt in May. In both battles the old line tactics prevailed. The first had been an utter disaster that ranked along-side the 5th Division's failure at Fromelles as a catastrophe of Australian arms.[35] In the second battle the 1st Brigade was detached from the 1st Division to act as a reserve for the 2nd Division. A portion of the German line was seized by the 6th Brigade in the opening assault. Thereafter the battle degen-erated into what military historians are fond of calling the 'soldiers' fight'—a situation where the outcome of battle rests entirely on the ability of the front-line infantryman to maintain his nerve and tough it out. At Bullecourt, as at Lone Pine, the 1st Battalion toughed it out with great courage. The vanity of the costly plan, however, was not lost upon the soldiers, as Ken McConnel recalled:

> A madder scheme was never conceived in the whole war. Bullecourt lay in a hollow overlooked on three sides by high ground occupied by the enemy, so that even if we took the place we should have a salient that would only be a death trap. One would imagine the obvious thing to do would be to withdraw from the ridiculous salient and gracefully acknowledge a failure, but no, the powers that be decided it would be detrimental to the morale of the troops to retire, so decided to hang on.[36]

Hang on they did. For two weeks the Australian and British divisions endured numerous counter-attacks before the Germans conceded the British gains.[37] The 1st Battalion held the line for three of those days. The confusion of battle, so evident in all the Battalion's previous experiences, was manifest from the outset at Bullecourt. Furthermore, cohesion and trust between officers, NCOs and other units was lacking, as the following account reveals. Sergeant Barwick described his company's approach to the front line:

> Captain MacKenzie sent up for me as he wanted to speak to me before moving off . . . 'Look here Barwick, he said, tonight you are going up to the line with a new officer, stick to him all you can and teach him what you know and you will be practi-cally in charge of the men for I can trust you.' He told us we were going into a Hell and he wanted to give me a good stiff drink of spirits but I never go in for that sort of thing . . . [Lieutenant] McKell was in charge of the Coy and he was already half-drunk and took us a long way out of our track, then [Sergeant] Jock Mackie got into holts with him and told him off properly . . . it was the biggest mix up I have seen in my life getting into the line, no one knew where anyone was and we wandered about all over the place under heavy fire at times too, the result was my officer got lost and took nearly all the platoon with him and I landed in the trenches with two men and

myself, the position of trench I was in was mostly 5th Brigade and they had the wind up properly for they had lost heavily as the numerous dead lying about showed all too plainly.[38]

Added to this confusion was an incident the following evening when the 1st Battalion exchanged fire with the 21st Battalion during a relief.[39]

Barwick's account reveals a number of weaknesses in the conduct of the 1st Battalion. Clearly the men most suited to command had not always been rewarded. McKell, a bank clerk whose father had been a magistrate, had possibly been one of the many officers selected on the merits of their pre-war occupation.[40] Barwick, on the other hand, despite being entrusted with the responsibility of being his officer's guardian, would remain a sergeant for the war's duration. McKell's performance was one not celebrated within the Anzac legend. The value of good NCOs to new or ordinary officers has already been discussed, and it proved detrimental to an NCO's prospects of advancement. If Barwick's assessment of McKell was correct, then the danger in the use or overuse of alcohol as a stimulant before an attack is also revealed.[41]

Of even more interest, in view of the confused nature of the approach to the line and subsequent relief, is Barwick's interpretation of an incident involving English troops later in the year. The manner in which the English troops blundered through a relief allowed Barwick to laugh at their expense. He termed their predicament a 'screaming farce' and described them as 'turning up in little mobs all hopelessly lost and out of touch . . . why not even their NCOs or officers knew for a start where they were going'.[42] He drew comparison between the initiative and individuality of the Australians and presumed docility of the English : 'They never question their leaders even if they are on the wrong track but will blindly follow him'. They were 'a mob of kids' headed by 'incompetent and useless officers'.[43]

Useless incompetent officer types were not restricted to the ranks of the English. A description by an Australian officer of a relief prior to the battle at Pozières serves as a further example of how Australian soldiers could be dismissive and derogatory about their own countrymen:

> Captain McLaughlan of the 5th L.H. (originally) . . . was as hopeless as ever . . . In the evening up came his beauties to relieve us. They certainly appeared to be a pretty good lot of men, but they didn't appear to have much discipline, and the machine gunners came up to make the relief without their guns. One platoon, or most of it, didn't turn up at all before we left, but McLauglan reported all correct, so we didn't enlighten him, but got a move on as soon as possible . . . It was the 47th Battalion which relieved us. Their Colonel seemed to be a particularly useless sort of beggar, and our old man hadn't much time for him.[44]

The mishaps that had befallen the English troops that Barwick had observed were not unique, as one 1st Battalion officer noted: 'the reliefs . . .

are carried out at night and the conditions are rather a strain on the nerves of inexperienced troops . . . and when hitches occur, as they always do . . . the situation becomes even more trying . . . I have seen some absolutely sick with funk.'[45] By Barwick's own testimony, and the confusion into which the 1st Battalion had been thrown during its approach march to Pozières, Australians too were capable of and prone to such 'screaming farce'. Barwick's disdain for the English highlights just how important their failure was to the advancement of Australian worth, despite the occurrence of similar incidents in the 1st Battalion's front-line experience.

Following the fighting at Bullecourt, the British press had been full of praise for the Australians' performance. The British press had, in fact, been praising the Australians since their arrival in France.[46] It was praise that Bean claimed embarrassed the Australians. It is arguable that some of that embarrassment may have stemmed from Australian soldiers being aware that not all had performed in the stoical and heroic image of the stereotype. Lieutenant Richards' account reveals the severity of the fight and the reactions of some of the troops to it:

> We have been right into the gaping jaws of Hell . . . where 1st Bn got into touch with Fritz he got Hell from our rifle and hand bombs also from our snipers. But alas!! there were blunders made by the 3rd and 11th and 12th Battalion that were shocking; they got away from the enemy bombing stunts like cattle stampeding. But looking at it from a personal view it was glorious for me . . . At 9.30 pm as word now came to Coy. Hdqs. that the 3rd Bn. were retiring. Sure enough I found to my dismay it was a fact. I did not think it possible for a crowd of Australians to throw up the sponge so frightfully. I got assistance from some 1st Bn bombers and after a while about 16 of the 3rd were coaxed and bullyed to come and build a barrier and make a stand . . . then this morning fully 200 men of the 11th and 12th Bns. come running out before the German bombing attack. I cursed and swore at the top of my voice, called upon them in the name of Australia to hold out.[47]

Richards, an Australian rugby international, may have had a greater sense of national pride than others. His humiliation at the actions of his countrymen, as well as the drastic measures employed to retrieve the situation, were evident in a second account he wrote of the fighting:

> went back along the roadside bank now lined by 170 or more 11th and 12th Bn men. 'What will Australia think when she knows you deserted your posts and let your brother soldiers down.' That shifted some back to their trench and I saw Lieut. Bruton in the end with his revolver drawn and preventing the men from going further back . . . It was a very exciting hour I can tell you and I would have enjoyed it were the men other than Australians.[48]

Australia was not called on to judge the men. The detail of the fighting was quickly lost to more general descriptions that celebrated the victory. The Australian effort at Bullecourt was the subject of much attention. As Bean noted, due to the British offensive having died down at most points, 'Bulle-court was occupying in the *communiqués* a prominence out of all proportion to its geographical extent. The whole world was now daily following the bare outlines of the struggle there.'[49] Bean himself was not deceived by that out-line. His language was not as passionate as Richards', yet it was clear that there had been some faltering on the part of the Australians. Bean did not speak of any retirement on the part of the 3rd Battalion. He did describe the men at one stage as being 'disinclined to advance' until led forward by an officer.[50] Of the 11th and 12th Battalions, Bean's account was more forthright. He described the 12th Battalion's bombers as having broken back and later: 'Panic had seized most of the garrison and . . . O.G.1 [the trench line occupied at the time] quickly emptied as far as the Central Road'.[51] It was the appear-ance of German *flammenwerfers* that had contributed to the Australians' demoralisation. The 11th Battalion history admitted that the first use of this weapon upon its men had been 'most demoralising'. It went on to describe the nature of the fighting:

> Bullecourt was one of those ding-dong battles which seemed to be all shell-fire and counterattacks, and there was no phase of the 11th Battalion's tour of the line that was particularly outstanding [a concession perhaps to its misfortune]. In all the attacks there were so many units mixed up, and the individual actions were so small, though desperately and fiercely contested, that it is hard to pick out any events of special significance.[52]

Did this battle offer many examples of initiative on the part of the soldiers involved? The examples given suggest not. They demonstrate that the men, far from possessing innate individual qualities, required leadership in battle. While some men were able to summon great courage to stand in the face of adversity, others displayed human frailty in the face of modern weapons. The resourceful digger was not much in evidence, certainly not in any appreciable numbers that justify assertion of resourcefulness as a general quality. There were of course some outstanding individual exploits. Corporal C. J. Howell, who organised a counter-attack in which he ran along the top of the trench bombing and later bayoneted the enemy, was awarded a Victoria Cross. The actions of the bombers, through whose efforts the hold on the trenches was extended, were also highly commendable. However, bombing teams were simply doing their job and formed a distinct and elite group within all British army battalions.

Although Bullecourt is generally regarded as an Australian battle, British divisions were also engaged in severe fighting on the Australian left, to the west and east of the town. On 7 May 1917 the 20th Brigade of the British 7th Division attacked and secured the German trenches immediately east of Bullecourt. The initial assault was conducted by the 2/Gordon Highlanders and 9/Devons. This attack secured the Australian left flank, eventually captured Bullecourt, and finally linked the 7th Division with elements of the 62nd Division which held the trenches west of the town.[53]

If the 11th Battalion described its service as being not 'particularly outstanding', the 1st Battalion stood in obvious contrast. The 1st Brigade and 1st Battalion received the thanks of GHQ for its good work.[54] The survivors took pride in the Battalion's performance, as Ken McConnel noted:

> Bullecourt had been one of the toughest fights the Battalion had seen but one which raised our morale and *esprit de corps* almost more than anything which had gone before. The feeling that we had hung on to a hopeless position for three days without flinching was something which made us feel jolly pleased with ourselves.[55]

The Battalion's good performance at Bullecourt, when combined with the favourable press reports of the Australian performance, naturally boosted the men's self-esteem as soldiers. Whether embarrassed by the attention of the British press or not, it is apparent that the troops were fast arriving at a belief in the truth of such eulogies and in their own superiority. For Archie Barwick the perceived British failure at Cambrai later in the year provided a perverse satisfaction:

> The English papers let themselves in nicely over this Cambrai affair, when the success was reported almost all the papers made a mouthful of it and they repeated it over and over again that this stunt was carried out solely by Imperial troops and no Colonials whatever were engaged . . . and what a gutser the Imperial troops came in the end it has turned out a dismal failure about the worst defeat in one way that has happened to Britain in this war and thank heaven no Colonials were in it . . . the London papers are rather sorry they spoke so hastily for it has only improved the Colonials' prestige.[56]

At Cambrai, the first day of the battle had provided the greatest and most significant gains to the British armies to that date. It also proved beyond doubt the value of the tank as an offensive weapon. The battle's failure—even though at the cessation of German counter-attacks the British gains had been significantly reduced though not fully recovered—lay in the inability of the armies to consolidate gains. This had been the problem throughout the war. In fact, it was a problem that had still not been fully overcome even in the battles that were to mark the final victory. A large part of this problem stemmed from the lack of stability in the Corps structures of the British army. This was a problem that was spared the Dominion troops. British divisions were moved from one corps to another regularly, with the result that divisional, brigade and battalion staffs were never exposed to the doctrines of one particular command. This compromised the soldiers' confidence, trust and training.

For instance one corps involved in the Cambrai offensive had, in one year, thirty divisions pass through it.[57]

By the end of 1917 the men of the 1st Battalion had no doubts about their self-anointed superior status over English troops. Lieutenant H. V. Chedgey, one of the authors of the Battalion's history who shared Barwick's emphatic belief in Australian superiority, wrote: 'the Colonials generally and the Scotch regiments are absolutely the best troops in the British army . . . Most of the Tommies are good, but many of them have no heart'.[58] Antagonisms between Australians (colonials) and Englishmen had existed prior to the war. Rugby and cricket tests were one obvious arena where the conflict was given a gentlemanly face. The war, however, brought about a harder edge to the competitiveness, at least on the part of the Australians. The high sense of nationalism and the sense of proving Australia's manhood on a world stage that many of the men carried to war heightened the rivalry. Moreover, the distance from home and inevitable homesickness that many suffered was further cause for the soldiers to assert their Australian identity. Like many minority groups they became insular and inward-looking as a defence against the isolation and unfamiliarity of their new world. Immediately after the Gallipoli campaign it was evident that the men valued their Australianness greatly. Criticisms of the English troops were one way of expressing this. Another was the pride the men exhibited in their Australian uniform. The issue of Tommy uniforms was considered an insult that brought much chi-acking of the unfortunates who had to don the clothing.[59] In France the soldiers took such matters even more seriously and refused to wear 'Tommy Stuff' altogether.[60]

The Australians were not alone in expressing pride in their national identity. The British soldier was equally adept and did not necessarily share the high opinion of Australians. British soldiers had expressed resentment at what they considered the inflated opinion that Australians had of themselves, an opinion only exacerbated by the excessive reportage of the Australians in the press.[61] Gilbert Hall, a British lieutenant, had rated the soldiers of all nations as inferior to those from Britain; of the Dominion troops he noted: '[they] were always happier if they had Imperial troops at the back of them because they were too impulsive and not steady under pressure'.[62] Assessments such as this are rarely acknowledged by Australian writers and historians.

Following the fighting at Bullecourt the Battalion was not engaged in a major assault until its part in the third battle of Ypres. The Battalion had been used in support in the advance along the Menin Road and had suffered heavily enough given its passive role. Its losses were 8 officers and 144 other ranks.[63] The battle for Broodseinde Ridge, during the third Ypres campaign, stands among the worst experiences of the 1st Battalion. After the fighting at

Pozières, Archie Barwick stated: 'one or two more such battles and we will be no more'.[64] Broodseinde was the second such battle, Bullecourt the first. The Battalion suffered nearly 60 per cent casualties, 299 from 500. The majority were inflicted during a German barrage as the Battalion was forming for the advance. It is a battle, too, that threatens to claim the dispassion of the researcher. At Broodseinde on 4 October 1917 many of the characters of the Battalion, diary and letter writers and those described therein, who have contributed their voices to this narrative, were killed. They were killed in the most random circumstances that underline the susceptibility of the individual to the destructive forces of industrialised war. Jack Vial, who thought Anzacs could do anything, is found curled up in death in a crater at the top of the ridge. Lieutenant McKell, drunk or otherwise, was killed by shell-fire, as was Harry Luders. The irrepressible Philip Howell-Price, bane of so many, died too. He was buried by an explosion and his body never recovered.[65]

Broodseinde had been another clockwork affair, a battle of timetables and limited objectives. The extensive operation planning—given the numbers of men involved, unlike Gallipoli—also linked the Australian commanders more firmly into the chain of command. They had come under the army command of General Plumer, whose methodical and meticulous planning laid the foundations for the success of operations against Messines Ridge. His planning of the other battles along the Gheluvelt Plateau (Menin Road, Polygon Wood and Broodseinde) were hardly distinguishable in human cost from General Gough's rushed and ill-advised attacks at Bullecourt.[66] Irrespective of the qualities of these two generals, the possibilities for independent action (not that it had been instigated at Gallipoli) by the infantry were even less likely. This was despite the diversity in weapons and despite growing emphasis on words such as 'initiative' and 'resourcefulness' in army manuals. The required advance of the Brigade at Broodseinde was only five hundred yards. The 1st Battalion formed part of the 1st Brigade's second wave and had to pass through the battalions holding the first objective. The second objective was 'accomplished according to programme, without any serious opposition'.[67] The authors of the Battalion history were almost moved to condemn the wisdom of the method: 'It seemed a heavy price to pay for a few hundred yards of ground. No doubt the "Heads" knew what they were about and had weighty strategical reasons to advance'.[68] There was some truth to this belief. Although the tactical experience of the Battalion was as bloody as any of its previous engagements, the tactics had contributed to an overarching strategy. The ease with which the British armies had demonstrated their ability to seize nominated points in the German line, such as Broodseinde Ridge, had prompted the German High Command to refer to 4 October as a black day.

According to Bean the British success along the heights of Ypres promised the possibility of a decisive victory in 1918.[69] Prior and Wilson have suggested that a more damning result was the loss of faith (the little there had been) by Britain's Prime Minister, Lloyd George, in the competence and trustworthiness of Haig's predictions. When Haig began to warn of an impending crisis through the build-up in German manpower following the collapse of Russia, Lloyd George, numbed by the barrenness of the Third Ypres campaign, remained unresponsive.[70] More immediately, however, the loss of so many within the Battalion emphasised the fatalistic sentiment conveyed in a trite saying among the men: 'All the good soldiers were killed sooner or later'.[71]

The battles of 1916–17 were so limited in their objectives and so tied to the timetables of the artillery barrages that the infantry advance required little initiative on the part of individual soldiers. Despite the variety of weapons available, and the extensive training given to the men, the infantry were generally not required to fight until they reached the trenchline objective. There, the fighting was sometimes desperate and generally confined to bombing and barricading by degrees until consolidation was achieved. Battle planning was not so much concerned with the tactics of fire and movement specific to the infantry arms, but rather with the co-ordination of the infantry advance with the artillery barrage. The covering barrage was deemed the most appropriate and safest method of assisting the infantry advance. The formation of anachronistic infantry lines or waves strangely complemented the grid-like lifts of the artillery. The weight of artillery that made possible the annihilation of infantry attacks made such tactics inevitable. Understandably, the infantry commanders were loath to forsake the artillery cover. At the same time their reliance on it reduced the possibilities of widespread initiative in the infantry formations. Commanders and men alike were bound to conform to the machinations of the modern battle.

The continuity of outstanding performance by Australian soldiers that is advanced through the legend is not supported by the actions of the 1st Battalion during 1916–17. The Battalion's performance was varied. It was nebulous at best at Pozières, mechanical and orchestrated at Broodseinde. It had failed at Bayonet Trench, and it was dogged at Bullecourt. This doggedness, admittedly, fulfilled the courage and resolution that Monash considered necessary for the successful carriage of battle. Added to these were actions at Mouquet Farm and Menin Road where the Battalion had only passive support roles that required no fighting but in which it, nevertheless, suffered substantial casualties. It is difficult to accept the combined effects and experience of all these actions as proving the existence of alleged national traits such as initiative and resourcefulness, particularly when British and other Dominion units could lay claim to similar experiences. The killing fields of France, nevertheless, were incorporated into the Anzac legend. They have been advanced as further proof, not only of initiative and resourcefulness, but also of the Australian endurance displayed at Gallipoli, thus giving rise to the conviction: 'The tradition of Anzac had certainly been upheld'.[72]

The massive casualties suffered make a mockery about claims of endurance. As we have seen, the modern battle shattered men. Survival was a matter of luck and the keeping of one's 'wits' had little, if any, effect on a man's capacity to survive. The huge losses served also to undermine the *esprit de corps* of the Battalion. The manufactured nature of the Battalion's *esprit de corps* was evident in the aftermath of battle where commanders and men invoked rhetoric that drew comparison with the Gallipoli veterans. The death and maiming of friends, combined with the miseries of the front line, touched the men at a personal level and consistently depressed them after each major engagement. The collective camaraderie that manifested itself as the Battalion's *esprit de corps* was at its strongest when the unit was able to rest and recuperate away from the danger of the front line. No 1st Battalion soldiers mention its existence or influence on their conduct in their more immediate accounts of the fighting. It is apparent that *esprit de corps* was something fashioned *out* of the front line and not readily identifiable *in* the front line. Its intangible nature precludes any complete dismissal of its influence despite the lack of empirical evidence to support its existence.

If a national character trait was discernible it may well lie, not in the physical prowess of the Australians, but rather in the inflated view the soldiers held of themselves. The manner in which Australia's First World War soldiers perceived themselves was, if not a national trait, something that has possibly evolved into a military tradition. In a study of America's Vietnam soldiers, Peter Bourne reflected on the ways of other nations' soldiers. He observed that the Australians emphasised their own qualities while criticising others: 'Closing their minds to all but the performance of their own unit against the Viet Cong they fought a private war in which their own military accomplishments take on a meaning and significance'.[73] In the First World War the Australians acquired a superiority complex in regard to the British, particularly toward the English soldier, that enhanced their own achievements. Despite a number of distinct Australian failures, perceived British failures fuelled the high opinion the Australians had of themselves. It was an attitude that had threatened to take hold at Gallipoli and one which developed in the period immediately preceding the 1st Battalion's arrival in France and flourished thereafter.

The major battles of 1916–17 in France and Belgium clearly demonstrate that there existed little scope for the practice of individuality on the part of the soldiers. It might be argued that greater generosity ought to be extended in discussing the qualities of initiative and resourcefulness in view of the limitations imposed by modern war. The horrific and appalling conditions of the Western Front are fully recognised. However, to attempt to extract positive views through a process of reduction would be to engage in a deliberate and misleading search for positive examples, one not dissimilar to the process of selectivity on which the legend-makers have relied. The fact is, few examples come to the fore to sustain claims that Australian soldiers were more individual and resourceful in combat than those of other nations. On the contrary, it is apparent that the Australian experience was a common one shared by the soldiers of many nations and one on which assertions of national character cannot be predicated with any validity. Despite this, the view of the 'digger' stereotype was and is still fostered.

5

1918: The 'digger' in victory

The final year of the war is almost as important as the events of 1915 in shaping the Anzac legend. Unlike Britain's popular memory, where the victories of 1918 were for many years lost to 'a curious feat of amnesia'[1] brought on by a general revulsion toward the ghastly battles of 1916–17, Australia saw in the final battles an emphatic and everlasting proof of its soldiers' high performance. Just as the original Anzacs had burst upon the stage with the fanfare of a grand opening, the later Australian divisions, filled mostly with 'rainbows' and 'hard thinkers' (as late reinforcements were often dubbed) closed with equal panache. Three phases mark the 1918 campaign. The circumstances of each of these phases are distinct, and the interpretations drawn from them form different strands of the Anzac legend that, when bound together, support the 'digger' stereotype. The first phase is the German breakthrough in March in which the British Fifth Army was broken. Stories of British stragglers being passed by the Australians marching forward to plug the gaps and halt the German advance punctuate many accounts of this period. Examples of British failures or lack of fortitude served to accentuate Australian stoicism in the face of adversity that reinforced the developing superiority complex of the Australians. Second is the phase following the blunting of the German advance in which the front stabilised and, according to the legend, Australian initiative and resourcefulness came to the fore under the guise of 'peaceful penetration', a euphemistic term to describe the Australian method of raiding against German positions. The final phase began with *der schwartz*

Tag (8 August), another of Germany's blackest days, on which the Australians in conjunction with the Canadians and British spearheaded a breakthrough and remained in the vanguard of the pursuit until the Hindenburg line was breached in September–October 1918. It is in the story of 1918 that the legend, at times, assumes its strongest and vainest guise in asserting that without the Australians the war could not have been won. Hyperbolical statements, such as 'without the Diggers the Allies would probably have lost the war',[2] conveniently ignore the many contributing factors that eroded the German war effort and contributed to its final defeat. Australia's five divisions in Europe did at times play an important—and in 1918 a vital—role in the final campaign; however, sufficient manpower was available to the Allies in 1918 (with the arrival of the Americans, even if the 'doughboys' were not as experienced) to compensate for the hypothetical absence of the Australians. Given the success of the Australians in 1918, particularly in the second phase of small-scale operations known as 'peaceful penetration', it is necessary that some context and background be provided before assessment is made of those actions—and more particularly, the 1st Battalion's role in them.

1st Battalion raids and patrols: success, failure and misadventure

It is reasonable to expect that the qualities of individual resourcefulness and initiative, which the legend asserts were intrinsic to the Australian soldier, would be more evident during raids and patrols than the major battles. The apparently flexible nature of raids and patrols would, presumably, suit the alleged natural abilities and temperament of the Australians. If these qualities were little supported by the major actions, it is still possible that they found expression in the smaller actions.

Raids against the enemy's trenches and patrolling of no man's land had become standard practice once the war of movement of 1914 stalled and stagnated into the static lines that characterised trench warfare. They were a feature of tactics on the Western Front in which the Australians had little opportunity to engage until they arrived in France in 1916. Raids were usually carried out for two reasons. First, it was a practical means, through the capturing or killing of enemy soldiers, to identify enemy units. The second reason was the High Command belief that by keeping the troops occupied in such activity, their fighting tenor and morale would be maintained, if not improved.[3] Sometimes, revenge inspired an additional motive for a raid, usually as a reprisal for some enemy transgression or success. Raids and patrols were something in which most troops were engaged or were expected to be engaged by the senior commanders.

Although raids and patrols can both be classed as small-scale actions, each had a separate function. The raid was specifically intended to damage the opposition materially and directly through the killing, capturing and identifying of enemy soldiers. The patrol, on the other hand, was generally undertaken as a means of reconnaissance, principally to gather information such as the location and strength of the enemy lines. Patrols were sometimes formed with an intention to engage the enemy if the opportunity arose. These fighting patrols were a feature of the 1917–18 period. As the war progressed, the tactics of the raid were refined to such a degree that the raids of 1918 bore little resemblance to those undertaken in 1915–16. Raids in the early period of the war resembled miniature set-piece battles and, as with the major set-piece battles, they provided little opportunity for displays of individual initiative on the part of the soldiers.

The 1st Battalion's first major experience of the raid in France came with their preparation for Haig's summer offensive. Raiding was ordered to be stepped up from 14 June 1916 as a preliminary to the Somme offensive and to placate the French who were appealing for an earlier start.[4] On the night of 27–28 June 1916 near 'Ontario Farm' west of Messines, a 1st Battalion raiding party consisting of five officers and sixty men conducted what was considered a successful raid. Raids of this size were generally carefully planned: for example, several days prior to the raid the Australians had practised on trenches modelled on those to be attacked. A heavy box barrage was laid down upon the German trenches in support of the raid. Its purpose was to hinder both the withdrawal and support of the defenders. Nine to fifteen Germans were reported killed and four captured, for the loss of one killed and ten wounded in the 1st Battalion.[5] According to one raider, the morale of the Australians was high after the success and he returned 'happy', believing 'the 1st Battalion had acquitted itself with honour'.[6] Another soldier, on the other hand, thought the raid was not worth the life lost. Sergeant Downer, who was described as 'popular', 'clean-living', an 'old hand', was killed.[7] Downer's death cast 'quite a gloom in the Battalion'.[8] Military success did not necessarily compensate for the sense of loss felt by men for their comrades. Ironically, this Australian success, which was reported in the *Sydney Mail*, was achieved in British uniforms. The despised Tommy clothing had been donned to prevent identification in case any of the men should be killed or captured.[9] The description of the raid that appeared in the newspaper was drawn from a letter by Private T. R. B. Wilkinson to a friend. Wilkinson's description was in contrast to the idealistic style of Bean's writing about the raid on German Officer's Trench (see Chapter 3). It was a balanced account that was free of the heroic rhetoric of the official war correspondent. Its value to the practitioners of Empire loyalty was that it described what was proclaimed 'a great success'.[10]

The reporting of successes perpetuated a belief in the superiority of Australian and British arms over the enemy. The outcome of some raids, however, was failure, providing little support to the mythical qualities of the stereotype. It is perhaps for that reason that discussion of raiding failures has been limited in Australian war writings. One 1st Battalion raid, conducted a month prior to the 'Ontario Farm' raid and unrecorded in both the Battalion and official histories, almost ended in disaster when two parties of the unit, a returning raiding party and a wiring party, became confused, mistaking each other for the enemy. Consequently, each commenced to fire upon and bomb the other. Second Lieutenant Ken McConnel recorded the incident in his memoirs:

> Graham had brought his patrol out in Balaclava caps instead of hats as arranged. Mountcastle, the sentry, challenged, and Graham replied in a whisper, which the former being rather deaf, did not hear, and seeing what he took to be a lot of Huns advancing fired at Graham and put a bullet through his cap. This started the shooting party.[11]

This incident revealed a defectiveness in small action planning on the part of the Battalion, highlighted by a considerable lack of attention to detail. Graham's failure to adhere to original instructions in regard to the type of headgear was one aspect; but the most blatant mistake was the apparent placing of a slightly deaf sentry (presuming his disability was known) at a post shrouded in darkness where the ability to hear was of critical importance.[12]

McConnel had been involved in another botched raid that had been lucky not to end in disaster when his whispered order to 'lie flat' had been misinterpreted by some of the men as 'get back'. Their hasty withdrawal had drawn a severe fire on the raiding party but fortunately no casualties were incurred.[13] Another unsuccessful affair that was mentioned in the Battalion history was a four-man patrol conducted on 31 December 1917.[14] It resulted in two men being captured by the Germans. On returning to their own lines, the two soldiers failed to give the correct password. On failing the challenge, they were duly fired on. They retreated back into no man's land where they became disoriented and were eventually captured by the Germans. A similar fate befell an eight-man patrol of the 1st Battalion in January 1918. According to Lieutenant S. R. Traill, the patrol 'came a gutzer' when it struck an enemy strong-post and the leader, Sergeant Bull—a young sergeant—and three men were hit. Bull called for the remainder of the men to run, which they did, only to be fired upon by another section of the company (D) who had not been apprised of the patrol's existence. Although they gave the password twice and shouted 'We are Australians', another two men were wounded.[15] Such confusion was not uncommon and contradicts the stealth and skill attributed to the Australians through the legend.

It has been suggested that the Australians actually enjoyed raiding and patrolling, viewing that mode of warfare as an exciting but deadly game.[16] The suggestion that the men enjoyed such operations has little credibility. Although it was true that many of the men adopted a seemingly light-hearted manner prior to going out, such behaviour was more often a defence mechanism to mask the fear they felt. This process was especially evident in the accounts of some of the junior officers whose role it was to lead the raids and patrols. Raiding commanders, it was said, got 'either military crosses or wooden crosses'[17] and patrol leaders were referred to as belonging to the 'Suicide Club'.[18]

Tensions between officers and NCOs also found expression in these small actions. The fact that patrols and small raids were generally planned in the lower echelons of command made this more likely. In larger operations, both junior officers and NCOs were servants of orders planned beyond their immediate sphere of the platoon or sections. These tensions, as well as the fact that reported successes were not always what they seemed, are revealed by Private Harold Mercer:

> Managed to get on a 'Fighting Patrol' by asking the OC platoon, who was taking it out to put me on. He is a nice fellow, but has a reputation for windiness . . . When we were waiting to go out he did not appear: he had gone sick; and the sergeant, Vic Stevenson, was ordered to take the platoon out . . . We met nothing however, and did not stay out long. Stevenson, who was in a fully lively condition [possibly drunk], said if it wasn't good enough for the OC to go swimming in No Man's Land it wasn't good enough for him. He found a pillbox and we stayed there for an hour or so, when he took us back, having written out a report in which he referred to violent opposition etc![19]

Another account of a 'fighting patrol', conducted a week after Stevenson's patrol, is illustrative of the apprehensions often felt. Also, the timidity of the unnamed officer of Mercer's account contrasts dramatically with the bellicosity of Captain Edgely described by his accompanying sergeant:

> we had to patrol No Man's Land looking for stoush . . . luckily we found nothing . . . though had we followed the plan that Capt. Edgely planned out at first there would have been some fun and bullets flying, he had the crazy idea of going out with the Hale's rifle grenades and a Lewis-gun . . . to shoot the grenades into their stronghold and then turn the gun on them, the maddest thing I ever heard of, what gutsers we would have come . . . for the place simply stinks with machine-guns, he and Kelleway were going out first; I nearly died laughing to see the look on poor Kelleway's

face when Edgely was planning his scheme. Charlie is no hero and makes no bones about it either, he regards Edgely as a madman and I fancy the majority of the Coy have the same opinion, he's what you call a military marnae [sic. martinet?] therefore he's a nuisance to the troops . . . he ended up by calling it up and squibbing it himself, sent Kelleway out to see what was going on . . .[20]

The notion of 'squibbing' featured in another of Archie Barwick's accounts of one of Edgely's patrols and highlighted the likely outcomes that such action could have on a soldier's standing within the Battalion:

Capt Edgely had Sgt McNab up today for cowardice it appears he was sent on a liaison patrol . . . a mere nothing, but he squibbed it and went back and reported all correct, his officer had his suspicion so he questioned him and eventually put him under arrest he got a severe reprimand and a great lecture, he won't last long his platoon have no time for him and once that happens, good bye, it was his first time in the line and he made a sorry mess of it.[21]

These examples reveal a marked tension between officers and NCOs which clearly, at times, undermined the efficiency of the Battalion's military operations. They also highlight the importance of junior officers and senior NCOs in the conduct of raids and patrols. Such operations were generally led by a lieutenant or experienced sergeant, irrespective of its size or purpose. They were more often planned rather than *ad hoc* affairs. A set pattern was applied to patrols. For example, in a four-man patrol a diamond formation was usually adopted.[22] The patrol leader occupied the advance point with a trusted NCO or scout on his right or left. The remaining two men, the other flank guard and man at the rear, were generally detailed to provide covering fire or support for the other two. Descriptions of a number of patrols reveal that the two men in support were generally privates or corporals. It was the patrol leaders who encountered the most danger and who, generally, instigated the actions that achieved the success or failure of an operation. If initiative was displayed during raids and patrols, it was most likely to emanate from the leader.

Patrols and raids during the period of 'open warfare' in 1918 were generally conducted at the platoon level. The exact character of these small actions was dictated by the variables that confronted the various patrols, so that each was distinct in its own way. However a certain method, practised and learnt, underpinned these actions. A hypothetical example of an investment of an enemy-held farmhouse was supplied by General Monash:

The Lewis gun section would, from a concealed position, on one flank, keep the place under steady fire. The rifle grenadiers from the same or another flank would fire smoke grenades to make a smokescreen. One section of riflemen would endeavour to sneak up depressions and ditches or along hedges, so as to get well behind the farm and threaten it by fire from the rear. The other section of riflemen would choose some direct line of attack, over ground which offered concealment to them until they were close enough to take the objective with a rush.[23]

It was an operation that Monash considered required 'skill, resource and energy'.[24] The secret of the Australian success in open fighting, he asserted, was due to 'the extraordinary vigour, judgement and team-work which characterized the many hundreds of little platoon battles' which were fought along the lines he had described.[25] Given the uniform successes achieved by the Australians in this mode of warfare during 1918, it is likely that Monash's assessment was, in the main, correct. Other factors though, made these successes probable and open to exploitation.

In contrast to the general successes of 1918, the performance of the 1st Battalion in raiding and patrolling up to the early months of 1918 was variable. Success and failure were equally prevalent in such operations. Raids and patrols were high-risk operations and, accordingly, failure was common. In view of the praise generally ascribed to the Australians, it is pertinent to assess the merits of the 1st Battalion in relation to their participation in trench warfare. Success and failure in raids is one method of assessing the effectiveness of a battalion. Judged in that light, the 1st Battalion could not claim to be a highly efficient unit at patrolling and raiding prior to and during the early months of 1918. However, such a judgement ignores the fact that raiding and patrolling were highly hazardous enterprises. In his study of trench warfare, Ashworth chose to measure the *elan*, rather than the efficiency, of particular battalions by assessing their willingness to engage the enemy. His focus was on British units only. By examining the unit histories of three particular units, the 11th East Yorks Regiment, the 7th Royal Sussex Regiment and the 1/4th Duke of Wellington's Regiment, he assessed, through interpretation of descriptions of their trench tours, whether some units were more prone than others to the 'live and let live' principle, that is, participation in tacit truces or non-aggression pacts with the enemy. He suggested three main ways in which this system was expressed. Infantry groups could fraternise at sap-heads, machine-gunners could remain inert, and artillery could ritualise their aggression, that is, regulate their fire to particular patterns.[26] He categorised the sectors in which a unit was assigned in three ways. The intensity of a sector could either be 'active', 'quiet' or 'not known'. Through a similar examination of the 1st Battalion history, figures for the Australians can be integrated —acknowledging that there may be some discrepancies in interpretation— with Ashworth's study. In acknowledging the inexactness of this method and the possibility of discrepancies in it, conclusions that are drawn remain speculative.

Table 8: Assessment of active and non-active trench tours by various troops on the Western Front

Trench tours	1st Battalion		11th East Yorkshire		7th Royal Sussex		1/4th Duke of Wellington	
	no.	%	no.	%	no.	%	no.	%
Active	16	51.61	5	12.19	17	34	24	48
Quiet	10	32.25	22	53.65	22	44	20	40
Not known	5	16.12	14	34.14	11	22	6	12
Total	31		41		50		50	

The figures in Table 8 do not relate to the fighting associated with the larger battles but rather with the act of holding the line. The total number of front-line tours by the 1st Battalion, which usually ranged between four to six days, is lower because the figures for the English regiments incorporate tours in 1915, a year prior to the Australian arrival in France. According to Ashworth, the high percentage of quiet tours implied that tacit truces were a regular feature of a unit's life in the front line. In this application of the 'live and let live' system the 1st Battalion appear to have been participants, though less so than the English regiments examined. The additional twelve months that the English regiments served may have contributed to their higher total of quiet tours, in that their longer war service may have reduced their aggression, both in desire and in loss of effectiveness following high casualties from the 1915 battles.

The majority of the 1st Battalion's quiet tours can be associated with three distinct periods. The first is in the Battalion's introduction to the line during May–June 1916. This was a period of training and acclimatisation to the routines of trench life. The other quiet periods were during the winters of 1916–17 and 1917–18. As we have seen, in both winters the Battalion's morale and organisation was shattered by the protracted offensives that had preceded them. This may have been equally true of the English regiments. Ashworth does not address that point directly. He does, however, assert that extreme conditions did not necessarily quell a unit's willingness to engage the enemy and cites the first trench raid by the 1/Worcester Regiment as an example.[27] The fact that this was that unit's first raid marks it as an exception rather than the norm. It is likely that most troops saw the hibernating effects of winter as offering a measure of salvation following the bloodshed of the summer and autumn campaigns.

The units that Ashworth examined were members of what he termed non-elite divisions. Having established that a measure of 'live and let live' was widespread in non-elite divisions, Ashworth wondered about its prevalence in elite divisions, although he argued that there were few elite divisions in the British army by the end of the war. The 1st Battalion definitely considered themselves to be 'crack' troops.[28] They believed themselves to be more war-like than their English comrades and not given to the friendly proclivities they sometimes detected. When the Battalion relieved the 5th Yorks in a sector known as 'the Maze' in January 1917, Lieutenant Richards was astonished by the sight of 'two Germans waist high over their trench waving a bottle and beckoning to us, at the same time calling out loudly'.[29] Importantly, he went on to differentiate what he implied were the prevailing Australian and English attitudes toward the enemy:

> it is said that the Tommys commonly do this sort of thing with the Germans, and in consequence neither side fire at the other . . . But this is the Australians' first day in the trenches here, so I reckon that in a few days there will be no more looking down at one another, it will be war to the teeth.[30]

Richards' observation is confirmed by the Battalion history, which recorded: 'The events of the first few days showed us that a "friendly war" had been going on for some time, neither side being frightened to show themselves, confident that they would not be fired on. But this was soon changed and the old order of hate was resumed.'[31] This view was further confirmed by another 1st Battalion officer a year later: 'When our artillery took over they found that, as usual they had been playing the Saxon game of "You don't fire, and we won't". The cold footed hounds. The more one learns of the Tommies, the more one despises them.'[32] Such experiences naturally cultivated the Australians' belief in their superiority as fighters over the English. If we accept that the Australian divisions were among the elite or 'crack' divisions of the British army, and the Anzac legend, through its lack of distinction of individual units, purports that they were, we would expect that the 'live and let live' principle had no place in their front-line experience. On the contrary, 'live and let live' *was* a component of their trench warfare experience, even though the Battalion's upholding of it coincided with a general downturn in active operations. The 1st Battalion's participation in that process stands in opposition to the martial ardour and aggression that the legend asserts the Australian soldier possessed.

Although the Australians welcomed the respite that a 'quiet' sector offered, there is little evidence to suggest that during 'quiet' tours they openly fraternised with the enemy.[33] Certainly they did not express the same empathy toward the German soldier as they had toward the Turkish soldier in 1915. Ashworth has suggested that the use of the friendly term 'Jerry', by British troops, was one of the forms in which the soldiers expressed a 'consciousness of kind' with the enemy.[34] The more derogatory terms 'squareheads' and

'Huns' were most often used by the letter and diary writers of the 1st Battalion. Any feelings of empathy were more likely to be internalised by the men, because the public expression of such feelings could invoke hostility. For example, when a junior officer suggested that the Germans weren't such bad fellows, Captain Howell-Price—whose two brothers had been killed in France —retorted: 'The only good German is a dead one'.[35]

As was true of the major battles previously discussed in which the 1st Battalion participated, the raids and patrols conducted up to the end of 1917 provide little evidence to emphatically support the general qualities advanced through the 'digger' stereotype. The Battalion's performance in these operations was variable, although the men's own opinion of their performance was generally high. However, in 1918, the success of the Australians during the period of operations known as 'peaceful penetration' would further cultivate the image of the Australians as natural-born soldiers, not only in the eye of patriotic war correspondents but also among the soldiers themselves.

Phase 1: Holding the line—'Britain's Last Hope'

The German breakthrough in March 1918 was the greatest crisis of the war that beset the British army during the Australians' time in France. Its dramatic opening reinforced to the Australians, who had been spared the danger of the front line in the early months of 1918, their superiority over the English. On hearing of the Germans' success, Lieutenant Sydney Traill declared: 'Those Tommies can't fight for nuts'.[36] His estimation did not mellow with time. Five weeks later he again passed comment: 'The name of the Tommy stinks in a good many quarters now, for it is coming out that they retreated a long way further than they need, and that the staff was a hell of a failure—Damn them'.[37] It is doubtful that the Australian divisions would have fared any better than the English under the circumstances. Some of the most highly regarded British divisions, Maxse's 18th and 30th in particular, were overrun and fine reputations were blighted.[38] While it was true that some British units succumbed sooner than was warranted, it was also true that others, far from melting before the German assault, fought on courageously and exacted a heavy toll upon the enemy.[39] The Germans had, in fact, suffered grievous casualties during the offensive. On the first day, alone, they suffered 40,000, and by the end of June the total had escalated to 680,000, of whom 114,000 had been killed. These losses had drastic repercussions on the quality of the German army that saw Ludendorff demanding the call-up of 17-year-old youths.[40]

In regard to the alleged poor performance of the British, the Battalion history stands in refreshing contrast to the opinions expressed by its soldiers, a testament, perhaps, to the fairness of 'Judge' Stacy, one of its authors and Battalion commander at the time:

> the Germans had been moving forward, delayed only by the gallant rearguard actions of some of the British units, such as the 5th Scottish Rifles, whose splendid conduct in the midst of what was practically a debacle *has not been sufficiently recognised, at least by Australians*. Too much was afterwards said about the bodies of stragglers encountered by us on our way into the line, and not enough of the many little groups of Tommies who, frequently without any leader, were still maintaining a stubborn resistance when the 1st Australian Division took over the front. On our own Battalion sector the bodies of several British soldiers were found beside little mounds of empty cartridge cases, which clearly showed what that retreat had been.[41]

Even though the strategic situation was critical at this time, the Australians were not seriously pressed. Their position was largely defensive and consisted of a number of small outposts arranged in such a way that they provided mutual support. The one German counter-attack that was made against the Battalion was described as being 'easily repulsed by rifle and Lewis gun fire'.[42]

German aggression had, in fact, lost its edge by the time the Australians reached the field. Not least among the factors contributing to this were the exhaustion and indiscipline that had compromised the German onslaught.[43] The German offensive had ground to a halt by mid-April and by the month's end new attacks had ceased against the British front.[44] In the face of this, and despite much anxiety over what its fate might be, heavy demands had not been made of the 1st Battalion. Furthermore, the defensive posture assumed by the Battalion had provided no opportunities for its soldiers to express their individualism, defined through their ability to display initiative in the face of adversity and in the absence of officers, to the same degree as had many of the British defenders whom they relieved. The critical nature of the operations at this time and the reliance on the Australians to hold the line, irrespective of whether the fighting was less demanding than in previous engagements, added further to the men's soaring morale. This pride in Australia (as well as the completeness of a soldier identity) was epitomised by Private A. C. Traill: 'you will have seen by the English papers what a bulwark I have been during this her darkest hour, in fact I am feeling rather proud of myself, you know it is something to belong to one of these famous Australian battalions'.[45]

The gravity of the strategic situation in April and May 1918 was not lost upon the 1st Battalion. The men were acutely aware of the potential danger in which they were placed and talked of the inevitability of 'being cut-off and annihilated'.[46] The very nature of the situation had generated an excitement that increased their awareness of their soldierly duties; they joked of being 'Britain's Last Hope'.[47] The crisis gave meaning to their actions. The Australians would be saviours. By holding fast they could, in a very real sense, contribute to the saving of the British line. Previous battles had never delivered such a clearly defined and urgent task. More importantly, the crisis had heralded a brief return to a war of movement and open warfare. The oppressive atmosphere of trench deadlock and incessant artillery barrages had, for the moment, vanished. As the Battalion history noted, more scope for initiative was now presented to the junior commanders.[48]

Phase 2: Peaceful penetration

'Peaceful penetration' is a term used to describe the Australian method of raiding during April to July 1918. According to Bean the term, which had previously been used by the press to describe the spread of German trade into British territories, was first used by the 46th Battalion in orders for 30 April 1918.[49] The abilities that the Australians displayed in their dominance over the Germans during the period April to July 1918 have come to be seen as a general quality. Peter Simkins has suggested that the Australian successes in mid-1918 were attributable to their 'qualities of enterprise and *bushcraft*'.[50] Enterprise most definitely featured in the Australians' actions, but the skills of bushcraft were as alien to the average 'digger' as they were to his British counterpart. Other reasons can be added to explain the successful raiding and patrolling of the Australians achieved in mid-1918. The first was that an aggressive policy of raiding had been adopted throughout the Australian Corps at this time.[51] It was deemed essential to control no man's land and maintain dominance over the enemy, who were considered to be suffering from a lack of alertness, and it was ordered that two patrols, nightly, were to scout no man's land.[52]

The 1st Battalion was particularly prominent in the latter stages of this period and did, in fact (according to the official historian), provide the climax to these operations. The reason for this was that the 1st Battalion successfully raided the Germans in daylight rather than under cover of darkness. The Battalion commander, Lieutenant-Colonel Stacy, believed that 'great opportunities' existed during the day due to enemy inattentiveness that ought not be passed up.[53] Stacy had, to that point been concerned by his Battalion's lack of raiding success.[54] Despite active patrolling, the 1st Battalion had been unable to secure prisoners to add to the tally being recorded by other battalions. Stacy's anxiety over his Battalion's success most likely figured in his decision to attempt a daylight raid. The success of the first daylight raids vindicated his decision. Two patrols led by lieutenants Gaskell and Morley succeeded in capturing sixty-eight Germans and cleared a 250-yard section of the German's outpost line. A further twenty-five prisoners were secured as further patrols were pushed forward to reap the rewards of the initial success.[55]

Although the successes of 'peaceful penetration' brought acclaim to the 1st Battalion and AIF, they were not without their debilitating effects. A study of the 1st Battalion's sick evacuations between December 1917 and July 1918 provides a revealing insight to the men's health. The winter of 1917–18 had made severe inroads on the Battalion. Nearly 25 per cent of the Battalion's line strength was evacuated between 15 November 1917 and 11 January 1918, during which time the Battalion spent a spell in a quiet but waterlogged sector of the front line in the Wytschaete area.[56] While an outbreak of scabies and laryngitis accounted for nearly one-third of these (27.33 per cent), pyrexia of uncertain origin (PUO) was also responsible for 30 per cent. Pyrexia (fever or raised temperature) when unattributed to any other illness could be considered psychosomatic and a likely reaction to the stresses of active campaigning, though there exists no way of proving such was the case. Its correlation with the 1st Battalion's activities suggests it was a *bona fide* war neurosis or nervous disorder and not a non-battle casualty as it was usually classified. Evacuations and the prevalence of PUO diminished during the period of 11 April to 4 May 1918, suggesting the restorative benefit of good weather and lack of front-line activity. However, at the height of the Battalion's involvement in 'peaceful penetration' the anxiety that the soldiers had felt at the instability of their position during the German breakthrough now manifested itself physically following protracted engagement with the enemy. PUO constituted 70.9 per cent of evacuations during 19 June to 15 July 1918.[57] Australian soldiers were continuing to break down, psychologically and physically, even in victory.

A range of factors contributed to the Australian successes in mid-1918. The Australians were fortunate to have reached the front after the climax of the German breakthrough and, as has been noted, the German advance had lost its impetus. A further boon to the Australians and other Empire troops was that, in preparation for a renewed effort against the French, the Germans withdrew many of their most experienced units and supplemented them with inferior ones. The Germans facing the Australians were low in morale. A report by an Australian war correspondent noted:

> the German divisions here are steadily deteriorating with the increasing proportion of new and young drafts . . . As Australians judge them, some of the machine gunners may be relied on to fight to the last, the other infantry is strikingly inferior . . . Prisoners sometimes surrender easily, almost amicably.[58]

Not surprisingly, the Germans' defensive lines were being neglected and were subsequently less formidable than those previously confronted. The high tally of prisoners captured during this period needs to be considered against that fact.

Information about the poor quality of the German defenders was being regularly transmitted to divisional, corps and army headquarters through the intelligence reports of Australian units. In response, the Australians were directed to pressure the enemy through active patrolling and raiding of no man's land. This was a command initiative that the men were compelled to obey. A further benefit to operations was the fact that it was spring. The crops in the fields were standing tall, the area having previously been spared the ravages of war, and provided ideal concealment for any attacker. These things aside, there is no doubt that the Australians achieved a superiority over their opponents during the mid-1918 period. The uniform successes of the Australians during 'peaceful penetration' had not, however, been reflected in the Battalion's previous raiding performances. This fact suggests, aside from the crumbling German resistance, that the 'craft' of raiding had been gradually learned and the necessary methods honed over the previous years.

It might be argued that had the Australians the opportunity to engage earlier in the type of operations that characterised the mid-1918 period, they would have proved themselves similarly adept. It is impossible to state categorically whether this would have been the case, and in fact it is unlikely. Prior to 1918 the German army was still strong and, simply, did not allow such a situation to develop in 1916–17. The general morale of the German army during 1916–17 appears to have been stronger and more resilient than in 1918. This is certainly reflected in the demeanour and preparation of the enemy soldiers that the 1st Battalion encountered in mid-1918.

The crisis of 1918 was instrumental in descriptions of the quality of the AIF. Irrespective of all the glory attributed to the Australians during the period of 'peaceful penetration', it was clear that at its outset, the morale of the 1st Battalion was not at its best. Some of the Battalion's finest fighting leaders were struggling to maintain their devotion to duty. Lieutenant Richards, who had been pained by the sight of retreating Australians at Bullecourt, was one: 'I have written to several of my girl friends telling them of my war weariness and home sickness. This, however, (be it a fact or not) I have to fight it down, live right over the top of it to fulfil my position as a soldier.'[59]

War-weariness troubled the Australian commanders since it made the men susceptible to thoughts antithetical to a soldier's duty. Ultimately, the 1st Battalion mutiny that occurred in September 1918 proved that such concern was not unfounded. Officers were worried by the distribution of large quantities of a pacifist journal, *The Herald*, among the ranks, apparently 'being read with interest by Australian soldiers'.[60] There also existed signs that the men's discipline and pride in the Battalion had lapsed. In stark contrast to the eagerness and pride displayed in 1915, many men were appearing on parade without the Battalion's colour patch sewn to their uniform although ample numbers had been issued.[61] It was also apparent that harmony within the Battalion's officer–man relationships was as volatile as it had been throughout the war. In early April, Sergeant Barwick was of the belief that the men had been treated 'very shabbily', particularly by Captain Somerset whom he described as 'too regimental . . . [and] thoroughly disliked by the Coy'.[62] At that time, Barwick believed it was the Battalion's misfortune to have 'a rotten lot of officers'.[63] He had earlier commented: 'The coy is getting in a bad state . . . there is too big a strain placed on the men and it's time they [the officers] took a jerry'.[64]

Nevertheless, the period of 'peaceful penetration' did see a new buoyancy in the Battalion's attitude. The reasons for the brighter outlook are suggested in the Battalion history:

> The countryside was all verdant, with growing crops, and it was possible to move and look about under conditions far different from those of the old trench, or semi-trench warfare. And, the greatest boon of all, there was no mud. The fighting itself was far less of the mechanical type, and there was much more scope for initiative on the part of lower commanders in the posts. Last, but not least, the shell fire was not nearly so heavy . . .[65]

This statement by the Battalion's historians was a tacit acknowledgment of the stultifying effects of the modern battle on the enterprise of the individual and small-group formations. It also raises another important point. Until now, the theme of initiative has been viewed in the context of the individual. In this instance, use of the term 'initiative' has been qualified. It was not a general quality of all soldiers. The opportunity of displaying initiative lay, not with the common soldier, but rather with the junior commanders. The more general use of 'initiative' was, however, reinforced in eulogies of the AIF. Marshal Foch, who as Allied Commander-in-Chief had no direct experience of (or contact with) the Australians, praised their 'initiative and fighting spirit, their magnificent ardour' and called them 'shock troops of the first order'.[66] Rhetorical statements such as this further entrenched belief in the stereotype.

Commanders who were closer to the operations of the AIF were also prone to uttering clichés that perpetuated the 'digger' stereotype. Beneath the veneer of such praise, however, it was evident that the speakers were keen to offer logical reasons that underpinned the Australians' success. For example, in an address to Australian soldiers, Haig was reported by F. M. Cutlack as saying that, apart from their courage and initiative, it was by virtue of their discipline and organisation that they had become great soldiers.[67] Organisation referred to the leadership of the Australians. General Rawlinson, commanding Fourth Army, also praised the Australians for their 'diligence, gallantry and skill', but added that the successful application of 'scientific methods . . . thoroughly learned' had also contributed to their good performance.[68] The comments by Foch (1919) and Rawlinson (1918) were made in the flush of victory and referred specifically to the recent successes and contributions of the Australians. These men, too, were publicists of the Allied cause, as was Haig in his public statements. It should also be said of Haig, that in his capacity as the Commander-in-Chief of British armies in France, he was necessarily cautious and unlikely to be too critical in his comments about the Australians. He was aware of the Australian Government's concerns over British discipline, of its desire to consolidate the Australian divisions into an army under Australian commanders and, importantly, of the risk of jeopardising the conscription debates in Australia in 1916 and 1917, which, had either been successful, would have provided much-needed reinforcements to his command.[69] As well, there was a belief in Haig's GHQ that the 'more phlegmatic English and Scotsmen' preferred to remain aloof from public praise, in contrast to the Australians and Canadians who were considered to derive obvious pleasure from such reportage.[70] Given this belief, it is possible that Dominion troops were more likely than British troops to be praised publicly by senior British commanders. One of the more astute comments to be made about the Australian soldier of the First World War was that by Major-General John F. O'Ryan of the American 27th Division, who had fought alongside the Australians and liaised closely with them. O'Ryan also pointed to the excellence of another, rarely acknowledged, quality of the AIF: 'the Australians had become refined by an experienced battle technique supported by staff work of the highest order'.[71]

In sum, the comments of these senior officers point to something other than natural abilities to explain the success of the Australians in 1918. Moreover, the term 'initiative' when applied to the AIF developed from a *general* use by commentators early in the war to a *specific* and military-structured use late in the war. In particular, it was being applied to the qualities of the General Staff and combat leaders of the AIF.

Phase 3: 'Der schwarz Tag' (and Chipilly Spur)

By late July 1918 the period of stabilisation, marked by the successes of 'peaceful penetration', ended and the Allied generals prepared to strike what they hoped would be the decisive final blow. On the British front, the Australian Corps, Canadian Corps, and British III Corps were selected to spearhead a blow against the German line east of Amiens. At 4.20 am on 8 August the artillery barrage erupted, signalling the commencement of the British attack. By day's end, the German line had been broken on a fifteen-mile front and a wedge driven in to a depth of six to eight miles. The success of the operation was a great fillip for Australian morale. Yet again, criticisms of the British performance were advanced to underscore Australian achievement. Lieutenant Traill—no lover of the English, as we have seen—exhibited his disdain plainly in his description of the operation: 'all got their objectives except those miserable Tommies who failed as usual, at Chipilly . . . So far it is believed that the attack has been uniformly successful, with the exception of the Tommies, whom everyone guessed would fail'.[72] Traill's comments were grossly unfair. The failure of the British III Corps on the Australians' left flank was due to a number of factors, not least that its commander was suffering from overstrain. It had been attacked two days before the offensive began. The III Corps had lost ground but regained most of it in a counter-attack the following day. They were exhausted when the offensive was launched. Furthermore, the ground over which they had to advance was more difficult than that which faced the Australians. As a consequence they had been allocated only 36 tanks compared to the 288 assigned to the Australian and Canadian Corps.[73] The battle had still not provided a decisive break-through. It had been carefully planned and had targeted the weakest known section of the German line. Yet the Germans had still been able to arrest the advance, though not with the alacrity that had marked previous counter-attacks. The most significant aspect of the battle was the effect on the German High Command. The ease with which the Allies had gained their initial objectives foreshadowed likely future outcomes. They now accepted that the war could only end in German defeat.[74]

The various tactical, topographical and physical factors provide specific details about Australian successes which few chroniclers of the Anzac legend have considered. General John Monash was probably one of the most influential writers in this regard. His book *The Australian Victories in France*, published in 1920 and feted in the aftermath of victory, set the tone for Australians' view of their achievements in this phase of the war. Monash recorded the Australian contribution to victory in yards and materials.[75] As we have seen, the factors contributing to victory were many, and the variables not always equitable. The Australians had possessed advantages over both their British comrades and the enemy. To suggest that these gains were proof of the Australian soldiers' greater individuality and ability in battle is to ignore the diversity of influences that contributed to the final victory. In fact in the attack of 8 August, and to a lesser extent Hamel on 4 July (the two most emphatic victories won by the Australians during the war), the demands upon the infantry had been considerably reduced through the use of combined arms. Planning had won the day. Both battles reflected Monash's ideal battle. Nevertheless, it is also sobering to note that Australian casualties in the two-month period 8 August to 6 October 1918 amounted to 21,243. At Fromelles, Pozieres and Mouquet Farm, over a slightly shorter timespan, 19 July to 5 September 1916, the Australians had suffered 28,259 casualties. The improved methods applied during the battles of 1918 had certainly reduced the flow of blood. However, the casualties sustained proved that even in its inexorable slide to capitulation the German army could still exact a heavy toll.

The success of 8 August forms a critical juncture in the Anzac legend. Given the German High Command's response, the events of that day elevated the AIF's role to a central one in the forging of Allied victory. Furthermore, comparison of the yards gained by the Australians against those of the British divisions provided a seemingly measurable proof of Australian superiority. As well, the failure of the British to gain Chipilly Spur on the Australian left flank opened the door of opportunity for a group of 1st Battalion soldiers to undertake an action that would draw together all the central strands of the Anzac legend in seemingly incontestable proof of the 'digger' stereotype.

The general failure of the British drew extra hostility within the ranks of the 1st Battalion when one of its members, Lieutenant R. O. Samuels, who was undertaking a reconnaissance patrol near Chipilly, was supposedly shot dead by English troops.[76] According to Bean, though, Samuels was shot by a German patrol who were retiring from the village.[77] The confusion and willingness to blame the English was not surprising for two reasons. The first was that the Australians had built up such a negative view of the English that such alleged ineptitude was easily believed. Second, the village lay between the heights held by the Germans and the line held by the British. It was disputed territory and had been reported as being in the possession of the British. English patrols, whose reconnaissances would likely have been observed by the Australians watching on the opposite bank of the Somme, had visited the village. At the time of Samuels' patrol an English patrol had also entered the village. This incident illustrates sharply how rumour and preconceived notions could shape a soldier's interpretation of his war experience. A soldier's reactions and thoughts were shaped by the reality of the chaos of the battlefield; the fog of war. Actual experience was not shaped by facts that became known retrospectively. Facts gathered after the event were crucial, however, in the reshaping of experience as soldiers reinterpreted their war service in the light of new evidence. This is evident in many of the post-war accounts. Consequently, those accounts are not necessarily accurate descriptions of a soldier's actual experience.

The raid at Chipilly had its genesis in the complications that beset the British III Corps on 8 August. As a result of these difficulties, already discussed, the III Corps was unable to keep abreast of the Australian advance. The British right flank, which rested on the Somme River, had been unable to dislodge the Germans holding the high ground referred to as Chipilly Spur. Subsequently the Australian left flank was being enfiladed by the Germans on the spur and the advance of the Australian Corps was being compromised by this fire. At the time the 1st Battalion was in reserve with the rest of 1st Brigade. On the morning of 9 August, two 1st Battalion sergeants, Jack Hayes and Harold Andrews, ventured across a small bridge in search of souvenirs in the village, which they found to be unoccupied. The knowledge of this fact opened the possibility of a flank attack on the Germans defending the ridge, and Hayes and Andrews reported it to their Battalion HQ. Later in the afternoon, as a result of General Monash's increased anxiety at the failure of the British to have gained Chipilly Spur, Hayes was ordered by his commanding officer to take a six-man patrol across the river to assist, if possible, the advance of the 2/10th London Regiment, who were preparing for another assault on the position. This was done and on the request of the London's commander the Australians acted as scouts to the flank company of the regiment. In this capacity Hayes, Andrews, and their four compatriots formed two groups who, during a four-hour period (6 to 10 pm), rushed a number of German posts, capturing seventy prisoners and paving the way for the successful clearance of the spur. The performance of the Australians was praiseworthy and certainly embodied key characteristics of the 'digger' stereotype. It was, however, atypical of the general experience of raids and patrols by the 1st Battalion during the course of the war.

The first men, other than those in the front line, to learn of the patrol's success were the men in the Battalion's nucleus, the core that acted as a reserve for the front-line troops. Lieutenant Traill described the action as 'quite an epic'.[78] That Jack Hayes, the patrol leader, was one of his sergeants gave him added pleasure. His disdain for the 'blasted Tommies' was further irritated by the absence in the papers of the Australians' achievement.[79] The raid might have lost its place in the annals of Australian military history had it not been for the controversy that surrounded the capture of Chipilly Spur after the war. Monash, in his book, was either unaware of the details of the 1st Battalion patrol or felt its discussion was not necessary to his narrative. He attributed the spur's capture largely to the arrival and advance of the 131st United States Regiment on 9 August and a series of local operations by the Australians on the following day.[80] This view was subsequently challenged by the commander of the London regiment, who claimed the success without mention of the Australians. His claim was easily rebuffed. Captain Berrell of the London regiment had, in fact, provided Sergeant Andrews with a written acknowledgment of the Australians' part to present to their commander on return to their lines. The exploits of the 1st Battalion patrol at Chipilly are most seductive to the Anzac legend as they bring the tensions between Australians and English to the fore. An obstinate English officer was denying the Australian involvement, which grated on the Australian yearning for a 'fair go'. Moreover, the impressive display of Australian fieldcraft bore out the key qualities of the 'digger' stereotype and, opposed to the lack of initiative and failure attributed to the English soldiers, fed the Australian superiority complex.

As with the general successes of 'peaceful penetration' (for that matter, any military success), there were contributing factors to the Australians' achievements at Chipilly, most of which were noted by one of the patrol's leaders, Harold Andrews, in a seven-page letter to the Director of the Australian War Memorial in 1929. Among these was the fact that the Germans had been fighting for thirty hours and had resisted a number of British attacks, while the Australians were fresh, forming the 1st Brigade's reserve at the time. Consequently the Germans' attention was to their immediate front and not the flank and rear from where the Australians approached. The Australians had been able to gain this advantage under cover of a smoke-screen laid down by a battery of six-pounders that had allowed them to cross the ridge undetected.[81] It has been suggested that the patrol's success was of crucial significance to the Allied advance: 'The actions of six Australians had regained the initiative for the British Fourth Army north of the River Somme'.[82] It is debatable whether the Fourth Army had actually lost its initiative because of the difficulties experienced in capturing Chipilly Spur. It was only a local attack, though one of importance. It is unlikely that the Germans could have held their position much longer, given that the majority of the ridge had been captured the previous day. Furthermore, it was only a day later that the offensive broke down completely on both the Canadian and Australian fronts. Any initiative regained by the British north of the Somme was shortlived, given the general breakdown of the advance. Nevertheless, the inference is clear—a patrol of Australians had paved the way for a British army. None of these things detracts in any way from the audacity displayed by the six Australians. The exclusion of these facts has, however, presented an incomplete picture of what occurred. Australian audacity without the support of the guns would have amounted to little. In the absence of the complete picture a more stereotypical version of the Australians has been advanced.

Taken singularly, the exploits of the 1st Battalion patrol at Chipilly Spur certainly appear to support the qualities of initiative and resourcefulness of the 'digger'. The forcefulness of the patrol's actions as a conduit for the stereotype lies in its representation as a typical example of the actions of the

Australians in 1918. Eric Andrews has argued that there has been a tendency to antedate the efficiency displayed during these raids to the earlier life of the AIF.[83] The skills exemplified by the Chipilly patrol were most certainly not something inherent in the 1st Battalion's actions in the previous years. Nevertheless, the application of superlatives such as the 'amazing six Australians'[84] and statements that celebrated the patrol's action as being 'in the usual spirit of Digger adventure'[85] have, whether intentionally or otherwise, served to foster a general view of the Australians being independent and resourceful.

Superior 'diggers'?

Although many of the eulogies of the AIF were exaggerated, there is little doubt that the performance of the AIF in 1918 was highly regarded then and since. Nevertheless, the qualities of individuality and resourcefulness cannot be advanced as national characteristics reflected in the performance of the 1st Battalion or Australian troops generally. In his study of the 1918 campaign, John Terraine concurred with John Monash's assessment that the success of the Australians lay with the uniformity they were able to achieve throughout their five infantry divisions. Importantly, he pointed out that such formations (although he rated the Australians especially highly) existed in other armies—the French 'Iron Corps' as well as the Guard formations of the German and British armies.[86] If the abilities of the Australians could be replicated in the armies of other nations, then the qualities those armies displayed were more common than is generally acknowledged by proponents of the Anzac legend.

It is also evident that the common soldier of the 1st Battalion looked to his leaders for direction. They were indispensible to the successful conduct of operations. Their presence and performance in battle is, to some degree, reflected in the distribution of military awards within the Battalion. Although the examination of awards cannot prove or disprove the prevalence of soldierly qualities between particular units, it can reveal biases that are of importance within a unit. The nominal roll of the 1st Battalion identifies the names of 224 soldiers who recieved military awards and decorations. Those men constituted only 3.6 per cent of the total of soldiers who served in the Battalion during the war. Military awards—or, more importantly, the deeds that won them—belonged to a significant minority of the unit. In that context, the actions, qualities and character of the men who performed those military feats must be considered atypical of the Battalion's performance generally. Moreover, military decorations awarded throughout the Battalion were not evenly distributed between the various ranks. Officers were more likely to gain awards than NCOs, who were, in turn, more likely to win them than private soldiers, as Table 9 demonstrates.

Table 9: Distribution of awards in 1st Battalion by rank[87]

Rank	Award-winners (%)	Rank in total Battalion (%)
Commissioned officers	28.12	22.02
Non-commissioned officers	45.53	8.78
Other ranks	26.33	1.23
Total	99.98	N/A

Of the sixty-three officers who gained awards, eleven (17.46 per cent) were decorated while serving as other ranks (most were NCOs) prior to gaining their commissions. The exploits of these men in winning decorations marked them as likely candidates for promotion though that, in itself, was not necessarily enough to ensure the award of a commission. The overwhelming percentage imbalance in these figures between the ranks suggests several possibilities. One is that, as with the biases displayed in the selection of the Battalion's officers, a bias was practised in favour of officers in the distribution of awards. If this were the case, the lack of true egalitarianism within the Battalion is underlined. However, a more likely alternative is that the most courageous and inspiring men did, in fact, reside or gain promotion to the commissioned ranks, irrespective of the biases we know to have existed in the attainment of those positions. An officer's role required leadership in battle, and as such it carried with it a higher likelihood of 'heroic' action through personal direction and example setting in combat. The defined roles of leader and follower necessary to the officer–man relationship carry ramifications that run contrary to the assumptions of the 'digger' stereotype. While it is impossible to state categorically that men of other ranks lacked the dash and *élan* expected of the 'officer type', it was certainly true that their role in battle could be, and often was, passive and their participation dependent on their officers' leadership. That dependence erodes the applicability of the qualities of initiative and resourcefulness to Australian soldiers generally.

The existence of a leader–follower dynamic was certainly suggested in the last attack by the Battalion at Ruby Wood on 21 September 1918. This attack by the remainder of the 1st Battalion following the 'walk-out' by the mutineers, was successful with approximately 100 prisoners taken, 'though all of these did not reach the rear'. It is apparent that German resistance remained poor, as was the case throughout the 'peaceful penetration' period: 'The enemy were found in their dug-outs, from which they emerged with their hands up, apparently without any desire to resist'.[88] Lieutenant Sydney Traill, along with a sergeant, operated in advance of the men and was largely responsible for securing the objectives of Company A- bearing out the 1st Brigade CO's belief that Australian soldiers were just as helpless as any other soldier without leadership.[89] Traill's account also illustrates how fragile morale had become at that time and the fear that visited soldiers in the front line:

> The attack went on, we only had 500 yds to go, along the top of the spur, our objective being a series of trenches at the end of it . . . On we bowled and hopped into the trenches. Sgt Barwick [Len, not Archie—who was recuperating from a wound in England] and I went on to the next trench and had the time of our lives hauling Huns out of dug-outs and souveniring . . . Then we commenced to establish posts and re-organise. I had not a single man of A Coy. so started out to collect them . . . Got them at last and got some sort of defence system going, had a handful of men to cover a front of 500 yds, all treacherous cross trench system country too. It had the wind up us . . . I took a wrong turning, saw a Hun peering round a corner . . . that put a further vertical draught up us, for we did not know their strength nor if they were contemplating a counter-attack. It was an anxious time for us . . . there was no relief in sight. How we were to face the prospect of night we didn't quite know. Spirits were at zero.[90]

Traill's flagging spirits were undoubtedly partly due to the sensational events that had preceded the attack. The mutiny that occurred in the 1st Battalion on 21 September 1918 was the most obvious and significant breakdown of the officer–man relationship within the AIF during the war. It represented an inglorious end to what its commanders had always held was an illustrious battalion.

Mutiny: 21 September 1918

The refusal by part of the Battalion to carry out an order for an attack constituted the most serious military offence. It was clearly a case of mutiny and not one of desertion, the crime for which the offenders were eventually charged. While the men believed their refusal to participate in the attack was justified and reasonable on the grounds that they were being overworked, the officers clearly saw the whole affair as not only a stain on the reputation of the Battalion, but also a challenge to the whole concept of duty and discipline that underpinned the army, and one for which the senior Brigade and Battalion commander advocated the maximum penalties available.[91] Even though the Brigade commander's private thoughts show that the weariness of the troops was not without foundation—two days before the attack the condition of the Brigade had warranted a mention in his personal diary: 'Brigade not now up to concert pitch in attack'[92]—he showed no official sympathy for the plight of the mutineers. Lieutenant S. R. Traill's diary also confirms the poor state of the men: 'The men had had a hard time and their nerve was just about gone to shreds'.[93] Sit-down strikes over poor rations and promised holidays may have been treated with some tolerance by officers out of the line but a mutiny, in the face of the enemy, was absolutely unacceptable. No officers participated in the mutiny. Clearly a combination of factors coalesced to make a mutiny possible. The trigger in this instance was the cancellation of a planned relief on the night of 20 September and the rumour that the Battalion was to participate in another attack the following morning. What is of particular interest here is the nature of the response by both officers and men to one another. Their responses reveal a clear difference in the expectations that each held toward the other's behaviour. The men's belief that they were justified in their action revealed a gross underestimation of the consequences that would flow from it.

Displeasure among the men about the proposed attack quickly took hold within the ranks of D Company. Here the NCOs, who were privy to the men's attitude and physical state, were placed in a difficult position. Responsible for the management and conduct of their men, the NCOs were clearly alarmed by the level of dissatisfaction being expressed within the ranks. They took the precautionary step of approaching the company commander, Lieutenant Steen: first, to confirm if the rumoured attack was true, and second, to alert him to the condition of the men, which they believed was parlous and unsuitable to the conduct of successful operations. According to the court-martial testimony of Corporal Alyward, who testified to being 'dumbfounded' by the possibility of such an attack given the state of the men, Steen's response was to dismiss the NCOs' concerns with the statement 'I can't tell the Colonel this'.[94] The NCOs were told by Steen to return to their platoons and ready the men for an attack.[95] This, of course, placated none of the dissenters. Steen was later informed that the men would not abandon the line but would remain as a reserve for the other companies provided they were not involved in the 'hopover'.[96] This did not transpire and the men eventually made their own arrangements for relief. Of all the parties involved in this affair, the NCOs were the most cruelly served. Some were clearly inexperienced. Alyward, for example, had been a corporal only four months and had never been in charge of a platoon before. This worked against NCOs (and officers) in exerting control over the men and in the NCOs' representations with their seniors. It would seem that the decision by NCOs to accompany their men out of the line was a result of that inexperience as well as their loyalty to the smaller group. Lieutenant Mortlock gave evidence to the effect that some of the NCOs clearly stated that there was no point in their participating without their men.[97] Their plight was further complicated when they were assigned the responsibility of being spokesmen once the mutineers had reached the nucleus camp eight miles to the rear of the line. When the penalties for desertion were handed down by the court, the NCOs were dealt with in the harshest manner: most received terms of five to ten years' imprisonment, as opposed to three years handed down to the other ranks.

The loss of officers in D Company just prior to the attack could have been a factor in determining the men's conduct. The presence of more officers might have headed off the developing dissatisfaction. However, this excuse is open to some challenge. Representations had been made to Lieutenant Steen, D Company commander, in the afternoon of the 20th and he, along with Lieutenant Blake, was not wounded until 2.30 am, two and a half hours prior to the attack and nearly twelve hours after it was known that some of the men had refused to draw ammunition.[98] Blake may not have been an ideal officer to rely on for a resolution of the crisis. He had previously been described by a fellow officer as a 'little self-important man . . . [who] could do nothing better or higher in this world than talk about himself'. It is unlikely whether such a man, if this characterisation was true, would exhibit much sympathy for the men's concerns.[99] In Blake's defence, however, it appears that he was wounded soon after being assigned to D Company and had little time in which to influence the situation. The same cannot be said of Lieutenant Steen, who had ample time to alert their commanding officer to the developing crisis but chose to do so only when the situation had further deteriorated. The men of D Company, having made up their minds, were clearly not going to be persuaded otherwise, and Steen's dismissive response to the trouble did nothing to address it. Even an appeal by the most revered of the Battalion's officers, Captain H. H. Moffat, failed to move the men.[1] Moffat had been sent forward when the seriousness of the trouble became known at 1st Battalion headquarters. Bill Gammage, in describing the relationship of officers and men within the AIF, held Moffat up as an example of the 'type of leader that men would follow cheerfully to hell'.[2] Moffat was indeed the *beau idéal* of an Australian officer and man, but it should be recognised that he was atypical, a real-life version of the *Boy's Own* officer.[3] Yet even he was ineffectual in this instance. In view of Moffat's failure to change the men's minds, it is unlikely that the complaint of an anonymous mutineer in later years—that the Battalion Commander, Lieutenant-Colonel B. V. Stacy, could have come up and addressed the men—would have had any effect.[4] Clearly a situation had developed in which it was, as J. J. MacKenzie has noted, 'apparent that the actions of some officers did not give the men satisfaction'.[5]

During the French mutinies of 1917, a preferred method for the defusing of the demonstrations of the mutineers was to have officers known to the men speak to them gently in an attempt to see reason (as the commanders saw it). This succeeded in a number of instances.[6] To a small degree this was tried and failed in the 1st Battalion, evidenced by Moffat's inability to move the men. As much as Moffat is revered in the Battalion's history, his influence in this situation was limited. Although an original Anzac, it is unlikely that he was well known to many of the men. Of the mutineers, only two were 1914 men and only ten were 1915 enlistees. A more telling figure is that which shows 50 per cent of the mutineers had joined the Battalion after the Bullecourt fighting (mid-1917). Furthermore, nearly 50 per cent of the mutineers had returned from hospital to the Battalion during the six months preceding the mutiny. MacKenzie has suggested that these men would have been mindful of becoming casualties again and, by implication, more susceptible to mutiny.[7] The war of attrition had made its mark. The Battalion's cohesion and trust in its officers had been compromised by the losses it had incurred. Only a few men had undergone the natural progression from 1914 through to 1918. The majority were short on experience and not sufficiently imbued with the *esprit de corps* that is fostered to overcome the discomforts, dangers and dissatisfactions that are so much a part of war.

The British historian John Terraine considered that the 1st Battalion mutiny had been 'a mutiny of exhaustion'.[8] MacKenzie, too, concluded that battle fatigue, combined with the combat inexperience of the Battalion's reinforcements, placed them as 'perfect candidates' for being ineffective soldiers and susceptible to mutiny.[9] Battle fatigue was certainly a major contributing factor. Fatigue was ubiquitous in the Battalion's history—it reached chronic levels following Lone Pine and the Somme battles—and, therefore, it cannot be advanced as the sole reason for the outbreak of mutiny. The losses incurred throughout the war brought an added pressure to both men and officers. For a wounded man the make-up of the Battalion could, during his extended absence, be changed so much by casualties and sickness that it little resembled the unit that the he had left and thus made the process of reassimilation more difficult. As a consequence, a strong sense of unfamiliarity invaded the soldier's combat environment. This was revealed in the testimony of one of the mutineers, Private W. Robson. Robson had been absent from the Battalion for nearly two years, because of attachment to other duties and illness, and had only returned to the 1st Battalion two months prior to the mutiny. Unlike some of the other accused he was unable to gain a character reference because, as he stated: 'All the officers that knew me were not with the Battalion when I returned'.[10] Fatigue provided one of the triggers for mutiny in the 1st Battalion. Ultimately, however, it was a lack of communication, trust and intimacy in the officer–man relationship that was responsible for the final breakdown of discipline.

The known presence of fatigue within the unit was possibly a cause for much of the regret exhibited by the combat officers over the fate of the men following the mutiny, and many officers attested at the court-martial to the good, fine or excellent character of the soldiers charged. This bonhomie, according to Lieutenant Sydney Traill, weakened the prosecuting evidence. He believed some of the junior officers had been reticent in giving their evidence, a fact he attributed to the officers being 'frightened of not making themselves good fellows with the men. A common fault with officers these days.'[11] Traill had no doubt that the absence of the death penalty in the AIF was a major contributor to the indiscipline that afflicted it.[12]

The absence of a death penalty does not appear to have influenced the mutineers. Their decision was based upon a perception that they were being asked to do more than their fair share of the fighting, and it is doubtful whether they gave much thought to possible outcomes beyond the expression of their dissatisfaction to their own officers. A comparison of the occupations of the mutineers and non-mutineers (Table 10) suggests that the social background of the men was a factor in their decision to mutiny. Soldiers from labour-intensive occupations were more disaffected than other groups. The three groups, 'tradesman', 'labourer' and 'industrial and manufacturing', account for 62.89 per cent of the mutineers, as opposed to 43.99 per cent of the non-mutineers. The combined occupations of 'professional' and 'clerical' are even more pronounced, representing 16.66 per cent of occupations of the non-mutineers as opposed to only 4.03 per cent of the mutineers.

Table 10: Comparison of occupations of mutineers and non-mutineers in 1st Battalion, September 1918[13]

Occupation	Non-mutineers (%)	Mutineers (%)
Professional	5.33	0
Clerical	11.33	4.03
Tradesman	14	15.32
Labourer	18.66	33.87
Industrial and manufacturing	11.33	13.70
Transport	8	7.25
Commercial	3.33	2.41
Rural	18	12.90
Seafaring	2	2.41
Mining	0.66	4.03
Domestic	4	2.41
Other/Unstated	3.33	3.21
Total	99.97	99.54

Another sub-group that appears to have been more disaffected than others was the Catholics within the Battalion. Catholics represented 25.80 per cent of the mutineers compared to only 14.66 per cent of the non-mutineers. This figure is important as it runs contrary to the trend in Catholic enlistments that suggested Catholics had not been disaffected by the conscription debates or the Easter Uprising in Ireland. The reinforcement figures do not include 1918 enlistments, though there were few, and therefore do not take into account the possibility of a more general war-weariness. Also, allowance needs to be made for the fact that no commissioned officers mutinied. Thirteen commissioned officers are included in the non-mutineers and, as was revealed in Chapter 1, men of labour-oriented or Catholic backgrounds formed only a small number of that select group. The higher number of men from blue-collar occupations and Catholics, who were highly represented in that category, suggest that working-class soldiers were more receptive to demonstrating their grievances than those from white-collar backgrounds.

Notions of class were paramount in one soldier's recollection of the mutiny in the post-war period. Fred Farrall (who became an avowed socialist after the war), provides an excellent example of how the 1st Battalion mutiny was interpreted to fit his own social and political values, as well as highlighting the dangers in accepting the testimony of old soldiers.[14]

Late in the war, while on escort duty near Flexicourt, Farrall came upon the 1st Battalion mutineers in the prison compound there. Apart from reflecting his own political proclivities his comments also show how the perpetuated democratic and egalitarian ideal of the AIF could be invoked to interpret the soldiers' behaviour:

> I was stunned to see the whole of the 1st Battalion, or what was left of it, there, and to be told that they had walked out of the Hindenburg Line; or, in so many words, they had voted with their feet. When the men left the trenches, the officers had to follow, as they had no job left to do—i.e. directing the men—so they too were put behind the barbed wire. The lesson to be learned here is that, without an army of soldiers or workers, officers and employers alike are superfluous. This was the most militant action taken by the Diggers during that long struggle, though there were others. I think it should be noted here that the AIF was an army of a new type; firstly, it was a volunteer army, and secondly, within its ranks was a big percentage of trade unionists, and it was undoubtedly these influences that made it the most democratic body of men in that war.[15]

Although many returned soldiers and members of the public most likely shared Farrell's sentiment about the democratic 'digger', his account distorts what actually occurred. No officers were imprisoned or charged with desertion, and Farrell's claims would most certainly have been disputed by the hierarchy of the 1st Battalion Association, which had among its members most of the officers present at the mutiny. Significantly, only one of the names of the men charged with mutiny appears on the Battalion Association's membership listing. They were, it seems, considered *persona non grata* after the war.

The predicament of the 1st Battalion mutineers provides another example of an experience that, until recently, had been largely ignored. The voice of the mutineers is muted. None have left a record of their involvement other than anonymous comment in the 1979 film documentary *Mutiny on the Western Front*.[16] Consequently, the harm to military law and to the prestige of the Battalion that the mutiny represented has been ignored in favour of explanations more befitting to the national character. The mutineers have subsequently been depicted as displaying the individual, democratic and egalitarian qualities of the stereotype, as well as that of mateship in adversity, that are synonymous with the legend. The ambiguous and virtuous nature of mateship is illustrated in *Mutiny on the Western Front* when two veterans discuss the morality of the mutineers' actions. One is unsympathetic on the grounds that the mutineers had deserted their mates; the other argues that the men were exhausted and followed their mates out of the line. It is the sympathetic view that appears to have struck a chord with the show's audience. As one viewer wrote: 'Nobody who saw that film could regard them as cowards or criminals. Rather, they remain quiet heroes.'[17]

These were, of course, matters of little consequence to the commanders in the field at the time. With the mutiny over and the successful operations against Mont St Quentin all but completed, the 1st Brigade commander, Brigadier-General Iven Mackay, was able to address the regrettable incident and 1st Brigade morale at length. He reserved some of his harshest judgement for his officers and lamented in a stern and heartfelt lecture that 'the 1st Brigade is not what it was'.[18] For the 1st Brigade, it was well the war ended when it did. The mutinous spirit of the 1st Battalion was a contagious one that could have been easily fanned had more demands been made of Australian soldiers late in the war.

With the exception of 1918, it could not be said that the experience of the 1st Battalion in the conduct of battles, raids and patrols illustrated the abilities defined by the 'digger' stereotype. Too many mishaps occurred to support an argument that advances natural-born abilities. However, the prominence of the Australians in the pursuit of final victory in 1918 provides a compelling conclusion to the often average performances to that time. The magnitude of the successes achieved, and their interpretation, has advanced the standing of the Australian soldier. The 'digger' stereotype has continued to survive through its symbiotic attachment to the successes achieved in 1918. Those successes did, in a very general sense, support the mythical qualities of the stereotype. But this support is in essence only and it should be remembered that it was in 1918 alone—and only for a brief period of the 1st Battalion's war experience—that these qualities found expression in any quantitative form. The successes were achieved with few original members and, as has been suggested, were due to improved training and planning throughout the British armies and in particular through the aggressive doctrine of the AIF. Contrary to the reality, an illusion has been created that the qualities of the stereotype, evidenced by Australian performance in 1918, existed throughout the war.

6

Return of the war-damaged soldier

The reputation of the 'digger'—his apparent individuality, resourcefulness and superiority—were firmly established through the final campaigns of 1918. The post-war period was also important in promoting the reputation of the Australian soldier. Returned soldiers were subjected to the overtures of various political forces in which the positive qualities of the 'digger' were publicly and excessively lauded.[1] However, the image of the public 'digger' inadequately represented the experience of many of the 1st Battalion's returned men. Furthermore, only a minority of the Battalion engaged directly in the process of post-war mythologisation. This process was driven mostly by the conservative hierarchy that after the war dominated both the Battalion Association and writings about the Battalion. In the literature of the 1920s and 1930s the 'digger' emerged as an antipodean version of Charles Kingsley's muscular Christian hero, Amyas Leigh.[2] Quixotic notions of the 'digger' as warrior, crusader and knight coloured descriptions of Australian soldiers and evoked a sense of unparalleled combativeness, morality and individuality that is not sustained by close study of the 1st Battalion's war experience.[3] Nor were these idealistically heroic characteristics especially evident in the post-war experience of the Battalion's returned soldiers.

After the war the returned soldiers' military service and war experience became a focal point for the attention of families, community and government. The debilitating effects of a man's war service were a legacy with which many families had to deal. The broader community, too, had to deal with the problems associated with the repatriation of returned soldiers. At both levels, a process was begun which sought to rationalise and accommodate, rather than understand, the experience of returned soldiers.[4] The public commemorations and ceremonies that mark Anzac Day form part of this process, as do the private mythologies (that is, the known and often incomplete understanding of a soldier's experience) particular to the families of returned soldiers and the (unrepressed) memories of the men themselves . The returned men of the 1st Battalion were part of that collective experience. These ceremonies, memories and mythologies have perpetuated the Anzac legend.[5]

The stoicism that the 'digger' allegedly displayed in battle has also been attached to his post-war experience. After the war the Government moved quickly to acknowledge the changed condition of returned men. An early Repatriation Department report stated the case plainly: 'No man who passed through the battle zone returned to the Commonwealth in a normal condition'.[6] For the legend-makers and the soldiers themselves, the post-war period offered further challenges. Colonel A. G. Butler, the official historian of Australia's medical services during the First World War, examined the effects of rehabilitation of returned men as part of his work. He believed that the problems associated with the war-damaged soldier were largely those of personal morale: 'the mind must heal itself and a man must heal his own mind'.[7] A returned soldier could, Butler asserted, through the application of the 'AIF characteristics of courage and self-help' accommodate even the most debilitating injuries.[8] In support of his argument, he cited examples of men who had adapted their lives to new occupations despite their injuries. It was no accident that the examples chosen represented the broadest possible cross-section of professions: a bushman, a townsman, an artist, and one man who might be described as a jack-of-all-trades.[9] Having presented his microcosm of AIF personnel, Butler concluded: 'Here, in some ways most typically, we have the "Dinkum Digger".'[10]

The cases selected by Butler were, of course, the most inspiring ones that best supported the 'digger' stereotype. It was true that many soldiers did continue with their lives and made light of their injuries. Len Beckett, a 1st Battalion soldier who had an arm amputated, was a case in point. Beckett participated in a soldier settlement scheme at Bankstown and used to joke to his sons, the younger of whom had a leg affected by polio, that with five good arms and legs between them they would get by. Operation of the farm was not so easy. Moreover, the extra dangers facing disabled men were illustrated when the claw of Beckett's artificial arm caught on a plough and pitched him forward onto its blades. Beckett abandoned the farm in favour of less dangerous work as the community's postal clerk until the effects of the Great Depression forced the closure of the office in 1938.[11] As Beckett's experience reveals, the transition into post-war society would not be so readily defined by the positive outcomes that Butler proffered. The post-war experience of the 1st Battalion varied and formed a pot-pourri that defies any particular stereotype.

Return and repatriation

The return of the 1st Battalion to Australia was a fragmented one. Illness and wounds sustained in battle meant that soldiers were regularly being returned to Australia from the beginning of the war. The numbers ebbed and flowed depending on the severity of the outbreaks of disease and fighting. As well, the introduction of 'Australia leave' throughout the AIF in 1918 saw the return of many soldiers of the original cohort. Few of the first Anzacs were left in the ranks by the war's end, a point highlighted by the diminution of the original E Company, 1st Battalion, as Table 11 indicates.

Table 11: Attrition of men from original E Company, 1st Battalion

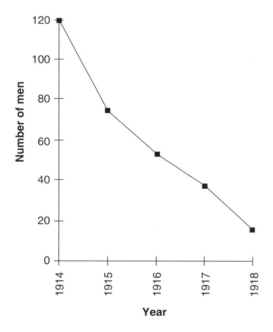

Of the 119 men represented by this company, only fifteen (12.60 per cent) were still on active service at the war's conclusion. Forty-four had been killed or died as a result of wounds or disease (36.97 per cent). Of the survivors, twenty-four (32 per cent) have been identified as having been granted war pensions for varying degrees of disability. From the experience of E Company it can be surmised that a similar percentage of the Battalion's survivors were granted pensions. Of the officers and men who served in the Battalion, 1165 died (18.72 per cent) and 2163 (34.76 per cent) were wounded. This represented a total casualty rate of over 50 per cent. The enormity of the casualties to the AIF and the numbers of men eligible for disability pensions presented immediate problems to families and the community at large as they attempted to match the grief associated with the death and disablement of so many soldiers with adequate levels of commemoration.[12] For the Government an added burden was the fiscal and ethical administration of the repatriation of the returned servicemen.

The repatriation process has been the subject of three major studies that provide different contexts through which the experience of the 1st Battalion's returned men can be viewed. Published works by Lloyd and Rees, *The Last Shilling*, and Garton, *Cost of War,* and an unpublished thesis by Richard Lindstrom reveal the divergence in opinion on the subject.[13] Lloyd and Rees argue that the management of the repatriation process was, through government weakness and returned soldiers' agitation, a generous one, indeed 'the most liberal system of veterans' assistance in the world [to those who qualified]'.[14] The large number of returned soldiers serving within the Repatriation Department's administration, they argue, made this generosity almost an inevitable consequence. Garton agreed that the repatriation scheme delivered 'enormous benefits to those who deserved recompense', although he suggested the various vested interests that existed within the system saw its administration viewed alternatively as 'humane and liberal' or 'heartless and tyrannical'.[15] He also argued that the system became a site for the articulation of and conflict over social and cultural values.[16] Repatriation welfare recipients were, he stated, subject to resentment and criticism from those excluded from the system. As well, Garton suggested that veterans, through the legitimate pursuit of their claims, became vulnerable to charges that in doing so they were betraying the spirit of those who had died—that is, their reliance on welfare contravened the independence of the 'digger' of the Anzac legend.[17] Lindstrom, whose study examined mainly shell-shock cases, also identified the variable functions of repatriation's administration as important to the returned soldier. He suggests that bureaucratic inconsistency often tainted a soldier's experience and sometimes adversely affected the outcome of a pension claim.[18] Moreover, Lindstrom argued that returned soldiers, or at least shell-shock victims, were not well served by the repatriation system due to the lack of scientific means within and available to the Department to assess psychological disorders.[19]

The greatest causes for complaint among 1st Battalion returned soldiers about their pension entitlements emanated from the inevitable red tape and delays inherent to bureaucracies. The delays to a claim for a transport concession for Tasman Douglass highlight the bureaucratic aspect of pension entitlement. Douglass was a resident of Lord Howe Island and was hampered by financial difficulties in purchasing a ticket for a flying-boat as part of his passage to Sydney to attend the fiftieth anniversary reunion of the 1st Battalion. As much as the Department of Veterans' Affairs recognised the apparent legitimacy of Douglass' claim, his unique circumstances unfortunately fell beyond the statutory limitations of the Department. It is evident from departmental correspondence that Douglass' request was treated with compassion and a number of enquiries were instigated on his behalf.[20] The compassion, in this instance, was in keeping with the sense of atonement and acknowledgment toward returned servicemen that the various soldier groups over the years had urged upon the public and government to adopt.

Less compassionate was the case of Stanley Davis, a former bugler in the 1st Battalion. Davis had his existing pension cancelled when a medical officer's report pertaining to the rejection of an additional claim was acted upon.[21] This action was a result of a clerical error more than a deliberate desire to cause hardship. In Davis' case, however, the fact that he was suspected of being a heavy drinker perhaps contributed to the error, in that his civil servant assessors may have cynically believed him to be unworthy of a pension grant. The use of alcohol as an anti-depressant and escape by soldiers suffering from war neuroses was unlikely to be viewed with sympathy by those assessing their claims. As Lindstrom has noted, the personal appraisal of a patient's character was an important and sometimes inconsistent part of the granting process.[22] Its existence also proved, in part, the adversarial nature of the repatriation process that so angered the RSL which sought, by appointing pension officers in sub-branches and at state level, to provide assistance to ex-servicemen applying for pensions and appealing against adverse decisions.[23] There was, too, as Garton has suggested, much conflict between what the Repatriation Commission deemed to be pensionable war-related illnesses and conditions and what the RSL campaigned for as acceptable.[24]

Soldiers whose service and medical records were explicit in the reportage of wounds and illnesses received on active service were likely to encounter few problems in the award of a pension. Stuart Burman, who was blown into a dug-out by a shell-burst while carrying a wounded man to a stretcher at Pozières and who also received a gunshot wound to his head, back and shoulders in 1917, did not apply for a pension until 1927—ten years later. His wounds and treatments had been well documented and the Department's medical officer had no reservations in accepting Burman's complaint of 'continual headaches and a feeling as if [his] head were inflated', causing irritability and bad-temper, as attributable to his war service. A character assessment that noted 'tells his story simply and without hesitation and appears to be thoroughly genuine' can only have assisted his case.[25]

Lack of medical detail on a soldier's service record and considerable passage of time preceding a claim made the award of pensions more difficult as it was sometimes hard to differentiate the natural physical and mental deterioration that could sometimes be attached to old age as from alleged war neuroses. Lloyd and Rees argue that this problem of attribution was compounded by the failure of Australian authorities to obtain Australian medical records (which listed most individual casualties, combat or otherwise) held in the Imperial War Office and which would have alleviated the problem of incomplete field service medical records, many of which had been lost or destroyed in the 'changing tides of war'.[26] Arthur Phillips, for example, applied for a pension in 1963. He based his claim on two counts: one, that he had been blown up by a shell and rendered unconscious while serving at Gallipoli on 18 May 1915 and, two, the strain of war service. Phillips' war record made no mention of any such incident. Unfortunately for the claimant, it did record the aggravation of a pre-existing foot injury while on active service, along with the suggestion that he had exaggerated the effects of the injury and the suspicion that he was malingering. He was not awarded a pension and had a later appeal against the decision dismissed.[27] The existence and tenor of such assessments (irrespective of the legitimacy of the Department's decision) confirm the division between the social and cultural values held by the Department as opposed to the various soldier-groups whose motivation was self-interest and who saw war pensions as compensation for a soldier's service rather than welfare assistance. The attitude and conflict between the two groups is revealed in a statement by the Repatriation Department's senior medical officer:

> A Departmental Medical Officer cannot be a 'nice kind doctor' by giving away public monies . . . Moreover the majority of the Department's clients were not heroes but plain men and many of them not as much wounded as they wished to be . . . your plea for a 'sympathetic' medical service sounds a bit like the criticism of the Soldiers' League . . . a demand that Departmental MOs should make dishonest recommendations for the benefit of soldier applicants.[28]

One 1st Battalion soldier awarded a pension without equivocation was Benjamin Hubbard. He suffered impaired vision in his left eye and was rendered totally deaf in his right ear as a result of a shell explosion on 18 May 1915—the same day that Arthur Phillips claimed to have been knocked unconscious by a shell.[29] Given that these men served in the same company, Hubbard's claim suggests the veracity of Phillips' statement of an experience that was subsequently viewed as unlikely by the Department. That the 18 May 1915 was a day of particularly heavy shelling is further confirmed by a diary entry by Colonel R. J. Millard, a medical officer at Gallipoli: 'at the trenches there was heavy shelling especially in the afternoon with big high explosive "Jack Johnsons" Carter of the 1st Battn was blown up by one of these and came to my dugout considerably "shocked".'[30] Of course, being such a memorable day may have made it a likely selection for any proposed dupe by a claimant against the department.

A problem that did present itself during the assessment of a soldier's claim for disability was that the injury claimed for had not always been reported. This is corroborated in the diaries and letters of some men, especially with regard to their being knocked down or buried by an explosion. The immediate effects of such incidents were not always considered as sufficient at the time for a man to abandon the front line. It is likely that such experiences, combined with other injuries and illnesses acquired during a man's war service, could culminate in severe post-war health disorders. That fact, along with the constancy of those effects, is suggested in the statements by and descriptions of many of the 1st Battalion soldiers' claims for pensions. Lawrence Riggs, who described his general health as 'allright' but for constant 'violent headaches' and 'insomnia', was described by the medical officer as 'extremely nervous and tremulous. Sleeps badly and frequently has nightmares. Is short of breath on exertion and very nervous in traffic. Is nearly one stone below his weight.'[31]

The post-war experience of many returned men, as these cases show, was negatively affected by the debilities incurred through their war service. As much as people, such as A. G. Butler, suggested and expected returned soldiers to overcome their disabilities, the nature of the injury or the state of debilitated health was often too severe. Such expectations, in hindsight, expose the moral turpitude of attitudes expressed by people like Butler. Men whom the Repatriation Department recommended as being unfit to take up land for poultry farming and described as 'mentally dull' could hardly be expected to—and, indeed, did not—fulfil the qualities of independence of the stereotypical 'digger'.[32]

Post-war mythologisation and the subjugation of reality

On the tenth anniversary of the Anzac landings the convergence of the treatment of returned soldiers and the public elevation of the deeds of the Anzacs formed the kernel of an address by Major-General Brand, the NSW State Commandant. Brand believed 'it was a hollow mockery for citizens to celebrate the glories of Anzac day unless they were prepared to fulfil their promises and do their duty to the men who had fought and suffered through the war'.[33] Furthermore, in a statement that suggested the existence of a substantial and perhaps burgeoning ignorance on the part of the Australian public, Brand, 'wished it to be known that the British division at Cape Helles had as difficult a task at landing as had the Anzacs, and the task of the British in maintaining their position was just as serious and difficult as was any task that the Australians accomplished'.[34] Brand was urging a public awareness of achieving balance in the treatment of returned soldiers commensurate to the sacrifice they had made to the nation's ideals as well as balance in the facts associated with the AIF's achievements.

The circumspection that Brand was seeking in relation to the AIF's achievements was essentially absent from the outset of its service. A further hurdle to the pursuit of a balanced appraisal of Australian performance was the speed with which the 'digger' stereotype was adopted as a truthful representation of Australian soldiers. An article in *Smith's Weekly*, written for the first peacetime celebration of Anzac Day, highlighted the elevated stature of the Anzacs:

> reckless and gallant in the spirit of their pioneer forbears . . . An army of warriors, these Anzacs, of, perhaps, the greatest physical perfection that the world has seen. Trained at the highest athletic pitch, briefly, but effectively, instructed in the use of unfamiliar weapons, untested in battle, these laughing paladins of the South . . . blooded their maiden steel in one irresistible rush . . . with the dawn light in their resolute laughing eyes . . . accomplished a feat of arms which placed Australia's name high upon the scroll of gallant adventure . . . only the accident of political change forced them to retreat after months of patient endurance, herculean labour, unflinching optimism, and, heroism unequalled . . . to these pioneers of Anzac will always belong the place of honour won in that dramatic preface.[35]

The high diction and *Boy's Own* rhetoric that permeates the article make nonsense of any attempt to achieve a reasonable appraisal of the qualities of the Australian soldier. Indeed, cautious analysis was hardly an issue with that publication. The contribution of *Smith's Weekly* to the stereotyping of the Australian soldier was significant. Its series 'Great Deeds of the AIF' was one example, as was 'The Soldiers' and Sailors' Parliament' page, which was committed to giving a voice to returned servicemen. While this forum did give opportunity for returned servicemen to express themselves, it also perpetuated the soldier stereotype through anecdotal snippets and cartoons of 'digger' humour. It would be tempting to discredit descriptions of the Australians as 'laughing paladins' and 'modern Crusaders'[36] as irrelevant to contemporary perceptions were it not for the fact that the stereotype and its associated prejudices are still perpetuated. The main source of prejudice is the questionable performance of the British. It is a theme that has become ingrained in Australia's popular memory of the war and one given an international audience through films like *Gallipoli*.

The 1st Battalion Association

The 1st Battalion Association is one organisation that must be discussed if the post-war contribution of the 1st Battalion toward the 'digger' stereotype is to be fully understood. The formation of post-war battalion associations added a cogent postscript to public perceptions of bonding and comradeship among old soldiers, and they certainly projected an image of solidarity as well as, through the publication of unit histories, giving expression to a battalion's war experience. Caution is especially necessary in accepting the Battalion Association as a being a natural continuation of the *esprit de corps* that supposedly underpinned Australian battalions, given the imbalance between officers and other ranks within the Association (see Table 12). In the same way that the RSL assumed the role of custodian of the identity and reputation of returned soldiers, so the Battalion Association assumed the role of custodian of the Battalion's honour in the post-war years.

Table 12: Comparison of rank as a percentage of Battalion Association members compared to rank as a percentage of total members recorded on 1st Battalion nominal roll[37]

Rank	Rank as a % of Battalion Association membership	Rank as a % of total Battalion	Battalion Association members' rank as a % of rank in total Battalion
Officers	9.96	4.56	31.46
NCOs	26.68	18.66	20.75
Privates	61.12	76.74	11.56
Unknown	2.21		
Total	99.97	99.96	N/A

A principal function of the 1st Battalion Association was the nurturing of imperial patriotism—so central to conservative mythologising of Anzac—through its conduct. It assumed responsibility for organising its members for the annual Anzac Day march in Sydney as well as providing members to attend AIF dinners and balls that were held periodically. The main events on the Association's calendar were the annual Anzac Day celebration, an event at which the official rostrums and podiums were dominated by Australia's conservative hierarchy, and the annual reunion of Battalion members. The date usually selected for the reunion was 18 October, the date the Battalion sailed from Sydney, or as near to it as possible. These reunions were generally described as well-attended. Over three hundred attended the 1932 meeting.[38] Other activities of the Association were often inspired by patriotic motives. During the Second World War the Association set up a comforts fund for the 2/1st Battalion, and after the war it provided regular food relief parcels to Britain, including a special package to Field Marshal Birdwood. A letter of protest was sent when a race meeting was proposed to be held on Anzac Day in 1951. Assistance was also provided to members who were experiencing difficulties in gaining pensions. The Association was not always able to assist with requests. When W. F. Kortegast applied for a loan of 30 shillings to purchase materials for the manufacture of first-aid kits, he was informed by the committee that funds were not available for such use.[39]

The composition of the committee, and the Association as a whole, suggests that the equality one would expect of an organisation purporting to represent an egalitarian AIF battalion was not in evidence. The Association's hierarchy was dominated by commissioned officers, with the lesser posts held mostly by non-commissioned officers. The committee personified the Battalion's wartime hierarchy. For example the 1932 office-bearers, elected unopposed, contained only three other-rankers, the treasurer, Private R MacKay, and auditors Sergeant J. Dewar and Private R. W. Boyce. The main posts were held by commissioned officers and a senior sergeant: Patron, Brigadier-General J. W. Heane; President, Lieutenant-Colonel B. V. Stacy; Vice-Presidents, Lieutenant-Colonel F. J. Kindon, Lieutenant H. A. Clow, Lieutenant G. Howard; Hon. Secretary, Regimental Quartermaster Sergeant H. H. Blunden; Solicitor, Lieutenant J. F. Mant. Of the twelve general committeemen appointed, ten were other-rankers.[40] Even if it is accepted that the senior officers were more equipped for the duties of their positions, one might query whether such an infrastructure would be particularly appealing to returned privates who did not necessarily hold their officers or war experience in high esteem. Those who found this structure objectionable would have been unlikely to have become involved in the Association. Examination of the membership list certainly supports the possibility that returned privates did not view participation or membership in the Association as highly as their former officers and NCOs. Officers were three times more likely to join the Association than a private, while NCOs were twice as likely to do so.

It may be deduced that men who had earned their stripes or had been granted commissions held a more positive view of their experience and drew from it a higher self-esteem and a greater sense of responsibility than those occupying the lower echelons. Moreover, the fact that the majority of officers were drawn from the middle and upper classes and white-collar backgrounds might, as Richard White has suggested, have made them more receptive to the ideals of Empire that were upheld through participation in military service at the time.[41] Privates, the majority of whom were drawn from labour-intensive occupations, may have equated the regimen of their war experience with that of their peacetime occupations and, as a consequence, were less likely to be enamoured of their war experience. The Battalion Association did not hold the same powers of affirmation for these men as it did for their superiors.

Given the hierarchical composition of the Battalion Association and the obvious imbalance in the relative representation of the divisions in rank, it is worth reflecting upon the relationships of these men. The Association was an extension of the wartime organisation it represented. It was run in a formal manner with the old officers in command. These officers, in the main, shared little common background with the soldiers of their commands. It is impossible to know exactly what the peacetime relationships of returned privates and NCOs might have been with their officers. The likelihood is that the two groups had little contact beyond the formality of the Association. In this respect membership in the Association may have been inspired by a sense of fellowship rather than any real comradeship spread across the ranks. For instance, the closest post-war friends of Lieutenant Ken McConnel had all been officers, who provided his best man and groomsmen for his wedding. After his marriage he rented a house from another 1st Battalion officer. While this is hardly conclusive proof of a great social divide, it does suggest a certain clannishness on the part of these officers. If that were the case, it did not necessarily preclude the existence of a genuine philanthropic interest in the welfare of their men. McConnel, for example, took an active interest in the building of a home for war veterans at Narrabeen[42] and Lieutenant John Mant, as the Association solicitor, was also said to have provided free legal advice and services to former Battalion members.[43]

Over a thousand names are on the Battalion Association's 1932 membership list. Not all were current members; some had died, and others had allowed their membership to lapse, due mostly to having changed addresses. Of the names on the membership list, a total of 903 corresponded with those on the Battalion nominal roll. This figure represents approximately 18 per cent of all those who served and survived the war.[44] The greatest significance of this figure is the 82 per cent of men who chose not to be members of the Association. These men represent an overwhelming majority. Some, in all probability, wanted to put the war and its memories behind them. Fred Kelly, who arrived at Gallipoli as a 1st Battalion reinforcement and later transferred to the unit's 'sister' battalion, the 53rd, never attended an Anzac Day march or joined an ex-serviceman's association. He considered himself lucky to survive. There was nothing grandiose about Kelly's perception of his war service. His time on Gallipoli he recalled as 'just routine', as the 1st Battalion's service was after the August offensive, and of the other fighting noted: 'You had to just stand there and take what ever came'.[45] Kelly had had enough of war; the Battalion Association held no appeal for him. Others substituted for membership in the Battalion Association by joining other returned soldier groups.

It was not uncommon for men to belong to more than one group, as a variety of returned serviceman organisations existed other than the Battalion Association. In fact, where the Battalion had formed the centre of most men's war experience, the post-war years provided a much broader soldier community through the establishment of soldier settlements and special-interest groups. The soldier settlements were not established upon service in any specific battalion or military organisation (other than the AIF) and as a consequence soldiers from many units formed new communities. Similarly, associations like the Limbless Soldiers' Association and Marrickville Anzac Memorial Club, which both contained 1st Battalion men, represented a variety of units in their memberships.[46] In contrast to the Battalion Association the hierarchy of the Marrickville club appears to have been more proletarian. It had as its president Sergeant Jack Hayes. The founders of the Marrickville club were far more concerned with providing recreation for the common soldier than preserving old orders of authority. Hayes also formed, with a number of soldier friends (only one of whom could be identified as an officer), a social club that met regularly in the Rocks in Sydney and produced its own newsletter, *The Dugout*.[47] The most likely other group that Association members would join was the local RSL sub-branch. The percentage of returned soldiers who joined the RSL appears to approximate that of the Battalion Association. RSL membership throughout Australia stood at 50,000 in 1933 and represented about 20 per cent of returned soldiers. Membership reached 82,000 at the outbreak of the Second World War after plummeting to a low of 24,000 (9 per cent) in 1924.[48] The RSL also created its own image of the 'digger' stereotype, depicting him as someone who epitomised patriotism and manliness.[49] The advent of other wars has provided new generations of returned servicemen and women; this has enabled the RSL to sustain its membership and perpetuate its image of the Australian soldier.

The ageing of the returned soldier population had obvious ramifications for the lifespan of the Battalion Association. By the 1970s the time had come for the Association, as the Battalion itself had done, to consign itself to history. The Association joined with that of the Second World War unit, the 2/1st

Battalion. While the original 1st Battalion Association virtually ceased to exist, one important and poignant tradition was passed on—Pozières Day, a memorial service held annually on a Sunday in July at St Columba Church, Woollahra.[50] This day had its genesis in the unveiling of a memorial cross at the church in 1935. The cross had originally been erected at Pozières to commemorate the 1st Battalion's dead in the battles of July and August 1916. The ground on which it stood was overrun by the German advance of March 1918 and the cross was not recovered until after the Armistice. Approximately 120 members of the Association attended the service.[51] The tradition is continued under the auspices of the Association of 1st Battalions, which incorporates the original Association, the 2/1st Association, and that of the 1st Royal Australian Regiment. Returned soldier organisations such as the Battalion Association and RSL undoubtedly provided a valuable refuge or focus for some of their members. This may have been more emphatic in the RSL which was instrumental in fighting for soldiers' rights and the preservation of soldiers' reputations in the post-war period.

For many returned soldiers the post-war period presented difficulties that had been little considered while on active service. However, the perceived void that peace would bring *was* considered, as one soldier revealed: 'it will be an awful shock when the war is over and a man gets the sack . . . the prospect has me a bit worried'.[52] War had taught Australian soldiers many skills, most of which were incompatible with peaceful civil occupations. Uncertainty would taint the perceptions of both the returned soldier and the society to which he returned. In his study of combat identity in First World War soldiers, Eric Leed describes two distinct public perceptions in which the war experience of the returned soldiers is interposed. In the first instance, the war unified many of the competing public interests in a common objective so that the citizen-soldier embarked on his journey to war with the knowledge that he was part of a community in which many of the social barriers had been pulled down and so he 'voluntarily submerged his private ego into a national persona'.[53] A soldier's front-line experience ruptured this mutuality of sacrifice.[54] There, contrary to the traditional images of war, he discovered that the industrial world imposed itself upon him in a way that it had not done in his civilian life and that the mechanised destruction that pervaded life in the trenches was a mirror image of industrial production.[55] A significant disjuncture occurred to the soldier's sense of belonging with his return home to a society that had maintained its *status quo*. Disillusionment afflicted the soldier as he struggled to equate his sacrifice and loss of individuality with a society that had not perceptibly altered.[56] At this point the second public perception of the returned soldier is applicable. The soldier was relegated from a heroic man to a superfluous one: 'The veteran, with his dangerous powers and his penchant for violence, was a threat to the society of his origins. He was someone who had to be reintegrated, reacculturated, reeducated.'[57]

The relegation from hero to superfluous man was not an immediate consequence of a soldier's return: it was a gradual process. In Australia, public disturbances by ex-soldiers and demonstrations on their part for a fairer go saw a degree of negativity and intolerance emerge toward the plight of returned men, even though the deeds of the 'diggers' were still heroically portrayed in the nation's literature. Returned Australian soldiers were certainly not the sole cause of this perceived malaise of the inter-war years but they were undoubtedly a symbolic reminder of the country's war trauma and continuing problems that stemmed from the Great Depression. The outbreak of the Second World War, however, allowed veterans of the First World War to be embraced again by grafting the new generation of soldiers to the old (of the Anzac legend) as the nation again girded itself for war.

The breakdown of 'digger' durability

Notwithstanding the problems associated with returned soldiers and their assimilation with Australian society, the continued observance of Anzac Day and remembrance of the sacrifices made in the nation's participation in other wars has provided a significant constant. The celebration of the qualities of the Australian soldier forms an integral part of this remembrance. Irrespective of whether Anzac Day was politically inspired or a spontaneous affirmation of public sentiment, and despite fluctuating public interest, it has endured. In this respect the legend that it enshrines has been a positive and healing force. The existence of the Association of First Battalions is symbolic of the integration of the various conflicts in the nation's remembrance. More recently, the manner in which the Battle of Long Tan has been elevated into the annals of Australia's military folklore exemplifies the addition of the Vietnam experience to the ongoing celebration of the success and endurance of Australian soldiers.[58]

Endurance is one attribute of the 'digger' stereotype that the legend celebrates. It is a word that escaped but could easily have been included in Paul Fussell's list of 'high' diction.[59] By definition a person's endurance implies a specific quality, a power or ability to withstand. Some soldiers did consciously overcome their fear and imposed a measure of control on their actions that allowed them to function in battle. Others simply could not overcome the physical strain and emotional stress and broke down accordingly. The breakdown in the men's physical and mental health did not evaporate with the war's conclusion; indeed, the large number of disability pensions awarded was a poignant testimony to that.

Signs of breakdown had begun to manifest themselves during the war throughout the AIF, particularly in 1917 and 1918 when incidents of accidental injury and self-inflicted wounds showed a marked increase. Self-inflicted wounds jumped 50 per cent in 1917, from the previous year's figure of 126 to 186, and doubled to 388 in 1918. Harold Mercer, a 1st Battalion soldier who had observed two men being wounded by a German aeroplane, commented: 'Charges for self-inflicted wounds are very frequent now—and the wounds need not be wilfully self-inflicted. These men might suffer for failing to obey an order to "take cover".'[60] These figures were paralleled by even more incidents of accidental injury, which have been previously ignored in assessments of self-inflicted wounds. Accidental injuries more than doubled in 1917, from 289 to 753, and increased fourfold in 1918 to 2588.[61] They accounted for 7.39 per cent of field ambulance admissions in the AIF.[62] Accidental injuries were categorised as a separate form of non-battle casualty to self-inflicted wounds, which were considered to represent a moral defect and therefore entered as 'Disorders of the mind'.[63] It is unlikely that any 'real' circumstances existed to make soldiers more accident-prone as the war progressed. It is arguable that many of these injuries were orchestrated by soldiers anxious to escape the dangers of the front line. It is not surprising that soldiers sought to avoid the horror of the trenches in this way. A 'Blighty' had long been viewed as an acceptable 'ticket of leave' and due reward for a soldier wounded at the front. For soldiers left unscathed after battle, similar relief was only offered through participation in more fighting which brought with it a greater chance of being killed. These soldiers, as well as those returned quickly after slight wounds, could easily have felt aggrieved by their lack of 'good' misfortune, particularly when they were aware of the good luck of others. For example, Private Frederick Buchan received a letter tendering the following consolation from a friend: 'You were stiff at not getting over here, I never had much of a wound and it is alright again now but I've been over here 3 months now, and am going on 14 days leave tomorrow'.[64]

Wounds, especially superficial ones, offered only temporary escape. A more final solution was the taking of one's own life. Suicide was not unknown to the officers and men at the front line. The rationale of those afflicted by thoughts of suicide, particularly those who enact it, remains a mystery. Its unfathomable nature and the bewilderment it evoked are evident in two incidents described by Archie Barwick. The first occurred early January 1917:

> A most peculiar thing happened this afternoon in full view of us all Lieut Rowbottom, of D Coy, hopped out of the trench and deliberately walked straight out

towards the German trenches and they were only 80 yards apart, when he got half way over he stopped and picked up a German rifle, then the expected happened for a rifle crack rang out but he missed him and Rowbottom signalled a washout then another crack and Rowbottom spun round like a top and collapsed, by this time nearly every man in the trenches was looking on . . . what on earth could have made him do such a mad act beats me, I think the cold must have affected him or he done it for mere bravado, however, it cost him his life.[65]

Rowbottom's actions, given the certainty of the German response, certainly appeared suicidal. It is impossible to know what prompted him, and one can only share Barwick's confusion. Less complicated was another death described by Barwick on his passage home to Australia, Christmas Eve, in fact: 'I could see something out of the ordinary had happened . . . it came out in an awestruck whisper, they said our C.O. Major MacPherson had just blown his brains out in his cabin'.[66] The major's suicide was a portent of the confusion and despair that accompanied some soldiers home.

Ken McConnel was one who attempted to understand the confusion that lay at the heart of such desperate acts. McConnel himself was the victim of four nervous breakdowns after the war. In one sense his personal ambition and commitment to his family were fundamental to his ability to restart his life after each episode of breakdown. In that respect his actions supported the stoical attributes of the 'digger' stereotype. On the other hand, contrary to such qualities, he was simply unable to stave off a nervous breakdown when it manifested itself: 'A ghastly depression settled upon my brain and I felt unable to think. I would sit in my office for hours and achieve little or nothing, and one day broke down and cried like a baby.'[67] By his own admission, suicide was no stranger to his thoughts. It is apparent from his response to the suicide of his cousin and former fellow officer, Rollo Somerset, that some other 1st Battalion officers had not only had thoughts in that direction but had followed them to their fatal conclusion. Rollo Somerset ended his life when he climbed on top of a pile of brushwood, set it alight, and then shot himself. McConnel wrote:

> Rollo's death by suicide was the *fifth* of a series of tragic similar endings which had occurred to men of whom I had grown fond of as fellow officers of the First Battalion. In all cases they had been unable to adjust themselves to a normal existence and a normal married life after the extraordinary mixture of stress, despondency, boredom and licence which had become part of their lives for four or five years of their early manhood. No one who had passed through that same experience could blame them. They were good fellows and fine men, some of whom had shown themselves to have tremendous character; yet life in the humdrum pattern of daily affairs was just too much for them to tackle for long, and at five, ten, fifteen, twenty years the tendons of tolerance had snapped, and they had sought what is oft called

the coward's way out. But is it? What right has anyone to make such an accusation unless he has had an exactly parallel experience of life?[68]

McConnel had identified what is probably the greatest difficulty for those attempting to understand a returned soldier's psyche, the absence of a parallel experience. Equally, a returned soldier's own recognition of his unique experience had the potential to make him less receptive to the well-intentioned overtures of 'outsiders'.

McConnel and Barwick describe experiences that, through the private nature of their recording, have lain dormant and hidden from the general knowledge and literature of the war. The observations of these men are important as they reveal experiences from which contrary judgements to the orthodoxies of the Anzac legend can be made. Incidents of suicide most definitely fall beyond the pale of the celebrated qualities of the 'digger' stereotype. In fact, behaviours observed or experienced that did not support the 'digger' stereotype were unlikely to become general public knowledge. Returned men who believed they had not performed creditably or in a manner befitting the stereotype were unlikely to volunteer their private experience for public consumption and possible ridicule. The positive image that the 'digger' stereotype conveys was not always in evidence. Examination of the service records of some of the 1st Battalion reveals characters who present themselves as atypical diggers (compared to the stereotype) but nonetheless real ones. James Molloy, one of the 5th Reinforcements who landed at Gallipoli on the eve of the Lone Pine attack and was subsequently wounded, spent the remainder of his war service in hospitals being treated for a variety of maladies as well as being pursued by the authorities for numerous unauthorised absences without leave.[69] In this context, the offence of absence without leave carries a greater significance than the connotations of revelry associated with it in Australia and Egypt. Soldiers like Molloy were clearly making a conscious decision to avoid service in the front line. The award of prison sentences to such offenders was probably a counter-productive measure, providing a safe haven for men otherwise fit for duty. By the end of 1917, Australian soldiers had the highest ratio per capita among men occupying military prisons in the British armies.[70] The men of the 1st Battalion were no strangers to prison life. If the record of inmates for the military prison at Lewes is representative of the prison population generally, then the 1st Battalion was well represented. Sixty-one 1st Battalion men (including Molloy) passed through the confines of Lewes between November 1917 and January 1920 (forty-two of whom were confined prior to the Armistice). Absence without leave and desertion accounted for nearly all the offences; only five of these men were being detained for other crimes.[71]

An even more colourful character was Professor Leo Galli. He was among the first wounded soldiers to be returned to Australia from Gallipoli. Following his return to Australia he spoke at recruitment rallies while supposedly awaiting a commission in the Italian army (it does not appear to have eventuated).[72] His return was, however, marked by controversy. He was suspected of being a deserter and malingerer. Accused by a 1st Battalion officer, Lieutenant W. W. Paine, he was subjected to re-examination by the medical board, which, despite its suspicions, cleared him for return.[73] These incidents, like awards for bravery in action, were not necessarily common experiences but they, along with others previously described, do provide contrary realities to the more positive examples promoted through the legend that ought not be ignored, especially when the character of Australian soldiers is advanced as being representative of national traits.

Another contributing factor to the perpetuation of the 'digger' stereotype was the sycophantic utterances of the various post-war political factions as they attempted to woo the soldier vote.[74] Their appeals centred upon the perceived heroic qualities and sacrifices of the 'digger'. George L. Mosse, in describing the effect of the war on Germany, noted:

> The cult of the fallen was of importance for most of the nation . . . Yet it was the political Right and not the Left which was able to annex the cult and make the most of it. The inability of the Left to forget the reality of the war and enter the Myth of the War Experience was a gain for the political Right.[75]

The same was true of Australia. The Right, whose values were ensconced in Australia's military and educational institutions (and which had been shared by the Australian Labor Party prior to the war), had succeeded in appealing to the masculinity of young men and inducing them to embrace a sense of duty that required them to fight for their nation when the time came. Few people had envisaged what fulfilment of that expectation would entail. With the war's end Australians were left to make sense of the nation's contribution. The broken health, both physical and mental, of many returned soldiers was visible to many. The reality of their condition was quickly transfigured by the cult of the fallen. Post-war Australia believed its manhood had taken part in some sort of Homeric odyssey and set about paying appropriate homage.[76]

It was in the war literature published in the late 1920s and early 1930s that the extent of elevation of the Australian soldier as a figure worthy of public veneration was most apparent. The exalted status of the 'digger' was graphically illustrated on the frontispiece of a boxed edition produced by the Australian War Memorial titled *Australian Chivalry*.[77] On it a medieval knight attired in the garb of a crusader is depicted applying a brotherly handshake to a bare-chested Anzac. The symbolism of the muscular Christian and the muscular individual that the 'digger' had become is emphatic. The imagery is further advanced on the book's duo-tone title page, with the crusader gazing upon a 'digger' standing nonchalantly upon a duckboard smoking a cigarette. This image was symptomatic of the almost religious status that the celebration of Anzac had achieved during the 1920s and 1930s. It was also the period when the first volumes of the *Official History* appeared and the publication of battalion histories flourished.

As the alleged qualities of the Australian soldier were woven into the commemorative services on Anzac Day and national literature, it became less likely that alternative experiences would be aired, much less considered. Returned soldiers who held contrary views were placed in an invidious position. Criticism on their part would likely be construed as unpatriotic and disrespectful to the sacrifice of their fallen comrades. The public vilification and libel that accompanied any opposition to the official line are underscored by the experience of John Reid, whose opposition to the introduction of a compulsory patriotic oath and flag ceremony in NSW schools met with blanket condemnation from the editors of Sydney's major daily newspapers.[78] For returned soldiers harbouring contrary views, the best course of action was to remain silent.

Although a majority of the men who served the Battalion did not participate in the post-war Association, we cannot conclude that they held a negative view of, or were indifferent to, the public acclamation of their war experience. However, it is likely, for the men were their own most effective censors.

Silence and family remembrance

Those closest to a returned soldier's methods of self-imposed censorship were his immediate family. Even during the war the men were aware of the negative effects the war might have had on their relatives and some sought to subvert the grim reality in their letters home. From interviews (and questionnaires) with some of the children of the 1st Battalion soldiers it is apparent that a similar censorship extended into the post-war years. The war was rarely spoken of in the family home other than through the transmission of humorous stories. Memory and oral history represent a problematic and contested area for historians, as they can effectively screen and distort actual experiences. The silences, selected memories and childhood memories of the 1st Battalion soldiers and their families as modes of censorship (as well as their functional nature) are, nevertheless, of interest. It is likely that the silence of a father was motivated by a desire to protect the family, as well as himself, from the disturbing memories of the war. As interesting as the men's experiences might be to enquiring historians, negative experiences or those revealing graphic horror held little appeal in the maintenance of a family and the upbringing of children. In most cases the shutters on a father's war experience remained closed for life. There were exceptions: one man recalled how, as a child, he could almost place his small fist into the cavity of his father's chest wound. He also remembered the time and place that his father revealed to him that he had killed a man. In this instance, the father's admission followed his son's return from overseas service in the RAAF during the Second World War.[79] The son's war service had provided the key to entry into his father's memories. Daughters, with the assumptions of what was fit and proper for their gender to bear, were less likely to gain similar intimacy.

Although returned soldiers could hide, through their verbal censorship, the reality of their war experience, the intimacy of the family home made it more difficult to hide its physical and psychological effect on behaviour. Judith Allen has studied the negative effects on women of returned soldiers in Australia. She found that crimes of violence against women increased, as did crimes against society in general, and noted that in the face of such incidents the courts tended to display a liberal degree of clemency toward the fallen heroes.[80] The courts' actions represent a public and official 'blind eye' policy toward behaviour contrary to that of the stereotypical 'digger'. The existence of domestic violence as an aspect of post-war family life is not evident in the responses to the questionnaires distributed or in the interviews conducted during this research. It is unlikely that incidents of domestic violence, due to their deep personal nature, would be volunteered. It is evident from the responses of those prepared to share their family's experience that a positive view was held of their upbringing and family relationships. Again, as with those who have donated letters and diaries to public institutions, this represents an unavoidable bias in this study's methodology. Nevertheless, the interviews and questionnaires showed that the effects of the men's war experience did sometimes encroach upon their family lives. It is clear, however, from discussion with one interviewee that some degree of trauma did affect some of the families of returned 1st Battalion men. Arrangement was made for a questionnaire to be forwarded to one woman who was known to have had a difficult upbringing. The questionnaire was returned anonymously; only the final question, 'What has your father's war service meant to you? Has it influenced you in any way?', was answered, and cryptically: 'Yes. It made it impossible to have a normal life.'

Sergeant John Murphy is remembered as having to dash from the family house on occasions to clear his head, a problem attributed to his war service. His absences would sometimes last for hours. One pleasure to come from his affliction was the long walks the family would take along the beach as restorative and rehabilitative treatment for their father's ailment. Murphy was not remembered as ever having joined a post-war soldier group and marched in only one Anzac Day parade for the benefit of his children.[81] John Reid was another 1st Battalion soldier susceptible to similar attacks. Following Reid's death, a teaching colleague recalled in an obituary how Reid had once 'swooned off' at the tea table and noted that the occurrence was 'an all too frequent reminder' of his war wound to the head.[82] Another obituary reflected on Reid's post-war distress, but it also elevated and transformed his suffering to a status worthy of the 'digger' stereotype: 'he was to face the future with debilitated health accompanied by unnecessary pain and discomfort. The story of his manner of doing this is an epic of determination and true manliness.'[83]

John Reid's pursuit of an academic career in the post-war years, as well as the courage he displayed in publicly denouncing the inappropriateness of imposed patriotism in schools, suggests someone determined to voice a contrary opinion. Whether it constituted an epic of determination or fulfilled the precepts of manliness was of little consequence to the personal agonies he suffered. However, it was important to the continued public perpetuation of stereotypical 'digger' qualities. No amount of resolve could stave off the inevitable surrender of some men's minds and bodies to the effects of their war service. Nor could the victim necessarily predict the time and place that war's spectres would choose to appear. Susan Conrade, the daughter of Charles Withy, a former 1st Battalion officer, provides an example of one unexpected visitation. During a visit to the Australian War Memorial in 1949, while in the company of her father, Conrade recollected a dramatic change in her father's countenance when viewing a diorama of the fighting in France: 'The look of total horror on his face was something I have never seen before and is a memory I will always keep. He did not need to say anything—it was all there in front of me.'[84]

In view of the potential life-long impression that incidents such as Withy's response could impose upon family memories, it is worth considering the effects of a man's war service on his family. Of the twelve people who participated in this research, none indicated any negativity in their view of their fathers. Most expressed pride in their fathers' service for the country. In some instances, where commissions had been awarded, the fact that their father had risen from the ranks to commissioned-officer was mentioned. Consideration of the biases that existed in the award of such commissions was not evident, principally because it is an aspect of the AIF that is not generally known. In fact precise knowledge of the Battalion's experience was largely absent, even though most respondents were aware of the existence of the

Battalion history. For instance, few knew of the mutiny within the Battalion, although it is mentioned in both the Battalion and official histories and has featured on the front page of the *Sydney Morning Herald*. This lack of awareness highlights the assertion that official histories are rarely read by the public, as well as the transitory nature of one-off headlines.[85] Those whose fathers had served in the war appear to have no great desire to penetrate beyond the fact that they had participated in the war. The more general stereotypical notions sufficed, even if they did not equate with what they saw in their fathers, because it was those which their fathers had chosen to convey through both their muteness and their considered anecdotes. Indeed, some respondents recognised fully that the glorified version of the stereotype bore little resemblance to their fathers. As one man stated: 'They were just ordinary men'.[86] Equally important to the continued acceptance of, or absence of challenge to, the stereotype was the sense of identity that the children of returned men perceived in their fathers. Their fathers were and had always been returned soldiers. None remembered any defining moment when they discovered that their father was a returned soldier. They were always aware of their fathers' status and identity through conversations experienced and overheard and through observation of their fathers' activities and friendships. It was a constant in their lives, a fact of life, and one that most felt no need to question or challenge.

It is not surprising that people whose fathers had served the nation would not feel compelled to challenge the foundations on which a large part of their lives had been built. For most, their father's service provided a deeply personal connection with the First World War that required no investigation and that also defined their own identity.

Given the long period of germination that the Anzac legend has had in the national conscience, it is not surprising that alternative perspectives have been slow in emerging. In the face of a rigorous and deliberate effort on the part of the early interpreters of the AIF's war service and achievements, to which the 1st Battalion Association and other 1st Battalion members contributed through their writings, shibboleths have been allowed to obscure some realities of important aspects of that experience. In the face of the myth-making process some returned soldiers and their families have been subdued in advancing differing interpretations even when a soldier's own experience, or that with which his family was confronted, suggested contrary meanings. One need not be critical of these people nor the public generally for a continued acquiescence in or reticence to challenge the 'digger' stereotype advanced through the legend; their responses are, after all, shaped in part by the interpretations presented by historians, writers, journalists and film-makers. Although these opinions are diverse, they still, in the main, perpetuate the qualities of egalitarianism, initiative and resourcefulness attributed to the Australian soldier. They do so because the actual experience of Australian soldiers is considered less important than the advancement of a positive national self-image. Consequently the descriptions and interpretations of the Anzac legend continue, through their selectivity, to project positive images of ourselves as a nation while at the same time distorting the experiences of the nation's First World War soldiers.

Conclusion

From its inception to its final action in battle, the experiences of the 1st Australian Infantry Battalion were many and varied. While traits such as egalitarianism, resourcefulness and initiative are assumed and maintained in the nation's popular memory as a truthful representation, not only of Australia's First World War soldiers but also, of the national character, they were not sufficiently evident in the experience of the 1st Battalion to justify their advancement as characteristics general to Australian soldiers or the nation. Moreover, much of the experience of the Battalion was not necessarily peculiar to Australian soldiers.

It would, of course, be unreasonable to assume that the composition, experience and behaviour of the 1st Battalion epitomised that of all Australian battalions. We know, at least in terms of composition, that the 1st Battalion, raised in New South Wales, differed significantly from the Western Australian units examined by Welborn. The most obvious difference is the proportion of Catholics in the officer ranks and the percentage of British-born in the ranks. The ramifications, if any, of these differences on behaviour across AIF battalions remains an area for exploration. An underlying assumption of this book has been the likelihood that the experiences of AIF battalions, though often similar—as general studies such as those by Gammage and Adam-Smith have demonstrated—were, nevertheless, distinct. Variations within and across battalions, in fact, diminish the force of the Anzac legend, which assumes an implicit homogeneity of behaviour.

In some instances, the attitudes of the men in the 1st Battalion appear to support, at least superficially, some of the qualities of Australian soldiers expressed through the 'digger' stereotype. They carried to war a distinct concept of egalitarianism. They assumed their volunteer status and the democratic notions they held would be sustained in the military organisation they were joining. They anticipated that an overt egalitarianism would dictate the army's response to their civilian identity. In these respects they were mistaken. Contrary to the democratic ideals that many enlistees brought to war, the autocratic and adversarial methods of military discipline were a feature of Australian army life. Resentments were expressed through frequent and varied acts of indiscipline. Direct confrontation with officers and NCOs marked many of these incidents. Refusal to obey orders, insolence, bad language and, in extreme cases, violence toward officers underpinned many of the soldiers' 'crimes'. It is not suggested that these offences represented the overriding experience of officer–man relations in the Battalion. Officers were conscious of gaining the men's respect, which was essential if an officer were to perform his duties at an optimum level of efficiency. Respect served a dual purpose. First, it could circumvent difficulties arising from a volunteer's concept of egalitarianism, since the impositions of military discipline and necessity were more palatable when demanded by a respected officer. Second, if an officer were to lead soldiers in battle, he had to be seen as equally willing to undertake the same risks as his men. This measure of worthiness was the key to the establishment of 'rough equality' between the ranks.[1] The establishment of 'rough equality' did not necessarily mean that officers treated the men as equals; indeed, and especially given the selection biases within the 1st Battalion, there is little evidence to support such a notion. Rather, it meant that officers sought to treat soldiers fairly and compassionately within the parameters allowed within their command. It was not something which was uniformly achieved by officers of the 1st Battalion. Moreover, the need of officers to earn their men's respect was not, as Sheffield's and Liddle's research into the British Expeditionary Force has demonstrated, something that was peculiar to the AIF. Line officers of that force were as desirous of obtaining that essential key to the officer–man relationship. Within the hardship of the front line, practice of 'rough equality' reminded officers and other ranks, upper or middle class and working class, that a measure of humanity flourished in what was generally seen as a 'modern hell' where men's resources were relentlessly crushed by the indomitable forces of industrialisation.

There is no conclusive evidence from the 1st Battalion's experience to suggest that a state of harmony ever prevailed in the officer–man relationship. To the contrary, the conflicts within that relationship in the 1st Battalion formed a significant and unpleasant undertone to battalion life, one which persisted throughout the war. That undertone is little considered in the formation of the 'digger' stereotype and as an aspect of battalion life it has been largely ignored in Australia's First World War historiography. Such tension should be expected in such a large group of men operating under the most trying conditions. It is not contended that officer–man relations in the 1st Battalion were never cordial and functional, nor that the officers were widely disrespected. However, tensions between officers, NCOs and other ranks were, at times, marked and chronic. This sometimes faltering relationship in the 1st Battalion provides a contrary image to the legend's depiction of the friendly mutuality that is assumed as axiomatic within the AIF.

The mutiny in September 1918 provided an emphatic—and dramatic—example of the depths to which officer–man relations could plunge. Apart from the obvious nadir that the mutiny represented in the 1st Battalion's officer–man relations, it also revealed the compromising effects of physical and mental fatigue and general war-weariness upon the soldiers of the front line. In the face of such distress, the fragile nature of the much-vaunted *esprit de corps* of Australian battalions is exposed. From a commander's point of view, it would have been hoped that a soldier's pride in his unit would have overcome the deep dissatisfaction that developed in the Battalion and would have prevented such a serious breach of discipline. On 21 September 1918 at Ruby Wood, despite being addressed by the much-revered Captain Moffatt, a majority of 1st Battalion soldiers in the front line could not be swayed by appeals of loyalty to either their unit or their officers.

Despite the mutiny and the many tensions between officers and men, expressed through their diaries and letters (and evident in relevant unit war diaries), it must be acknowledged that many of the soldiers who recorded such negative views nevertheless embraced the myth of egalitarianism that emerged about the AIF. Although the actual experience of many of the soldiers often ran counter to the myth, the men have assisted its transmission into the legend. In the post-war years, through their selective memory and through publications such as the unit history and various articles (which gave only abridged and protected versions of the Battalion's war experience), returned soldiers helped obscure the reality of their war experiences. In this process, the Battalion Association, with its disproportionate participation of officers to other ranks—and subsequent archetypal conservatism—was a powerful conduit. There exists little evidence in the primary sources about the 1st Battalion—contrary to the expressions of post-war solidarity between the ranks—to suggest that officer–man relations were especially egalitarian. We can conclude that officer–man relations within the 1st Battalion were considerably more strained than is suggested through the Anzac legend and that resentment by Australian soldiers was not confined to British officers, as the legend prefers, but their own as well.

It is not denied that officers and men shared common goals. The defeat of Germany was clearly one shared by both, although the extent to which officers and soldiers were motivated by a sense of righteousness in the cause of Empire or by a more pragmatic desire for the war to end is problematic. One aspect of the 1st Battalion's experience that was shared by some officers and men, and was pivotal to the high opinion they held of themselves as soldiers, was the anti-British sentiment that they expressed. Their low regard for the quality of the English Tommy, and the contempt with which they viewed British performance (and, on occasion, of the class system that was seen as underpinning the British army), operated on two levels. First, when morale was at a low ebb after a military reverse had occurred—such as at Gallipoli, generally, or at Bayonet Trench, specifically—poor British performance or examples of British failures were invoked to shore up the Australians' self-belief in their own soldierly qualities. This pattern of thought was expressed in two ways: either the British had let them down, or the British had also failed to do what the Australians had unsuccessfully attempted. Second, following Australian successes, the men boasted of their achievements through comparison with British failures, particularly those involving English troops. Irrespective of how unfair this was of English performance, it was a potent process in shaping the Australian soldier's nationalism and (soldier) identity. Given the conciliatory post-war comments of men such as Major-General Brand, C. E. W. Bean and the authors of the 1st Battalion's history—and given the sense of antipathy that is felt by contemporary British writers—it is apparent that an anti-British sentiment was incorporated to a significant degree into the national consciousness. These writers all drew attention to British participation in events generally considered the exclusive domain of Australian soldiers.

Much of what the 1st Battalion experienced, especially in combat, was common to all soldiers of the First World War. Despite the commonality of soldiers' experiences, the Anzac legend has advanced a view that Australian soldiers were more resourceful and possessed more initiative than other soldiers (particularly the English). Their displays of these alleged qualities are seen as key aspects in the definition of the national character. They were held to symbolise the power of the individual—a distinctly Australian individual—to overcome adversity. In the light of the 1st Battalion's behaviour, such assumptions must be viewed with far greater circumspection. The modern battle as it appeared in the First World War, with the role of the infantry generally subordinate to the success of the artillery bombardments, ensured a common and limited role among the infantrymen of all armies. That is not to say that Australian soldiers performed better or worse under this regimen than the men of other armies. Indeed, it has never been my contention that Australian soldiers were not competent and dedicated fighters when set a task. On the matter of courage and competency, my argument has been deliberately ambivalent; while I do not seek to deride the 'digger', I do contest the legitimacy of some of the myths constructed around (and even by) the 'digger'.

In 1918 the 1st Battalion participated, as did other Australian units, in successes that do appear to support notions of Australian resourcefulness and initiative. Although these qualities are often assumed to be characteristics of a national identity, there are insufficient examples within the experience of the 1st Battalion to support such a claim, as the Battalion's performance at the landing on Gallipoli and in the battle at Pozières—two of the defining moments in the reputation of Australian soldiers within the legend—clearly reveal. However, the successes in the raids and battles of 1918, particularly Chipilly Spur, have been combined to present a view of illustrious performance in all Australian units that was absent during the battles of the previous three years. The Australian Corps under John Monash did achieve noteworthy and important successes in 1918 that undoubtedly contributed significantly to the final Allied victory. The successes of that year, at least as far as the 1st Battalion's experiences reveal, were fought out against a backdrop of increasing war-weariness mixed with tension between the ranks. Those successes should not be seen, as they have tended to be, as vindication of Australian soldiers possessing innate soldierly qualities above and beyond those of other nations. Rather, they reflect the success of a tactical system practised throughout the British armies and, in the case of the Australians, of the unswerving commitment of a commander, Monash, who was willing to drive his troops to the limit to achieve final victory.

Unfortunately, within those successes, it is impossible to determine whether soldiers were driven, as well, by some self-fulfilling prophecy or whether, as Russel Ward might have suggested, they were motivated by how 'they ought "typically" behave'. Such notions find little expressions in the diaries and letters of the 1st Battalion men. The extent to which nationalism and unit morale sustained and inspired Australian battalions in combat cannot be adequately measured. The 1st Battalion was proudly Australian from the beginning to the end of the war and keenly aware of its national distinction within the British armies. The soldiers exhibited less consistency in their allegiance to the Battalion. For the Gallipoli veterans the 1st Division appeared to hold a greater resonance for their soldier identity. This divisional attachment diminished with the expansion of the AIF and influx of later reinforcements when a specific unit tradition was created to encourage *esprit de corps*.

Morale fluctuated throughout the war and the men's level of *esprit de corps* was largely determined by their immediate concerns, the level of comfort or discomfort, their despondency and depression caused by the fortunes of war and concern over their chances of survival. Morale plummeted after major actions—with the notable exception of Bullecourt, where pride in the unit's performance momentarily reached its zenith. Nevertheless, the intangible nature of *esprit de corps* will ensure that it remains contested ground between traditionalists, who assume its positive influence, and revisionists, who are less sanguine regarding its influence on First World War battlefields. A high level of *esprit de corps* within the Battalion was not so apparent from the immediate battle accounts. These were more likely to document the horror of the moment, the fear and dread felt in battle, rather than quixotic notions of the regiment. In contrast, retrospective accounts tend to highlight unit pride as an important factor in the men's war experience. As such it appears to be something (re)invented away from the front line. That in itself does not prove that the soldiers lacked a pride in the battalion or that they were not motivated by it. It does, however, reveal the great difficulty that exists in identifying or disproving its existence.

Many factors contributed to the successes in which the 1st Battalion participated. Improved planning, better training methods, advances in technology and deteriorating German morale all contributed to Australian and Allied success in 1918. These are aspects of the war that remain largely unexplored in Australia's First World War historiography. An examination of the effects of technology on the operations of the Australian divisions, similar to that done on the Canadian Corps, would be instructive to further understanding of the achievements of the AIF.[2] Similarly, an analysis of the performance of the Australian General Staff could provide insights into the operational planning of the AIF. Indeed, a broadening of study into the performance of Australian officers (combat and staff) generally, would be a welcome addition to Australia's historiography, which has, in the main, been dominated by the fortunes of the front-line 'digger'. It could be expected that such studies would provide a more balanced view of the command and actions of Australian soldiers in combat. This book has attempted to address those themes, at least in part, wherever they directly affected the performance of the 1st Battalion.

The qualities of egalitarianism, initiative and resourcefulness under-pinned much of the immediate post-war writings about the AIF and portray-als of the 'digger'. The 1st Battalion Association and some of its soldier-writers contributed unashamedly to this process. However, the per-sonal post-war struggles of returned soldiers (most of which were kept guarded by the soldiers and their immediate families) are at odds with the warrior image of the past and present. As the soldiers' accounts, pension records and testimonies of family members reveal, ill-health, permanent inca-pacity, alcoholism, unemployment and severe depression—sometimes cul-minating in suicide—were conditions that characterised some of the lives of returned 1st Battalion men. The overwhelming weight of some of these inter-nal and external problems was too much for some men to bear. That is not to say that all men were incapable of coping with the problems that confronted them in the post-war years. Many men and their families would endure the mental and physical debilities that invaded their lives—silently and stoically. In presenting an uncomplaining face to the world they, perhaps uncon-sciously, supported the quality of endurance advanced through the emerging 'digger' stereotype. It was ironic that the ceremonial tradition of the Anzac legend, through its powerful and symbolic celebration of the 'digger' and Empire loyalty, effectively muted the voices of dissent and veiled the many individual sufferings and unpleasant memories of returned 1st Battalion sol-diers and their families. Whether this was a contributing factor in the deci-sion of some of the Battalion's returned men not to participate in the activities of conservative post-war soldier groups such as the Battalion Association remains problematic.

Overall, the experience of 1st Battalion soldiers was more complex than, and significantly different, from the sanitised experiences painted by the 'dig-ger' stereotype of the Anzac legend. In relation to two central features of the legend—egalitarianism, and resourcefulness and initiative—the experience of the 1st Battalion suggests they were far less pervasive than has been tradi-tionally believed.

NOTES

Introduction

1 See the anonymous entry for 'Anzac Legend' for a useful discussion of the legend and related writings, in Peter Dennis *et al.*, *The Oxford Companion to Australian Military History*, pp. 47–8; Michael McKernan guesses that the author of this entry is Jeffrey Grey. See his book review in *Eureka Street*, vol. 6, no. 1, January–February 1996, p. 53.

2 C. M. H. Clark, *A History of Australia: 'The old dead tree and the young tree green'*, vol. IV, p. 132; Phillip Deery, Labor Interlude in Victorian Politics: The Prendergast Government, 1924, pp. 31–41.

3 L. L. Robson, 'The Australian Soldier: Formation of a Stereotype' in M. McKernan and M. Brown (eds), *Australia: Two Centuries of War and Peace*, p. 330; Dale James Blair, 'The Glorification of Australian Masculinity and the Reshaping of Australia's Great War Experience', pp. 33–4.

4 C. E. W. Bean, *Anzac to Amiens: A Shorter History of the Australian Fighting Services in the First World War*, p. 181.

5 The full text of the speech is in 'Funeral Service of the Unknown Australian Soldier, 11 November 1993, Eulogy delivered by the Prime Minister of Australia', *Journal of the Australian War Memorial*, no. 24, April 1994.

6 For a perceptive account of the emergence of this stereotype in Australia's war literature see Robin Gerster, *Big-Noting: The Heroic Theme in Australian War Writing*. Also, L. L. Robson, 'The Australian Soldier: Formation of a Stereotype' in McKernan and Browne (eds), *Australia: Two Centuries*, pp. 313–37.

7 J. Beaumont (ed.), *Australia's War, 1914–18*, p. 161. This chapter provides a fresh and challenging overview to the legacy of the Anzac legend and the various stages of its transmission.

8 A. Marwick, *The Nature of History*, p. 14.

9 This argument was advanced by Reuben Potter in a discussion on American remembrance of the Alamo, cited in Eric von Schmidt, 'How Is the Alamo Remembered?', p. 66.

10 Alistair Thomson, 'Steadfast Until Death'? C. E. W. Bean and the Representation of Australian Military Manhood'.

11 Robin Prior and Trevor Wilson, *Command on the Western Front: The Military Career of Sir Henry Rawlinson, 1914–18*. Also, *Passchendaele: The Untold Story*.

12 Bean, *Official History*, vol. VI, pp. 935–40; Bill Gammage, *The Broken Years*, pp. 228–9; Patsy Adam-Smith, *The Anzacs*, pp. 319–21; The eight battalions were the 19th, 21st, 25th, 29th, 37th, 42nd, 54th, and 60th.

13 Gammage, *The Broken Years*, p. 228.

14 John Laffin, *Western Front, 1917–1918: The Cost of Victory*, p. 153; See also Jeffrey Williams, Discipline on Active Service: The 1st Brigade, First AIF, 1914–1919, p. 121.

15 Lt A. W. Edwards, 'My War Diary', AWM/PR 89/50, p. 3.

16 Pte Reg Donkin, AWM/2DRL 069, 3DRL 3618; Cpl J. K. Gammage, AWM/PR 82/003.

17 Gammage, *The Broken Years*, pp. 40, 59–60, 90; John Robertson, *Anzac and Empire: The Tragedy and Glory of Gallipoli*, pp. 59, 73, 121–3.

18 Report: 'Relations between American Expeditionary Force and British Expeditionary Forces 1917–1920', prepared in the Historical Section, Army War College by Lt-Col. Calvin H. Goddard June 1942, p. 8, 7200-E [file copy] Pt. 1 No-5, U.S. Military History Institute, Carlisle, Pa.

19 Peter Simkins, 'Everyman at War: Recent Interpretations of the Front Line Experience', p. 312, emphasis in original.

20 This includes works by 47 1st Battalion and 7 non-1st Battalion letter and diary writers held in the Australian War Memorial's personal records collection; 23 1st Battalion chroniclers identified in newspapers and private collections; 9 1st Battalion chroniclers held in the Mitchell Library's manuscript collection; and 21 Repatriation Department personnel case files of ex-1st Battalion soldiers held at Australian Archives (Sydney).

21 Desmond Morton, *When Your Number's Up: The Canadian Soldier in the First World War*, pp. 277–8.

22 1st Battalion Offences Book, AWM 9/1/2.

23 Sgt. A. A. Barwick, Mitchell Library, Box ML MSS 1493/1, Items 1–9, 10–12, 13–16; Cpl P. Q. J. Collins, AWM/3DRL 6121.

24 L. L. Robson, review in *Meanjin Quarterly*, October 1974, pp. 320–2.

25 B. V. Stacy et al., *The History of the First Battalion, AIF, 1914–1919*. Hereafter cited as *First Battalion*. Demand among the Battalion's five thousand survivors was clearly not high and only two hundred copies were made available.

26 *Reveille*, 29 June 1929, p. 21.

27 Fussell, *The Great War and Modern Memory*, p. 175. Original reference cited as *Stillwell and the American Experience in China, 1911–1945*, p. 557.

28 Smyth was an ex-Sudan War veteran and Victoria Cross winner and commanded the 1st Brigade from May 1915 till the end of 1916. He also provided a foreword to the 3rd Battalion history, see Eric Wren, *Randwick to Hargicourt*, pp. vii–ix.

29 *First Battalion*, p. 5.

30 Ibid.

31 *Reveille*, 1 October 1932, p. 13.

32 Ibid., 30 September 1929, p. 25.

33 Ibid., 31 January 1930, pp. 28–32.

34 Ibid., 31 July 1930, p. 32.

35 Ibid., 31 December 1930, p. 17.

36 Ibid., 31 March 1931, p. 36.

37 Lt-Col. Neil C. Smith, *The Red and Black Diamond: The History of the 21st Battalion, 1915–1918*, introduction (no pagination).

38 Ron Austin, *Cobbers in Khaki: The History of the 8th Battalion, 1914–1918*, p. viii.

39 Ibid., p. vii.

40 *Sunday Age*, 8 November 1998.

1 Formation of the 1st Battalion

1 C. E. W. Bean, *Official History*, vol. I, p. 43.

2 Bob Millington, 'Are We in Danger of Forgetting our History?', p. 5.

3 *SMH*, 21 August 1914.

4 Brisbane *Courier Mail*, 21 April 1995, Weekend p. 4.

5 Private Stan Ayoub of the 1st Battalion was one such Syrian volunteer. His rescue of a man drowning in the Suez Canal was reported in *Sydney Mail*, 30 August 1916; *SMH*, 14 August 1914, 'The Syrians: Will fight for Great Britain'. Turkey did not enter the war until 31 October 1914, though her allegiance to Germany was never doubted.

6 Lt H. M. Lanser, letter, 16 May 1915, AWM/PR 00394.

7 John Reid, letter, 22 April 1915, in possession of Mrs Heather Cooper, Sydney.

8 For an account of the Sydney *Bulletin's* contribution to the cultivation of Australian culture see Henry Lawson's comments cited in Stephen Alomes and Catherine Jones (eds), *Australian Nationalism: A Documentary History*, pp. 94–7.

9 *SMH*, 14 October 1914.

10 Letter, 13 January 1915, MLA 2660.

11 Ken Inglis, *The Rehearsal: Australians at War in the Sudan, 1885*, pp. 102, 128.

12 Laurie Field, *The Forgotten War: Australia and the Boer War*, pp. 180–6; R. L. Wallace, *The Australians at the Boer War*, pp. 349–53.

13 Richard White, *Inventing Australia: Images and Identity, 1788–1980*, p. 127.

14 Russel Ward, *The Australian Legend*, p. 1; J. G. Fuller, Popular Culture and Troop Morale in the British and Dominion Forces, 1914–1918, pp. 259–62.

15 Peter Dennis *et al.*, *The Oxford Companion to Australian Military History*, pp. 147, 175.

16 Craig Wilcox, 'False Start: The Mobilisation of Australia's Citizen Army, 1914', p. 4.

17 *SMH*, 14 August 1914.

18 *SMH*, 21 August 1914.

19 Bean, *Official History*, vol. I, p. 60: 'The 1st Division contained 2263 young trainee soldiers, 1555 older militiamen, and 2460 who had at one time served in the Australian militia; there were also 1308 old British regulars and 1009 old British territorials in its ranks. But 6098 men had never served before.'

20 Ibid., p. 54, emphasis added.

21 *SMH*, 3 September 1914.

22 *Sydney Mail*, 3 September 1914.

23 *SMH*, 4 September 1914.

24 *Newcastle Morning Herald*, 1 September 1914.

25 *SMH*, 12, 20 August 1914.

26 A low percentage of AMF volunteers (17) has also been detected in the composition of the Victorian-raised 8th Battalion. See Austin, *Cobbers in Khaki*, pp. 4–5.

27 For a description of this early mobilisation, see Wilcox, 'False Start', pp. 4–9.

28 Sgt-Maj. T. Murphy, 1st Battalion, 'A Soldier's Diary', *Anzac Memorial*, The Returned Soldiers Association, Sydney, 1917, p. 308.

29 Lt B. W. Champion, typed copy of diary, p. 1, AWM/2DRL 512.

30 C. E. W. Bean, *Anzac to Amiens: A Shorter History of the Australian Fighting Services in the First World War*, p. 537.

31 F. M. Cutlack (ed.), *War Letters of General Monash*, p. 233.

32 Figures are based on the examination of the attestation papers of 63 lieutenants and 60 sergeants.

33 Robson, 'The Origin and Character of the First AIF', pp. 748–9. See also John F. Williams, *The Quarantined Culture*, pp. 249–51.

34 Street's religion is recorded on the 1st Battalion embarkation roll and on his attestation papers, Personal dossier, Australian Archives [ACT].

35 Alan Clark, *The Waratahs: South Coast Recruiting March, 1915*, pp. 43–57.

36 R. Floud, K. Wachter and A. Gregory, *Height, Health and History: Nutritional Status in the United Kingdom, 1750–1980*, pp. 135–8.

37 Stephen Garton, *The Cost of War: Australians Return*, 1996, p. 155.

38 Bean, *Official History*, vol. I, pp. 56–7.

39 The importance and British composition of Australian NCOs is explored in an unpublished paper by John Connor, 'The British Part in the Making of the Anzac Legend'.

40 Peter Bourne, 'From Boot Camp to My Lai', in Richard A. Falk (ed.), *Crimes of War*, New York, 1971, cited in Richard Holmes, *Firing Line*, pp. 45–6.

41 Holmes, *Firing Line*, p. 46.

42 Five were aged 31–35 and seven were 36–40.

43 Sgt. A. A. Barwick, Diary No. 1, pp. 7–8, MSS 1493/1, Item 1, Mitchell Library.

44 Bean, *Official History*, vol. I, p. 41.

45 1st Brigade Diary, appendix no. 28, Confidential Report by Col. MacLaurin, appendix 'A', AWM 4.

46 *First Battalion*, p. 14.

47 Barwick, Diary No. 1, pp. 4–5. Barwick's diaries provide one of the few detailed accounts of this period by 1st Battalion members.

48 Champion, diary, p. 24.

49 *Delegate Argus*, 9 September 1915, 'What about our Thousand?'

50 Clark, *The Waratahs*, p. 42.

51 Confidential Report on the Raising and Equipping of the First Infantry Brigade, Australian Imperial Force, by Colonel MacLaurin, in 1st Brigade Diary, appendix no. 28, AWM 4.

52 S. Welborn, *Lords of Death*, p. 190.

53 *SMH*, 25 August 1914.

54 Ivan Chapman, *Iven G. Mackay: Citizen and Soldier*, p. 105.

55 A. B. Paterson, *Happy Despatches*, p. 91.

56 J. G. Fuller, Popular Culture and Troop Morale in the British and Dominion Forces, 1914–1918, pp. 254–9.

57 Bean, *Official History*, vol. I, p. 54.

2 'Class is everything'

1 It seems that this anecdote first appeared in British trench journals. British perceptions are discussed in Fuller, Popular Culture and Troop Morale in the British and Dominion Forces, 1914–1918, pp. 68–71. Peter Liddle has attacked Fuller's findings that the other ranks were distant and unknowable to their officers, and has argued that the officer–man relationship was not as distant as is so often supposed. See Peter H. Liddle, *The 1916 Battle of the Somme: A Reappraisal*, pp. 153–6.

2 John Lahey, 'The World's Most Democratic Army' in 75th Gallipoli anniversary souvenir in the *Age*, 20 April 1990. See also Bill Gammage, *The Broken Years: Australian Soldiers in the Great War*, p. 244.

3 G. D. Sheffield, The Effect of War Service on the 22nd Battalion Royal Fusiliers (Kensington), 1914–18, with Special Reference to Morale, Discipline, and the Officer–Man Relationship, pp. 67–8.

4 Peter Simkins, *Kitchener's Army: The Raising of the New Armies, 1914–16*, chs 3, 8. See also John Keegan, *The Face of Battle: A Study of Agincourt, Waterloo, and the Somme*, pp. 223–4. For a revealing account of the training and character of a New Army division (the 18th), see John Baynes, *Far from a Donkey: The Life of General Sir Ivor Maxse, KCB, CVO, DSO*, ch. 12, pp. 123–34. See also Colin Hughes, *Mametz: Lloyd George's 'Welsh Army' at the Battle of the Somme*, pp. 26–31.

5 Sgt E. R. Larkin, letter, 13 January 1915.

6 *Sydney Mail*, 13 September 1916.

7 Eric Leed, *No Man's Land: Combat and Identity in World War I.*

8 Carl von Clausewitz, *On War*, pp. 254–5; it was published posthumously under its original title *Vom Kriege* in 1833.

9 Confidential Report on the Raising and Equipping of the First Infantry Brigade, Australian Imperial Force, by Colonel MacLaurin, in 1st Brigade Diary, appendix no. 28, AWM 4. One thousand and thirteen men are listed as having embarked for overseas service with the 1st Battalion.

10 Pte Herb Bartley, 'First Day in Camp', *Delegate Argus*, 3 June 1915.

11 Harry Sharpe, 'The Australian Way', *Town and Country Journal*, 15 September 1915.

12 Craig Wilcox, Australia's Citizen Army, 1889–1914, pp. 334–7.

13 *Town and Country Journal*, 7 July 1915, p. 23. For a most benign account of the men's grievances and subsequent events see Ernest Scott, *Official History of Australia in the War of 1914–18: Australia During the War*, vol. XI, pp. 228–30.

14 *Town and Country Journal*, 1 December 1915, p. 12.

15 *Ibid.*, 16 February 1916, p. 12.

16 *Daily Telegraph*, 15 February 1916; *SMH*, 15–19 February 1916. The dead soldier was Trooper Ernest William Keefe. A post-mortem examination revealed that he had been struck by only one bullet and that no other wounds existed other than that made by the bullet: *SMH*, 17 February 1916.

17 *SMH*, 15 February 1916.

18 *SMH*, 16 February 1916.

19 *Commonwealth Parliamentary Papers*, General 2, Session 1914–1917, Interim Report, Further Interim Report, and Report on Liverpool Military Camp, New South Wales, by His Honour Mr. Justice Rich, pp. 273–97.

20 *SMH*, 16 February 1916.
21 *Daily Telegraph*, 15 February 1916.
22 *SMH*, 18 February 1916.
23 *Town and Country Journal*, 26 April 1916, p. 16.
24 Ridley to his mother, 22 January 1916.
25 Capt. D. V. Mulholland, letter extracts, France, 27 June 1916, AWM/2DRL 40.
26 Pte F. W. Muir, letter, *S.S. Afric*, 'At Sea', Thursday, AWM/2DRL 316, item 2.
27 *The Kangaroo*, 26 October, 24 November 1914. These two editions are contained in Lt H. M. Lanser, AWM PR 00394, File No. 3.
28 David A. Kent, 'Troopship Literature: A Life on the Ocean Wave, 1914–19', p. 8.
29 Ibid., p. 10.
30 *Kangaroo*, 24 November 1914.
31 Pte R. Donkin, diary, 7 December 1914, AWM/2DRL 069.
32 L.Cpl W. Swindells, Diary No. 1, 5 December 1914, AWM/PR 00251.
33 *Delegate Argus*, 2 September 1915.
34 Jeffrey Williams, Discipline on Active Service: The 1st Brigade, First AIF, 1914–1919, p. 8.
35 Herbert Matthews (unit unidentified), letter, 21 December 1915, *Finley Mail*, 31 March 1916.
36 Herb Bartley, letter, 29 July 1915, *Delegate Argus*, 26 August 1915.
37 Swindells, Diary No. 1, 7 November 1914.
38 H. J. Cave, letter, 26 December 1915, ML MSS 1224.
39 Cpl P. Q. J. Collins, undated postcard, AWM/3DRL 6121.
40 Suzanne Brugger, *Australians and Egypt, 1914–1919*, pp. 43–4.
41 Ibid. See, in particular, ch. 2, pp. 30–47.
42 Ibid., p. 44.
43 Donkin, diary, 8 December 1914.
44 Pte F. W. Muir, letter, 10 December 1914, p. 10, AWM/2DRL 316.
45 Swindells, Diary No. 1, 8 December 1914. For another favourable impression of the local police, see letter by Pte W. Simms (1Bn) to his father published in *SMH*, 27 January 1915. This soldier's identity was confirmed by matching his father's name with that cited on the 1st Bn embarkation roll entry for W. Simms.
46 *St George Call*, 24 April 1915.
47 Sgt J. Ridley, letter dated 5 November 1915, AWM/3DRL 6428.
48 In his study of New South Welsh identity in the 1880s, Stephen Shortis has suggested the possibility of a distinct colonial identity being conveyed through the rhetoric used in public debates. After examining public responses to two events—the affairs in New Guinea in 1885 and the death of General Gordon at Khartoum—he noted that a definite colonial pride emerged based on New South Wales' position as the premier colony and a belief that it had a responsibility to lead by example. Shortis acknowledged the limitations of his research and suggested that further research was required to investigate possible differences between the public response and private utterances: see "Colonial Nationalism": New South Welsh Identity in the mid-1880s', pp. 31–51. Certainly the private utterances of identified 1st Battalion chroniclers contradict the existence of a similar identity.
49 Muir, letter, 10 January 1915.
50 Williams, 'Discipline on Active Service', p. 19.

[51] Ibid., appendix I, p. 127.

[52] Letter, 18 April 1915, AWM/1DRL 310.

[53] Swindells, Diary No. 2, 2 April 1915.

[54] Cited in Williams, 'Discipline on Active Service', p. 21.

[55] Swindells, Diary No. 2, 30 January 1915.

[56] Ibid., 4, 1 March 1915.

[57] Ibid., 8 March 1915.

[58] Ibid.

[59] Bean, *Official History*, vol. I, p. 134.

[60] Sgt John H. Kirby, letter, *Dan Dorigo Gazette and Guy Fawkes Advocate*, 24 October 1914.

[61] Donkin, Diary, 23 March 1915.

[62] Lt K. McConnel, war memoir, p. 5, AWM/2DRL 29.

[63] *Sydney Mail*, 7 July 1915.

[64] Pte Robert Grant, 'World War One memoirs', p. 10, AWM/PR 89/180.

[65] Richard Jebb was a traveller and chronicler of the emerging Dominion nations in the first decade of the century; see John Eddy and Deryck Schreuder, *The Rise of Colonial Nationalism: Australia, New Zealand, Canada and South Africa First Assert their Nationalities, 1880–1914*, pp. 1–2.

[66] The most forceful language in the article, over which the men most likely took offence, was: 'But there is in the Australian ranks a proportion of men who are uncontrolled, slovenly, and in some cases, what few Australians can be accused of being—dirty. In a certain number of cases it is noticeable that these men are wearing the South African ribbon', cited in Dudley McCarthy, *Gallipoli to the Somme: The Story of C.E.W. Bean*, p. 91.

[67] Major Davidson, notation on copy of the poem in AWM/1DRL 235.

[68] McCarthy, *Gallipoli to the Somme*, pp. 91–7.

[69] Herb Bartley, letter, *Delegate Argus*, 26 August 1915.

[70] Pte A. E. Rostron, diary, 15 October 1915, AWM/2DRL 106.

[71] Pte Andria Locane, diary, 20 December 1915, AWM/3DRL 6217.

[72] Rostron, diary, 22 October 1915.

[73] Sheffield, however, notes that within the 22nd Royal Fusiliers, some men did address their officers by their first names: The Effect of War Service, p. 67.

[74] Barwick, Diary 7, 19 December 1916.

[75] McConnel, undated letter, Golding to McConnel, typed transcript of letters, p. 4, AWM/2DRL 29.

[76] Golding's age was given as twenty-one on the 1st Battalion's embarkation roll and McConnel was nineteen on enlistment. Both enlisted in 1914. The letter was written after the fighting at Pozières.

[77] 1st Battalion Offences Book, AWM 9/1/2.

[78] McConnel, letter, 27 August 1916, Howell-Price to McConnel, typed transcript, p. 3.

[79] A short discussion of the development and role of language in British society is contained in Jose Harris, *The Penguin Social History of Britain; Public Lives, Public Spirit: Britain, 1870–1914*, pp. 22–3.

[80] A useful discussion of the existence of that ethos in Australian schools is contained in Michael McKernan, *The Australian People and the Great War*, ch. 3, pp. 43–64.

[81] Sheffield, The Effect of War Service, p. 60.

[82] Harold Mercer Papers, Diary, 31 December 1917, p. 33, ML MSS 1143.

83 Sheffield, The Effect of War Service, pp. 56–7; Denis Winter, *Death's Men: Soldiers of the Great War*, pp. 60–2.

84 Letter, 2 November 1916 in AWM/2DRL 29.

85 Special Memo: Confidential for Officers only, Headquarters, 1st Anzac Corps, 11 November 1916, AWM 27/354/39.

86 Letter, 27 August 1916, AWM/2DRL 29.

87 1st Australian Infantry Brigade report, 6 August 1916, AWM 26, Box 53/22.

88 Bean, *Official History*, vol. I, pp. 51–3; Ann M. Mitchell, 'Sir Henry Normand MacLaurin', in *Australian Dictionary of Biography*, vol. 10: *1891–1939*, pp. 327–9; AWM 8, Embarkation Roll for 1st Battalion.

89 Bean, *Official History*, vol. I, p. 54.

90 Dobbin to Bean, letter dated 9 September 1920, AWM 43 [A214].

91 McConnel, typed memoirs [3 of 3], p. 13, AWM/2DRL 29; McConnel, personnel dossier, AA[C], attestation papers.

92 McConnel, family memoirs, letter to his mother, 27 February 1916, held by Mrs Barbara Fitzherbert (Sydney).

93 List 3: Rank and Name of any Reinforcement Officers now with Battalion who have not been absorbed with recommendation as to disposal in each case, AWM 27/302/102.

94 Richards, personnel dossier, AA[C], Casualty Form—Active Service.

95 *First Battalion*, p. 40.

96 Australian Imperial Force circular, 'Rules governing the promotion of Non-co officers', issued with List No. 4, 15 October 1915, AWM 27 /360/19. It is possible that these instructions were framed to limit the practice of preferred selection within battalions (which was apparent in the 1st Battalion).

97 Typed extracts from letter, 7 December 1915, AWM/2DRL 0005, p. 8.

98 List 6: No. Rank and Name of NCOs and men, serving with present Battalion, who are recommended for appointment to commissions, AWM 27/302/102.

99 Sgt J. Ridley, letter, 17 January 1916, AWM/3DRL 6428, [1 of 4].

1 Ibid., 6 February 1916.

2 War memoirs, p. 13, [3 of 3].

3 Lt T. J. Richards, AWM/2DRL 794, typed copy of diary, book 4, 11, 12 January 1917, pp. 61–2.

4 Lt A. W. Edwards, 'My War Diary: The Seventh Platoon of The First Australian Infantry Battalion', p. 120, AWM/PR 89/50.

5 Letter to his mother, 9 July 1916, held by Mrs Barbara Fitzherbert (Sydney).

6 Philip Howell-Price, letter, 1 August 1916, AWM/PR 89/50.

7 Champion, Diary, 13 May 1916, p. 70; 22 November 1916, p. 123. Champion's promotion followed soon after the action at Bayonet Trench in which the Battalion incurred heavy losses.

8 Lt R. B. Finlayson, diary, 27 June 1916, AWM/1DRL 287. An example of the ranks attained by bank clerks is found in the *Bank of New South Wales Roll of Honour*, Sydney, 1921. Of five 1st Battalion men previously employed by the Bank of New South Wales, four were commissioned as officers: see pp. 19–20 (2nd Lt Alford), p. 90 (Pte Cuddeford), p. 100 (Lt Downton), p. 327 (Capt. Prior), p. 397 (Capt. Walker). Bank employees were also highly represented in the western battalions of the Canadian Expeditionary Force; see Desmond Morton, *When Your Number's Up: The Canadian Soldier in the First World War*, pp. 98–9.

⁹ Dinning to his father, 30 January 1916 held by Miss Nancy Joyce (Sydney).

¹⁰ A. A. Barwick, Diary No. 6, 13 October 1916, p. 41.

¹¹ Ibid., Diary No. 4, 30 July 1916, pp. 49–51.

¹² Letter, 7 March 1916, MSB 176, MS 10143 (La Trobe Library, Victoria).

¹³ Lt O'Keefe, 'Type of Fighting in France—Trench Warfare', AWM/PR 85/253.

¹⁴ Champion, Diary, 26 July 1916, p. 95.

¹⁵ Edwards, War Diary, p. 110. Perhaps the most prominent victim of such treatment was Albert Jacka who was incensed by his initial non-selection to attend officer training after the Gallipoli campaign. His prospects of promotion improved markedly with the arrival of a kindred spirit, Colonel Peck, in his battalion: Ian Grant, *Jacka, VC: Australia's Finest Fighting Soldier*, pp. 52, 92–7.

¹⁶ Lt Sydney Robert Traill, Diary, 21 March 1918, p. 40, AWM/2DRL 711.

¹⁷ Barwick, Diary No. 8, 15 February 1917, p. 123.

¹⁸ Champion, Diary, 22 November 1916, p. 123.

¹⁹ Batmen occupied a special purgatory within a Battalion's structure. As an officer's ser- vant they could be patronised by their superior while at the same time scorned by other soldiers for the service they were providing. A discussion of this point in relation to the 2nd AIF is contained in Mark Johnston, *At the Front Line: Experiences of Australian Soldiers in World War II*, p. 140. For some derogatory descriptions of batmen within the 1st Battalion see the diary entries in Barwick, Diary 8, 4 January 1917, pp. 7–8 and Lt S. R. Traill, 18 February 1918, AWM 2DRL 711.

²⁰ Richards, book 4, 13 December 1916, p. 37, AWM/2DRL 794.

²¹ Lt C. A Sweetnam, undated postcard to Master A. Sweetnam, AWM/3DRL 7033.

²² Dinning, letter to his father, 30 January 1916.

²³ Private Frederick Buchan, Service Record, AA[ACT].

²⁴ *Delegate Argus*, 9 September 1915. Bartley was eventually promoted to the rank of sergeant.

²⁵ John Gammage, diary, 6 August 1915, AWM/PR 82/003.

²⁶ Gammage, diary, 9 August 1915. Respective casualties for the battle have been estimated as being over 6000 Turks and 2300 Australians. See Fewster *et al.*, *A Turkish View of Gallipoli*, p. 100.

²⁷ Gammage, diary, 9 August 1915.

²⁸ Brigade casualties appear in Bean, *Official History*, vol. II, p. 566.

²⁹ Donkin, diary, 18 May 1915.

³⁰ Ibid.,12 August 1915.

³¹ Ibid. The argument with Sasse was over the delivery of mail—six newspapers—which Donkin claimed to know had been recieved but which Sasse claimed otherwise.

³² Donkin, diary, 13/14 August 1915. His death was described in a letter by Private Roy Anderson, 15 December 1915, contained in AWM/2DRL 069.

³³ Donkin, Service record, AA[ACT].

³⁴ AWM 9/1/1.

³⁵ R. G. Casey, Diary, 25 May 1915.

³⁶ Ashworth cited in Sheffield,'The Effect of War Service', p. 74.

³⁷ Dobbin, personal service record, AA[ACT].

³⁸ 1st Battalion Offences Book, AWM 9 1/2.

³⁹ Barwick, Diary No. 12, 8 April 1918, p. 87.

⁴⁰ Sgt N. H. Langford, Narrative, 10 June 1916, p. 67, AWM/2DRL 666.

41 Mercer, diary, 24 April 1918, p. 161.
42 M. D. Field, 'Information and Authority: The Structure of Military Organization', p. 17.
43 McConnel, diary, 22 May 1916.
44 Private D. Horton, Essay, p. 32, AWM/1DRL 359. 'Government stroke' referred to the easy pace at which work was done, supposedly typical of those working in the government. It was originally used to describe the slow work-rate of convict road labourers. See G. A. Wilkes, *A Dictionary of Australian Colloquialisms*, p. 159.
45 Lt T. J. Richards, Diary No. 4, 9 February 1917, p. 83, AWM/3DRL 8050.
46 Barwick, Diary No. 9, p. 32.
47 Mercer, diary, 19 December 1916, pp. 11, 13, ML MSS 1143.
48 Lt S. R. Traill, typed copy of diary, 22 February 1918, p. 27, AWM/2DRL 711.
49 See graph of Australian Death Sentences in Christopher Pugsley, *On the Fringe of Hell: New Zealanders and Military Discipline in the First World War*, p. 351. A total of 121 death sentences were imposed on Australian soldiers during the war, 117 of these in France, p. 298.
50 Samuel Stouffer, *The American Soldier: Combat and its Aftermath*, vol. 2, pp. 125–8.

3 Gallipoli

1 *SMH*, editorial, 'The Anzacs' Unbroken Spirit', 25 April 1994.
2 For a description of the rapidity and manner in which this occurred, see Ken Inglis' two-part article, 'The Australians at Gallipoli', pp. 219–30, pp. 361–75. Bill Gammage suggests the seeds of the tradition were planted in the public response to the Boer War; see his chapter, 'The Crucible: The Establishment of the Anzac Tradition, 1899–1918', pp. 147–66; also R. Ely, 'The First Anzac Day: Invented or Discovered?', pp. 41–58.
3 *Sydney Mail*, 12 May 1915. For a discussion of Bartlett's role in the establishment of the Anzac legend, see Kevin Fewster, 'Ellis Ashmead Bartlett and the Making of the Anzac Legend', pp. 17–30.
4 Fewster, 'Ellis Ashmead Bartlett', p. 19. Bartlett went ashore for half an hour later in the evening of 25 April. Bean, by contrast, went ashore at 9.30 am and remained with the troops for the duration of the campaign.
5 First despatch, GHQ, MEF, 20 May 1915, published in *Ian Hamilton's Despatches from the Dardanelles etc*, p. 43.
6 John Masefield, *Gallipoli*, p. 19.
7 MacKenzie, *Gallipoli Memories*, p. 81.
8 See Table 6. The importance of height in the establishment of Australia's soldier stereotype is referred to in L. L. Robson, 'The Australian Soldier: Formation of a Stereotype', pp. 317, 323.
9 Cited in K. S. Inglis, 'The Australians at Gallipoli—I', p. 223. Monash carried a copy of Fitchett's book to war and used it at Gallipoli and France to stimulate the interest of the men in their military traditions, p. 228.
10 Jonathan King, 'Our Last Anzacs', pp. 12–17. Emphasis in original.
11 Geoffrey Moorhouse, *Hell's Foundations: A Town, Its Myths and Gallipoli*, pp. 10–11.
12 Robert Rhode James, *Gallipoli: A British Historian's View*, p. 3.
13 King, 'Our Last Anzacs', p. 15.
14 *Age*, 25 April 1997.
15 Many of the 'eye-witness' accounts published by returned soldiers were characterised by their patriotic celebration of the militaristic and heroic conquests of the Australian

soldier. For a lengthy discussion of these, chs 3–4 in Gerster, *Big-Noting: The Heroic Theme in Australian War Writing*. For some discussions of examples directly related to military history of the problems and nature of oral history see Graham Dawson, 'Playing at War: An Autobiographical Approach to Boyhood Fantasy and Masculinity', pp. 44–53; Patrick Hagopian, 'Oral Narratives: Secondary Revision and the Memory of the Vietnam War', pp. 134–50; Peter Liddle and Matthew Richardson, 'Voices from the Past: An Evaluation of Oral History as a Source for Research into the Western Front Experience of the British Soldier, 1914–18', pp. 651–74.

16 E. John Solarno (ed.), *Drill and Field Training*, pp. 4–5.

17 John Baynes, *Far from a Donkey*, pp. 142–43.

18 *First Battalion*, p. 39.

19 1st Brigade Diary, Lecture by GOC to all Officers of Brigade, Appendix 19, p. 40, AWM 4.

20 Donkin, diary, 19 February 1915, AWM/2DRL 69.

21 *First Battalion*, p. 22.

22 A description of the circumstances of the Brigadier's statement is contained in the 3rd Battalion history; see Wren, *Randwick to Hargicourt*, p. 38.

23 Donkin, diary, 25 February 1915.

24 Les Dinning, letter, 7 February 1915, held by Ms Nancy Joyce, Sydney.

25 P. A. Pederson, 'The AIF on the Western Front: The Role of Training and Command', p. 169; Bean, *Official History*, vol. I, p. 139.

26 Fewster *et al.*, *A Turkish View of Gallipoli*, p. 55.

27 Elmar Dinter, *Hero or Coward: Pressures Facing the Soldier in Battle*, p. 1.

28 Donkin, diary, 4 March 1915.

29 Maj. William Davidson, letter, 22 April 1915, AWM/1DRL 235.

30 Pte Robert A. Grant, 'Memoirs of World War One', pp. 13, 15, AWM/PR 89/180.

31 Extracts of letters from Alan Mitchell to his father, *The King's School Magazine*, December 1915, pp. 477–8.

32 Grant, 'Memoirs', p. 15.

33 Lanser, letter, 16 May 1915.

34 The *Australian Imperial Force: Staff, Regimental, Gradation Lists of Officers* for 1914 and 1915 provide notations of previous service for the two officers, Major Kindon (South Africa) and Captain Davidson (India).

35 The 7th Battalion's experience at Fisherman's Hut is described in Bean, *Official History*, vol. I, pp. 324–32.

36 *First Battalion*, p. 25.

37 For detail of the landing instructions 'Operation order No. 1' see, AWM 4, 1st Australian Division Diary (m/f roll 803), also, 1st Australian Infantry Brigade Diary, Appendix No. 6. See also F. W. Taylor and T. A. Cusack, *Nulli Secundus: A History of the Second Battalion, AIF, 1914–1919*, p. 59. The objective of the covering force was the third ridge. Few men other than isolated parties ever reached the position. There is little evidence in the diaries and letters of 1st Battalion soldiers that suggest the officers or men had any conception of the objectives of the battleplan. Denis Winter has argued that three separate plans were issued in the fortnight prior to the landing: the first was finalised on 13 April, the second on 21 April, and the third and actual plan (for which no actual orders are known to have survived, according to Winter) was framed between 22 and 24 April. The final plan, Winter suggests, deliberately placed the Australian landing at Anzac Cove and not by accident as the legend would have it. See Winter, *25 April 1915: The Inevitable Tragedy*, pp. 125–49.

38 Eric Wren, *Randwick to Hargicourt*, p. 47.

39 For a recent, graphic account about the fate of one of these parties see Greg Kerr, *Lost Anzacs: The Story of Two Brothers*, pp. 1–3.

40 Hamilton's address is described by Lt R. A. Cassidy, letter undated, AWM/2DRL 0315, and Pte F. W. Muir, letter, *South Coast Times*, 13 August 1915, photocopy in AWM/2DRL 316, item 1. For a good description of the *Minnewaska's* journey and the Battalion's disembarkation see Bean's diary for 23 to 25 April, quoted in Fewster, *Gallipoli Correspondent*, pp. 54–74.

41 Hamilton's address, distributed among the troops, was posted home by some of the men either separately or as a novel piece of writing paper.

42 The 2nd Brigade had commenced landing at about 5.30, one hour after the initial landing.

43 Muir, *South Coast Times*, 13 August 1915.

44 *St George Call*, 12 June 1915.

45 'Great Deeds in the AIF, No. 17', *Smith's Weekly*, 12 September 1930.

46 Pte V. E. Jones, letter, 2 May 1915, AWM/PR 00360.

47 Grant,'Memoirs', p. 16. Swannell's departure was most probably due to his being instructed to reinforce the line on Baby 700. See *Official History*, vol. I, pp. 295–6.

48 *First Battalion*, p. 27.

49 Jones, letter, 2 May 1915.

50 Muir, *South Coast Times*, 13 August 1915.

51 *First Battalion*, p. 29.

52 Tony Ashworth, *Trench Warfare, 1914–1918: The Live and Let Live System*, p. 41.

53 Diary, 25 April 1915, AWM/3DRL 6418.

54 Cited in Christopher Pugsley, *Gallipoli: The New Zealand Story*, p. 136.

55 Carter, diary, 25 April 1915.

56 *First Battalion*, p. 31.

57 Letter, 11 May 1915, held by Mrs Heather Cooper, Sydney.

58 Unidentified article provided by Nancy Joyce, Sydney.

59 *First Battalion*, p. 28.

60 Incidental to the reportage of casualties was the fact that, due to the Battalion's primacy in the sequential listing of the army's battle order, relatives and friends of 1st Battalion men did not have far to look to ascertain the names of those wounded or killed. Private W. V. Knight (710), 1st Battalion, headed the first published Australian casualty list from the Dardanelles, *Daily Telegraph*, 3 May 1915.

61 *Henty Observer*, 19 June 1915, 'From the Firing Line'. The soldier is possibly R. S. Davey of the 1st Battalion. Private O'Leary (1st Bn) also spoke of this: 'These men never had a look in. They were shot down before they even had a chance to fire a shot or plug a Turk', in *Globe and Sunday Times War Pictorial*, 11 December 1915. Examination of the embarkation of subsequent reinforcements reveals that few of the men who returned to Australia returned to the fray.

62 Carter, diary, 26 April 1915.

63 The advance that Carter describes is probably that described in the preface of the third edition *Official History*, vol. I, pp. xvi–xviii. It was made across Lone Pine toward Owen's Gully but was enfiladed from the right and broke. The Australians reformed on the main defensive position along Bolton's Ridge.

64 Carter, diary, 26 April 1915.

65 *Official History*, vol. I, p. 527. Turkish counter-attacks on that day were repulsed with comparative ease, bearing out the advantage that well-placed defenders had over attacking troops.

66 Carter, diary, 29 April 1915. Carter, like the Battalion's CO (Dobbin), was eventually evacuated from the Peninsula suffering 'debility', the term given to a state of exhaustion which doctors suspected was psychological in origin. A. G. Butler suggested that 'as a link between the mental and physical sphere it may be held to afford perhaps the most tenable aetiological and scientific basis for the concept of the "burnt out" soldier', Butler, vol. III, p. 838. Anxiety (nervousness) and hysteria formed the two major classes of war neuroses and were paramount in the classification of shell-shock. For a discussion of the effects and treatment of shell-shock see chs 3, 4 and 6 in Richard Lindstrom, The Australian Experience of Psychological Casualties in War, 1915–1939, pp. 112–59, 183–223; Stephen Garton, *The Cost of War*, pp. 143–75.

67 Swannell's death is described by Henry Lanser, letter, 16 May 1915. Total losses of all ranks in the Battalion during this period amounted to 366. The figures given in the Battalion's history are: Killed, 3 officers and 33 other ranks; Wounded, 15 officers and 248 other ranks; Missing, 67 other ranks. By noon on 30 April the total casualties given in the *Official History* were: Killed, 3 officers and 36 other ranks; Wounded, 13 officers and 201 other ranks; Missing, 1 officer and 174 other ranks; Total casualties to that stage were 428: vol. I, p. 536.

68 Bean, *Official History*, vol. I, p. 297.

69 Donkin, diary, 25 April 1915, p. 22.

70 *Official History*, vol. I, p. 387.

71 1st Battalion Diary, 25–29 April 1915, AWM 4.

72 *First Battalion*, p. 32, emphasis added.

73 E. M. Luders, diaries (no page numbers or dates), ML MSS 2782, item 1. Similar sentiments are expressed in the soldier diaries of other units. Frank Loud (9th Battalion) noted: 'Our officers are not the best like us they are not trained and a most vital thing they on the whole know nothing of men', cited in AWM, 'Collection Notes: A New Gallipoli Diary', p. 70.

74 John Reid, letter, dated 7 May 1915.

75 This shift in the tactical thought of the Australian commanders is discussed in Chris Roberts, 'The Landing at Anzac: A Reassessment', pp. 29–33. For further discussion of the problems of tactical command associated with landing, see Winter, *25 April 1915*, pp. 183–204.

76 Jones, diary, 2 May 1915.

77 Swindells, Diary No. 2, 24 April 1915. Swindells' entries describing the landing and subsequent days appear under this date and it is obvious that no daily entries were made between 25 April and 5 May.

78 Reid, letter, 7 May 1915.

79 Eric H. Ward, diary, 30 May 1915, ML Doc 1300.

80 Major W. Davidson, letter, 13 May 1915, AWM/1DRL 235.

81 Reid to Mr Dinning, letter, 11 May 1915.

82 Muir, letter, 13 May 1915.

83 Birdwood papers, letter (pencilled copy), 24 May 1915, AWM/3DRL 3376, 419/10/7.

84 Davidson, second of two letters dated 14 June 1915.
85 For a fuller description of this relief and of the doubts of the Australians, see *Official History*, vol. I, ch. 23.
86 Barwick, Diary No. 1, p. 111.
87 Luders, diaries; Sgt-Maj. T. Murphy also wrote uncritically of the Marines, noting they had been 'cut up': 'A Soldier's Diary', *Anzac Memorial*, p. 317.
88 Muir, letter, 19 June 1915; this letter also appeared in the *South Coast Times*, 20 August 1915.
89 Bean's diary entry for 5 May 1915, cited in Fewster, *Gallipoli Correspondent*, p. 87.
90 Birdwood papers, letter, 28 June 1915.
91 Nigel Steel and Peter Hart, *Defeat at Gallipoli*, p. 138.
92 Ibid., p. 143.
93 For an account of this attack see Bean, *Official History*, vol. II, pp. 1–44; Ron Austin, *The White Ghurkas: The Australians at the Second Battle of Krithia, Gallipoli*, pp. 91–146.
94 Bean diary entry, 20 May 1915, cited in Fewster, *Gallipoli Correspondent*, p. 110; Gammage, *The Broken Years*, pp. 91–2.
95 Donkin, diary, 24 May 1915
96 Barwick, Diary No. 1, pp. 127–8.
97 *Official History*, vol. II, pp. 241–2, p. 325; *First Battalion*, p. 35.
98 Letter, *Globe and Sunday Times War Pictorial*, 4 September 1915. Higbid's figures for the total casualties are slightly higher than those given officially and cited previously.
99 L. Cpl John Gammage, typed copy of diary, 6 June 1915, AWM/PR 82/003. Original diary held in PR 83/117. Bean's account attributed the mistake to a newcomer on sentry forgetting an order for no shots to be fired until the party's return: see *Official History*, vol. II, p. 327.
1 The despatch appeared in the *Riverina Recorder*, 23 August 1916, under the title 'Hero of Anzac: A Scouting Episode'. See also Bean's account in *Official History*, vol. II, p. 327.
2 *Riverina Recorder*, 23 August 1916. Its publication was clearly a fillip for flagging spirits at home as it appeared at a time when Australian casualty lists were especially long following the fighting at Pozières. According to the attestation papers of Elart and Morris, they were 25 years and 24 years and 9 months, respectively. If true—and one must consider that some soldiers did lie about their age—their recorded ages hardly suggest they were among the youngest in the Battalion.
3 *Reveille*, 30 September 1931, pp. 7, 30–1. See also Brian Tate, 'The Gallipoli Samurai', East Ballina, NSW.
4 John Gammage, diary, 9 August 1915.
5 All quotes are from a letter dated 13 September 1915, AWM/2DRL 189.
6 Bell, letter, 21 October 1915.
7 Carter, diary, 8 August 1915.
8 Cited in Pederson, 'The AIF on the Western Front', p. 169. Original reference cited as C. B. B. White, 'Some Recollections of the Great War', 1 April 1921, White papers, AWM/3DRL 6549.
9 Cited in Fewster *et al.*, *A Turkish View of Gallipoli*, p. 100.
10 Dinning,, letter, 3 November 1915.
11 Ibid., letter, dated 24 October 1915.
12 Barwick, diary no. 2, pp. 257–8. This diary was written some time between 27 April and 10 May 1916 when the Battalion first entered the line in France.

13 Champion, diary, p. 25.
14 *Rock Mercury*, 18 November 1915.
15 Letter, 21 October 1915, emphasis in original.
16 See Table 7.
17 Champion, diary, p. 24.
18 Birdwood papers, letter dated 4 September 1915. For a description of the sickness of the army see *Official History*, vol. II, ch. 13. For the Battalion's strength see *First Battalion History*, p. 36.
19 L.L. Robson (ed.), *Australian Commentaries: Select Articles from the Round Table, 1911–1942*, p. 50. The *Round Table*, was the London journal of a group of men formed principally from the entourage of Lord Milner (the British high commissioner) following the creation of the Union of South Africa in 1909. The group's specific aim was to promote and influence discussion on the future of the Empire and its dominions.
20 Ibid., p. 48.
21 Extract of letter, 20 December 1915, AWM/2DRL 0005.
22 Carter, diary, 19 December 1915.
23 J. A. Bell, letter, 27 January 1916.
24 'Anzac Spirit', *SMH*, 24 April 1922.
25 *Gallipoli: One Long Grave*, pp. 161–2.

4 *'Mechanical slaughter' on the Western Front, 1916–17*

1 Phillip Gibbs, despatch reprinted in the *Advocate*, 22 July 1916.
2 C. E. W. Bean, *Two Men I Knew: William Bridges and Brudenell White: Founders of the AIF*, p. 137.
3 This service was first held in 1935.
4 John Keegan, *The Face of Battle: A Study of Agincourt, Waterloo, and the Somme*, pp. 209–10.
5 John Laffin, *Guide to Australian Battlefields of the Western Front, 1916–1918*, pp. 90–1. The 1st Battalion did not participate in the fighting for the ridge. Their fight had preceded it and was limited to the capture of the village.
6 Pte D. Horton, essay, p. 2, AWM/1DRL 359.
7 Ibid., pp. 2–3. The essay was written and submitted for a divisional essay contest and its content may have been influenced by its audience, the judges presumably being officers within the division.
8 Sgt. N. H. Langford, 'Narrative of Experiences, 1914–19', p. 3, AWM/2DRL 666.
9 McCarthy, *Gallipoli to the Somme*, pp. 217–18.
10 Lt G. H. Leslie, 'Wartime Reminiscences', p. 11, AWM/PR 88/67.
11 'Notes from an officer in France', AWM 27/310/16.
12 Paddy Griffith, however, has argued that there was rather more attention to the tactics of fire and movement in the infantry formations during that period than is generally acknowledged: *Battle Tactics of the Western Front: The British Army's Art of Attack, 1916–18*, pp. 47–64.
13 Bell, letter, 2 February 1916; AA[C], Personal Dossier.
14 Champion, diary, 13 June 1916.
15 Barwick, Diary No. 3, 26 June 1916.
16 Ibid.

17 Charlton, *Pozières 1916*, p. 48; See also Correlli Barnett, *Britain and Her Army: A Military, Political and Social Survey*, p. 394.

18 Ibid., pp. 1–4.

19 Champion, diary, 13 July 1916, [2 of 3], p. 87.

20 McConnel, diary, 12 July 1916.

21 Horton, essay, p. 3.

22 Sgt. L. R. Elvin, diary, 18 July 1916, AWM/2DRL 209; Pte Andria Locane sid 'the place was a mass of dead bodies still unburied and the smell here was worse': diary, 19 July 1916, AWM/3DRL 6217, item 1.

23 According to the Battalion's historians, 'in the summer of 1916 . . . [it] had reached a high standard of efficiency and discipline': *First Battalion*, p. 52.

24 Champion, diary, 19 July 1916, pp. 87–9. This description is an elaboration on the detail entered in his diary, 19 July 1916; *First Battalion*, p. 53.

25 General Sir John Monash, *The Australian Victories in France in 1918*, pp. 245–7.

26 Liddle, *The 1916 Battle of the Somme*, p. 25.

27 G. D. Sheffield, '*Blitzkrieg* and Attrition: Land Operations in Europe 1914–45', p. 61.

28 Trevor Wilson, *The Myriad Faces of War: Britain and the Great War, 1914–1918*, p. 42.

29 Lt. S. R. Traill, typed copy of diary, 25 March 1918, p. 42, AWM/2DRL 711.

30 Bean, *Official History*, vol. III, p. 720.

31 Desmond Morton, *When Your Number's Up: The Canadian Soldier in the First World War*, p. 180.

32 This denial of and consequential loss of initiative in relation to the Somme offensive is discussed in Martin Van Creveld, *Command in War*, pp. 161–7.

33 For an overview of the plan of battle see Martin Middlebrook, *The First Day on the Somme: 1 July 1916*, pp. 67–79; John Keegan, *The Face of Battle*, pp. 207–45.

34 English failures are mentioned by McConnel, typed diary, 22 July 1916 (AWM): 'The Tommies have had two goes already, and have had to retire again both times, for want of support or something'. No mention of the English failures appeared in his original diary (held by Mrs Barbara Fitzherbert).

35 Pte Andria Locane, diary, 15 April 1916.

36 Jon Cooksley, *PALS: The 13th and 14th Battalions, York and Lancaster Regiment: A History of the Two Battalions raised by Barnsley in World War One*, p. 227. The limitations of the High Command's tactical doctrine are discussed by Dominick Graham, '*Sans Doctrine*: British Army Tactics in the First World War', pp. 76–82.

37 Robert Blake (ed.), *The Private Papers of Douglas Haig, 1914–1919*, p. 155.

38 'First Australian Division: General Staff memorandum, No. 54', AWM 4, m/f roll 810.

39 'Report of Reconnaissance carried out on 17 July 1916 by Xth Corps General Staff', AWM 45 [35/7].

40 Charlton, *Pozières 1916*, pp. 132–3. Sally ports had been used to good effect by Congreve's XIII Corps on 1 July. The attention to detail in that Corps had given the British a uniform success on a two-mile front. For an account of the XIII Corps' planning and attack, see Terry Norman, *The Hell They Called High Wood: The Somme 1916*, pp. 38–60; The 36th (Ulster) Division, too, had opted to send its men into no man's land under the cover of the supporting barrage. The 36th advanced further than any British Division on 1 July but had to withdraw due to being unsupported on both flanks: Philip Orr, *The Road to the Somme: Men of the Ulster Division Tell Their Story*, pp. 165, 175, 200–1.

41 See Walker's report on the operations of the 1st Australian Division at Pozières, 3 August 1916 in 1st Division Diary, AWM4, m/f roll 810.

42 McConnel, war memoirs, 23 July 1916, [3of 3]; see also diary, 23 July 1916, [2 of 3].

43 Champion, Diary, 23 July 1916, p. 90.

44 McConnel, war memoirs, 23 July 1916.

45 McConnel, diary, 22 July 1916.

46 Hayes, diary, 22 July 1916. 1st Battalion soldiers did kill prisoners on occasions but so to did British and German soldiers. For an example of German soldiers killing prisoners, see Martin Middlebrook, *The Kaiser's Battle: 21 March 1918: The First Day of the German Spring Offensive*, pp. 215–16.

47 Horton, essay titled 'Pozières: by Cadmus', p. 18, ML MSS 1991.

48 Elvin, diary, 25 July 1916. It was little wonder that, after relief, Elvin found himself 'Tired and sore at heart' and next day 'nervy and weak' (Diary, 26 July 1916).

49 Barwick, Diary No. 4, 24 July 1916, p. 12.

50 Bean, *Official History*, v. III, p. 590.

51 Confidential Report, BHQ, 27 July 1916 by Brig.-Gen. N. M. Smyth, commanding 1st Inf. Brigade, AIF, appendix 21, AWM 26, Box 53/19.

52 Champion, diary, 26 July 1916, p. 92.

53 Lt C. J. McDonald (3rd Bn), AWM/2DRL 146.

54 Champion, diary, 26 July 1916, p. 93.

55 Bean, *Official History*, vol. I, p. 606. This theme also appears in Bean's Gallipoli diary. He noted that: '[Lt.-Col.] Maclagan puts down our lasting out to Tuesday night to the determination of the stronger men to hold like grim death at all costs. There were enough strong men to do it!': 'Regimental Records I', p. 16, AWM 38, 3DRL 606, item 25 [2].

56 Ibid., p. 607.

57 The 1st Australian Division suffered a loss of 5285 officers and men in the attack on Pozières: Bean, *Official History*, vol. III, p. 593. Some divisions of Fourth Army had, in fact, managed to advance double the distance of the Australians in some sections of their advance between 1 and 4 July. For example, 7th and 19th Divs (XV Corps) and 18th and 30th Divs (XIII Corps) in the Fricourt–Montauban sector. See sketch 3, p. 18 in *Military Operations*, vol. 2. Their objectives had also been greater in depth than the Australians at Pozières.

58 A useful reference work of the fighting for specific villages and towns during the war and the units involved is Gerald Gliddon, *'When The Barrage Lifts': A Topographical History and Commentary on the Battle of the Somme, 1916*. The references to Contalmaison, pp. 105–12, and La Boiselle, pp. 249–56, are necessary for understanding the nature of operations in the advance toward Pozières that preceded the village's capture.

59 Peter Dennis *et al.*, *The Oxford Companion to Australian Military History*, Table 1, p. 655.

60 Bean, *Official History*, v. III, pp. v–vi. But see Lt. Richards' comments later in this chapter.

61 Bean, 'Sidelights', p. 209.

62 For an example of this attitude see the article headed 'Insanity and the War' in the *Henty Observer*, 18 November 1915.

63 Hayes, diary, 25 July 1916.

64 McConnel, diary, 23 July 1916, p. 38.

65 Bean, *Official History*, vol. III, p. 593; *First Battalion*, p. 59.

66 Middlebrook, *The First Day of the Somme*, Appendix 5, p. 330.

[67] Bean, *Official History*, vol. III, pp. 442, 593, 724.

[68] Pte A. C. Dunlop (2 Bn), diary, part 4, 28 July 1916, AWM/PR 00676.

[69] Barnett, *Britain and Her Army, 1509–1970*, pp. 381–2; Peter Simkins, *World War 1, 1914–1918: The Western Front*, pp. 73, 137.

[70] Tom Wintringham, *The Story of Weapons and Tactics: From Troy to Stalingrad*, p. 169; Simkins, *World War I*, p. 124.

[71] C. E. W. Bean, *Letters From France*, p. 108.

[72] John Vader, *ANZAC: The Story of the Anzac Soldier*.

[73] Bean, *Official History*, vol. III, p. 858. For a general application of this example see Peter Firkins, *The Australians in Nine Wars: Waikato to Long Tan*, p. 86.

[74] Champion, diary, p. 93.

[75] Locane, diary, 25 July 1916.

[76] Ibid., p. 59.

[77] Bean, *Official History*, vol. III, p. 599.

[78] Report dated 26 July 1916, AWM 26, Box 53/21.

[79] Dinning, letter, 10 August 1916.

[80] *Argus*, 2 October 1916.

[81] Birdwood papers, letter, 12 August 1916, to New Zealand's Defence minister, Col. the Hon. J. Allen.

[82] Cited in J. D. Millar, A Study in the Limitations of Command: General Sir William Birdwood and the AIF, 1914–1918, p. 145. Millar considered this remark an almost frivolous one given the Australian casualties at Pozières. Birdwood, however, regarded the Pozières fighting as comprising two distinct phases, the taking and the holding. He recognised the difficulty the troops had in holding on to their position, given the intensity of the counter-bombardment. His comments need to be considered against that fact. See Birdwood to Allen, 12 August 1916.

[83] Birdwood to Walker, 1st Anzac Corp, 27 July 1916, AWM 26, 2/51/27.

[84] Dinning, letter, 10 August 1916.

[85] Locane, diary, 24 July 1916.

[86] Diary, 18–22 August 1916.

[87] Garton, *The Cost of War*, pp. 150–5.

[88] *The Australian Medical Services in the War of 1914–1918*, vol. III, p. 102.

[89] Simkins, *World War I*, p. 116.

[90] *Pozières, 1916*, p. 216.

[91] H. J. Cave, letter no. 136, 17 August 1916, ML MSS 1224, CY3246; letter no. 135.

[92] Horton, essay, p. 6.

[93] Lt R. A. Cassidy, letter, 8 August 1916.

[94] Cassidy, undated letter.

[95] Cassidy, letter, 8 August 1916.

[96] The inherent tension in trying to balance journalistic integrity, the lies perpetrated at GHQ, the knowledge of the appalling casualties and the desire to remain patriotically committed to the war effort, are evident in a small article titled 'Pozières' in the *Bulletin*, 28 September 1916, referring to the 5th Division's failed attack at Fromelles.

[97] *Sydney Mail*, 13 September 1916.

[98] Horton, p. 27. A similar account of the words spoken are recorded in *First Battalion*, p. 59.

[99] Barwick, Diary No. 4, 29 July 1916, p. 34.

1 Ibid., p. 40; Diary No. 3, 7 June 1916, p. 206.
2 The problems and horror involved in these assaults are aptly described in Alex Aiken, *Courage Past: A Duty Done*, pp. 91–9.
3 For an account of these combined operations see James Edmonds, *Military Operations: France and Belgium, 1916*, vol. 2, pp. 135–49.
4 Champion, diary, 17 August 1916, p. 101.
5 'Report on operation of the 1st Battalion in the line 16 August 1916 to 22 August 1916' by Col. Heane, AWM 26/Box 53/24.
6 *First Battalion*, p. 60.
7 A week after this engagement the Battalion's strength was 22 officers and 454 other ranks. For an approximate figure of the unit's line strength prior to the engagement add the 104 casualties incurred. The casualties represent 17.93 per cent of the total strength of 580. See *First Battalion*, p. 60.
8 Undated letter in AWM/2DRL 29.
9 Champion, diary, 1 November 1916, p. 117.
10 Sergeant K. Rixon in a letter to Finlayson's mother, AWM/1DRL 287; Champion, diary, 25 February 1917.
11 1st Brigade Diary, AWM 4.
12 Pte A. E. Rostron, diary, 5 November 1916, AWM/2DRL 106. According to the Battalion history a third attack was attempted but was too weak to achieve success: *First Battalion*, p. 65.
13 Ibid.
14 Bean, *Official History*, vol. III, p. 907. Bean's account of the attack is on pp. 904–9. In his diary he directed some criticism to the OC of the supporting company, B Company, who had placed his supports in the jumping off trench rather than 'out in front where the attack wavered': AWM 38/3DRL 606, item 125 [1], p. 8.
15 Diary, p. 119.
16 Ibid., pp. 119–20.
17 Ibid., p. 121.
18 Maddocks, *Liverpool Pals*, p. 137.
19 'Statement by a Repatriated Prisoner of War', re: operation of 5 November 1916, AWM 30/B 5.1.
20 Barwick, Diary No. 6, 5 November 1916, p. 137.
21 Champion, Diary, p. 121.
22 Sergeant K. Rixon, undated letter, AWM/1DRL 287.
23 Richards, Diary No. 4, 13 December 1916, pp. 38–40, emphasis in original.
24 Bean, *Official History*, vol. III, p. 446.
25 Richards, Diary No. 4, 15 December 1916, p. 41.
26 Champion, diary, 20 October 1916, p. 114.
27 *Official History*, vol. III, p. 447.
28 *Pozières 1916.*, p. xiv.
29 Ibid., p. 292.
30 Barwick comments on his expectations of the upcoming referendum in Diary No. 6, 6, 19 October 1916, pp. 9, 66 and the result in Diary No. 7, 1 December 1916, p. 64; Richards, Diary No. 4, 13 December 1916, p. 38.
31 Richards, 21 January 1917, p. 67. Richards noted a similarly poor response a month later, see diary, 18 February 1917, pp. 89–90.

[32] The formation is mentioned in Lt A. W. Edwards, War Diary, p. 70; Champion, diary, 25 February 1917, p. 133. See also Appendix to First Anzac General Staff Circular: Assaulting platoon, dated 16 December 1916 in AWM 27 303/190–194. Maxse was aggressive in his attempts to educate all his commanders, from his division commanders through to his platoon commanders. See Baynes, *Far from a Donkey*, pp. 169–71.

[33] For an example of some of the topics covered by this training see 'Syllabus of Training for Week Ending, 26 May 1917' in 1st Brigade Diary, AWM 4. Some other examples of the type of literature being produced by the General Staff are: Appendix to First Anzac General Staff, Circular No. 48, and Divisional Headquarters General Staff, Memo. No. 2, 'Assaulting Platoon', 11 January 1917, AWM 27/310/45; Booklet, Instructions for Battle, May 1917, AWM 27/310/46; Booklet issued January 1918, The Training and Employment of Divisions 1918, AWM 27/310/46.

[34] For example see, 1st Division diary, microfilm roll 807, AWM 4.

[35] For an account of this battle and its genesis see Bean, *Official History*, vol. IV, pp. 252–354.

[36] McConnel, war memoirs, pp. 42–3, AWM/2DRL 29 [3 of 3]. Throughout the war the Germans almost invariably held the higher or better ground. They were prepared (often pre-prepared) to fall back on better positions. For the Allies, particularly the French, the land was sacred and had to be held at all costs (at least, such was the philosophy of the Allied General Staffs).

[37] In the operations about Bullecourt, units from four Australian divisions (1st, 2nd, 4th and 5th) and four British divisions (7th, 58th, 62nd and 4th Cavalry), were principally engaged. See Order of Battle in J. Edmonds, *Military Operations: France and Belgium, 1917*, p. 563. For description of the fighting see ch. XVIII.

[38] Barwick, Diary No. 9, 4 May 1917, pp. 103–6. The 5th Brigade had attacked in conjunction with the 6th Brigade. The 6th had gained a lodgement in the German trenches but the 5th's advance had been broken by fire on their right flank and they failed to gain their objectives.

[39] Ibid., 5 May 1917, pp. 108–9.

[40] McKell, attestation papers, Service Record, AA[ACT].

[41] McKell's condition was also mentioned by Ken McConnel in his account of the battle. McConnel, however, attributed McKell's condition to shell-shock: 'I looked up McKell and found him looking very shaky . . . He had had a bad time with shelling and was himself suffering from shock': McConnel, war memoirs, p. 44. McConnel, who had himself suffered severely through nerves, had some empathy for McKell.

[42] Barwick, Diary No. 11, 11 December 1917, p. 111.

[43] Ibid., p. 112.

[44] McConnel, diary, 3 July 1916.

[45] Lt H. V. Chedgey, letter, 23 September 1917, AWM/2DRL 178.

[46] For an account of the treatment of the Australians by the British press during this period, see Michael McKernan, *The Australian People and the Great War*, pp. 120–5.

[47] Richards, Diary No. 4, 3 May 1917, p. 134. The entry was probably made on 6 May.

[48] Ibid., 7 May 1917, p. 136.

[49] Bean, *Official History*, vol. IV, p. 507.

[50] Ibid., p. 495. The 3rd Battalion history speaks only of a segment of its line giving ground temporarily. See Wren, *Randwick to Hargicourt*, p. 241.

[51] Bean, *Official History*, vol. IV, pp. 514, 515.

[52] Captain Walter Belford, *Legs-Eleven: Being the story of the 11th Battalion (AIF) in the Great War of 1914–1918*, p. 445.

[53] Edmonds, *Military Operations 1917*, pp. 471–5; Bean, *Official History*, vol. IV, pp. 520–9.

[54] 'Complimentary message to First Australian Infantry Brigade from General Officer commanding FIFTH ARMY', May 1917, AWM 27 /354/126; *First Battalion*, p. 74.

[55] Memoir, p. 45.

[56] Diary No. 11, 21 December 1917, pp. 191–2.

[57] For criticism of this system, see Baynes, *Far from a Donkey*, p. 182.

[58] Lt H. V. Chedgey, letter, 15 October 1917, cited in Gammage, *The Broken Years*, p. 208.

[59] Champion, Diary, 27 January 1916.

[60] Barwick, Diary No. 6, 19 October 1916, pp. 67–8.

[61] Peter H. Liddle, *The Soldier's War, 1914–18*, p. 211.

[62] P. W. Turner and R. H. Haigh, *Not for Glory: A Personal History of the 1914–18 War*, p. 99.

[63] Bean, *Official History*, vol. IV, p. 789.

[64] Barwick, Diary No. 4, 23 July 1916, p. 8.

[65] The deaths of these men are mentioned in *First Battalion*, pp. 80–2. Vial's death is also described by Lt A. W. Edwards, 'My War Diary', p. 73.

[66] For some comparison and criticism of these generals' tactics see Robin Prior and Trevor Wilson, *Passchendaele: The Untold Story*, pp. 69–110 (Gough) and pp. 113–39 (Plumer); Dennis *et al.*, *Australian Military History*, pp. 657–60; Bean, *Official History*, vol. IV, pp. 544–5, 559; John Laffin, *British Butchers and Bunglers of World War One*, pp. 105–15; P. A. Pedersen, *Monash as Military Commander*, pp. 158–9.

[67] *First Battalion*, p. 82.

[68] Ibid., p. 83.

[69] Bean, *Official History*, vol. IV, pp. 876–7.

[70] Prior and Wilson, *Passchendaele*, p. 192.

[71] Edwards, 'My War Diary', p. 20.

[72] Peter Firkins, *The Australians in Nine Wars*, p. 86.

[73] Holmes, *Firing Line*, pp. 263–4.

5 1918: The 'digger' in victory

[1] Barnett, *Britain and Her Army*, p. 408.

[2] John Laffin, *Digger: The Story of the Australian Soldier*, p. 131.

[3] For a discussion of the context of raiding policy on the British front in France see Tony Ashworth, *Trench Warfare*, pp. 90–1, 176–9.

[4] Bean, *Official History*, vol. III, p. 258.

[5] Ibid., pp. 265–6; *First Battalion*, p. 51. A description of the preparation and raid by Pte T. R. B. Wilkinson was published in the *Sydney Mail*, 27 September 1916.

[6] Champion, diary, 20 June 1916, p. 78.

[7] Barwick, Diary No. 3, 29 June 1916.

[8] Ibid.

[9] *Sydney Mail*, 27 September 1916.

[10] Ibid.

11 McConnel, war memoirs, 11 June 1916.

12 The incident is also recorded by Sgt Langford, 'Narrative of Experiences, 1914–18' and he stated: 'Mr. McConnel and I often laugh over that incident since our return home', p. 11.

13 Annotated copy of 'family memoirs', entry for 22 June 1916, held by Mrs Barbara Fitzherbert, Sydney.

14 *First Battalion*, pp. 85–7.

15 Lt S. R. Traill, typed copy of diary, 20 January 1918, p. 11, AWM/2DRL 711.

16 Laffin, *Digger*, p. 89.

17 Richards, Diary No. 4, 21 December 1916, p. 46.

18 McConnel, diary, 29 May 1916.

19 Mercer, diary, 1 January 1918, pp. 37, 41, 43.

20 Barwick, Diary No. 11, 8 January 1918, pp. 220–1.

21 Ibid., 11 January 1918, p. 223.

22 Bean, *Official History*, vol. VI, p. 414.

23 General Sir John Monash, *The Australian Victories in France in 1918*, p. 250.

24 Ibid.

25 Ibid.

26 Ashworth, *Trench Warfare*, p. 39.

27 Ibid., p. 36.

28 Paddy Griffith asserts that in 1917, apart from the ten ANZAC and Canadian divisions, the BEF could claim over a dozen elite divisions that had originated in the British Isles: *Battle Tactics of the Western Front: The British Army's Art of Attack, 1916–18*, p. 81.

29 Richards, Diary No. 4, 28 January 1917, p. 75.

30 Ibid., pp. 75–6.

31 *First Battalion*, p. 67.

32 Lt S. R. Traill, diary, 6 March 1918, p. 32.

33 The son of one 1st Bn soldier stated that his father had told him that one Christmas the Australians had fraternised and shared their rations with German soldiers in no man's land: anonymous interview.

34 Ashworth, *Trench Warfare*, pp. 142–3.

35 Champion, diary, p. 121.

36 Lt S. R. Traill, diary, 22 March 1918, p. 41.

37 Ibid., 29 April 1918, p. 59.

38 For positive appraisals of these divisions see Gregory Blaxland, *Amiens 1918*, p. 31; For a discussion of the methods employed by General Maxse in training the 18th Division (methods that would ultimately influence training throughout the British armies) see Baynes, *Far from a Donkey*, pp. 122–34.

39 For an incisive account of British resistance and morale during the attack, see Martin Middlebrook, *The Kaiser's Battle: 21 March 1918: The First Day of the German Spring Offensive*, pp. 332–9. See also Blaxland, *Amiens 1918*, pp. 35–68.

40 Laurence Moyer, *Victory Must Be Ours: Germany in the Great War, 1914–1918*, pp. 244, 248.

41 *First Battalion*, p. 94, emphasis added.

42 Ibid., p. 96.

43 Robert B. Asprey, *The German High Command at War: Hindenburg and Ludendorff and the First World War*, pp. 385–6.

44 Ibid., p. 396.
45 Pte A. C. Traill, letter, 16 May 1918, AWM/2DRL 706.
46 Mercer, diary, 7 April 1918, p. 131.
47 Ibid., diary, 3 April 1918, p. 125.
48 *First Battalion*, p. 97.
49 Bean, *Official History*, vol. VI, p. 42, n. 24.
50 Simkins, *World War I*, p. 106, emphasis added.
51 AWM 27/310: Item 138, 10th Aust. Infantry Brigade, memorandum, 4 April 1918; Item 140, Third Australian Division, General Staff circular, No. 69A. Patrols; Item 142, 3rd Aust. Infantry Brigade, instruction stipulating increased size of patrols and function; Item 143, 1st Australian Division, General Staff memorandum, No. 41, patrols.
52 Memo 42, Headquarters, 9 July 1918, AWM 26/458/8.
53 Bean, *Official History*, vol. VI, p. 411.
54 *First Battalion*, p. 99; Edwards, 'My War Diary', p. 121.
55 *First Battalion*, pp. 100–1; Bean, *Official History*, vol. VI, pp. 411–19.
56 Based on figures given in *First Battalion*, the unit's strength is estimated at 616.5 men. On 31 October 1917 the Battalion's strength was 485 (p. 83) and by 23 March 1918 it was 748 (p. 90); these have been divided by two as an estimation of the unit's strength for November to January.
57 Figures and descriptions of the 1st Battalion's sick evacuees are extracted from AWM 26, Boxes 331/4, 331/5, 452/2, 456/7, 456/8, 458/2, 458/6, 458/7.
58 Despatch from Mr F. M. Cutlack, Assistant official correspondent with the Australians, War Correspondents Headquarters, France, 13 June 1918, AWM 10/4332/5/106.
59 Richards, Diary No. 4, 17 January 1918, p. 212.
60 Battalion Order No. 119, 28 March 1918, AWM 25, 707/9, File III.
61 Ibid., No. 137, 15 May 1918. This was reiterated in Battalion Order No. 139, 27 May 1918.
62 Barwick, Diary No. 12, 4 April 1918.
63 Ibid., 8 April 1918, p. 88.
64 Ibid., Diary No. 11, 17 January 1918, p. 234. The term 'jerry' referred to the need to change one's views. See Downing's *Digger Dialects*, p. 112.
65 *First Battalion*, pp. 97–8.
66 Statement by Marshal Foch, Paris, 7 April 1919, AWM 27/354/65.
67 Despatch from Mr F. M. Cutlack, War Correspondents Headquarters, France, 22 May 1918, AWM 10/4332/5/106; Haig had also written the previous year that the confidence of Australian officers before the Menin Road fighting was high because: 'Every detail had been gone into most thoroughly and the troops most carefully trained . . .': Diary extracts, 17 September 1917, AWM 3DRL 376.
68 Memo, To Australian Corps from General Sir H. Rawlinson, Commanding Fourth Army, 14 October 1918, AWM 27/354/65.
69 See, for example, Lord Derby's letter to Haig, 9 November 1917, in Robert Blake (ed.), *The Private Papers of Douglas Haig, 1914–1919*, p. 266.
70 Brig.-Gen. John Chateris, *At GHQ*, p. 245.
71 Maj.-Gen. John F. O'Ryan, *The Story of the 27th Division*, vol. I, pp. 339–40.
72 S. R. Traill, diary, 8 August 1918, p. 102.
73 For an account of the difficulties of the III Corps and its commander's exhausted state, see Robin Prior and Trevor Wilson, *Command on the Western Front: The Military Career*

of Sir Henry Rawlinson, 1914–18, pp. 324–326. The authors argue that under the circumstances III Corps should have been withdrawn and replaced with fresher divisions.

74 Asprey, *The German High Command at War*, p. 448.
75 Monash, *Australian Victories in France in 1918*, pp. 307–10.
76 S. R. Traill, diary, 9 August 1918, p. 103.
77 Bean, *Official History*, vol. VI, p. 649, n. 11.
78 S. R. Traill, diary, 16 August 1918, p. 106.
79 Ibid., p. 107.
80 Monash, *Australian Victories.*, pp. 148–9, 151–2.
81 For a detailed account of the raid see Lt H. D. Andrews, letter to the Director, Australian War Memorial, 29 December 1929, AWM/1DRL 43.
82 Barry Clissold, '. . . that six-man patrol', *Sabretache*, vol. XXXI, April–June 1990, p. 22.
83 Eric Andrews, *The Anzac Illusion: Anglo-Australian Relations during World War I*, p. 147.
84 Blaxland, *Amiens 1918*, p. 191.
85 Article by '*Sammy*' [Sgt. Norman Langford, 1st Bn], 'Chipilly Stunt: Brave Diggers', *Reveille*, 1 September, 1933, p. 23.
86 John Terraine, *To Win a War: 1918, The Year of Victory*, pp. 186–7.
87 Of the 224 award winners listed, 63 were officers, 102 NCOs and 59 other ranks. From the nominal roll of the Battalion, 286 officers served the Battalion, 1161 NCOs and 4774, other ranks (Total Battalion 6221).
88 *First Battalion*, p. 111.
89 AWM 4, 1st Brigade Diary, Lecture by GOC to all Officers of Brigade, Appendix 19, p. 40.
90 S. R. Traill, diary, 17 September 1918, pp. 125–6.
91 1st Australian Infantry Brigade diary, appendix, report by Lt-Col. B. V. Stacy, p. 48, AWM 4; Ivan Chapman, *Iven G. Mackay: Citizen and Soldier*, p. 114.
92 Lt-Gen. Sir Iven Mackay, diary, 19 September 1918, AWM/3DRL 6850, item no. 6.
93 17 September 1918, p. 124.
94 AWM 51/item 122/part 4, pp. 3–4.
95 Ibid., part 7, p. 1.
96 Ibid.
97 Ibid., p. 2.
98 Ibid., part 4, p. 2.
99 Richards, Diary No. 4, 4 December 1916, p. 31.
1 AWM 51/item 122/part 4, p. 2.
2 Gammage, *The Broken Years*, pp. 244–5.
3 His character is remarked on by a number of his peers, for example: 'Moffatt was essentially a man's man. Slow of speech and slow of smile his was a nature that attracted men, women, children and dogs . . . perfectly serene . . . Men like Moffatt do not die, their deeds live on for ever . . .'. See Edwards, 'My War Diary', pp. 21–2.
4 Television documentary, *Mutiny on the Western Front*, Mingara Films, 1979.
5 J. J. MacKenzie, A Disabling Minority: Mutiny in the First Battalion AIF, September 1918, pp. 52–3.
6 Leonard V. Smith, *Between Mutiny and Obedience: The Case of the French Fifth Infantry Division During World War I*, pp. 197–8.
7 MacKenzie, A Disabling Minority, Tables 3–5, pp. 61, 65.
8 Television documentary, *Mutiny on the Western Front*.

9 MacKenzie, A Disabling Minority, p. 63.
10 AWM 51/item 122/part 3, p. 6.
11 S. R. Traill, diary, 18 October 1918, p. 138. Of 102 of the men charged, where a character assessment had been made, 92 were described as being of 'good' character: AWM 51/122, parts 1–9, '1st Battalion AIF Field General Court Martial'.
12 S. R. Traill, diary, 18 October 1918, p. 138.
13 These figures are based on the examination of the attestation papers and embarkation records of 150 non-mutineers and 124 mutineers. A list of men who participated in the attack of 21 September 1918 was published in the Battalion Routine Order No. 199 in AWM 25, 707/9 part 112. The names of the mutineers appear in 1st Brigade Routine Orders, 8 October 1918, 1st Brigade Diary, AWM 4.
14 Alistair Thomson has argued that the post-war experiences of returned men were overlaid with time across their war experience to create gradually an experience adapted to their needs. Fred Farrall was one of Thomson's principal subjects: Anzac Memories, pp. 7–12.
15 Lois Farrall, The File on Fred: A Biography of Fred Farrall, p. 114.
16 Television documentary, Mutiny on the Western Front.
17 SMH, 7 August 1979.
18 1st Brigade diary, Lecture by GOC to all Officers of Brigade, Appendix 19, AWM 4.

6 Return of the war-damaged soldier

1 For a discussion of the battle for the support of returned soldiers see Terry King, On the Definition of 'Digger': Australia and its Returned Soldiers, 1915–1920, pp. 33–50.
2 Charles Kingsley, Westward Ho! One might argue, however, that the 'digger' was less inspired by religious principles. For a discussion on the heroic manner in which the 'digger' has been depicted in Australian literature see Gerster, Big-Noting, chs 3–4. Ch. 3 discusses the style of the Official History and ch. 4 discusses the contribution of ex-servicemen's war reminiscences and memoirs.
3 For an especially effusive example of this type of description see the article 'In Memory of the Landing of the AIF, April 25, 1915', Smith's Weekly, 26 April 1919.
4 For a discussion of the importance of the effect that private memory and public commemoration had in the context of the establishment of the repatriation process, see Garton, The Cost of War, pp. 31–73.
5 For general discussions of the perpetuation of the Anzac legend (and in the case of the conservative class, the usurpation of) see Richard White, Inventing Australia: Images and Identity, 1688–1980, pp. 135–9; John Rickard, Australia: A Cultural History, pp. 122–9.
6 Repatriation Department Interim Report to 30th June 1919, Commonwealth Parliamentary Papers, 1917–19, vol. IV, Melbourne, 1919, p. 5.
7 A. G. Butler, The Australian Army Medical Services in the War of 1914–1918, vol. III, p. 832.
8 Ibid., p. 839.
9 Ibid., pp. 839–42.
10 Ibid., p. 844.
11 Interview with Len Beckett, jnr, Sydney.
12 For examples of the differing degrees, usually due to financial considerations, with which various communities commemorated the 'fallen' see AWM/ORMF, newscuttings —Australian War Memorials.

13 Clem Lloyd and Jaqui Rees, *The Last Shilling: A History of Repatriation in Australia*; Garton, *The Cost of War*; Richard Lindstrom, The Australian Experience of Psychological Casualties, 1915–1939. See also Stephen Garton, 'Return Home: War, Masculinity and Repatriation', pp. 191–204.

14 Lloyd and Rees, *The Last Shilling*, p. 329.

15 Garton, *The Cost of War*, pp. 117, 97.

16 Ibid., p. 117.

17 Ibid.

18 For his discussion of the Repatriation Department's attitude to the granting of pensions see Lindstrom, The Australian Experience, pp. 173–9, 214–23.

19 Ibid., p. 183.

20 Repatriation file of Tasman Charles Douglass, H 9176, AA[NSW]. See Douglass to Department, 22 September 1964. See also letters from Deputy Commissioner to Secretary Limbless Soldiers' Association and to T. C. Douglass, both dated 30 September 1964.

21 Repatriation file of Stanley Howard Davis, M 11958, AA[NSW]. See medical report, 21 March 1921; also letter of complaint from Davis to Department, 11 April 1921. Davis was entitled to a partial pension due to the loss and damage to fingers of his right hand.

22 Lindstrom, The Australian Experience, pp. 173–4.

23 Garton, *The Cost of War*, p. 92.

24 Ibid., pp. 94–6.

25 Repatriation file of Stuart John Burman, H49838, part (1), AA[NSW]. Report by Dr C. K. Parkinson, 1 July 1927; Minute by Dr C. C. Minty, 21 July 1927; File M49838, part (1), Memo from Dr C. C. Minty, 26 April 1927.

26 *The Last Shilling*, p. 146.

27 Repatriation file of Arthur Sydney Phillips, M3109, AA[NSW], Form ES 167, statement, 21 January 1964; Medical History Sheet, pp. 10–11.

28 Garton, *The Cost of War*, p. 109.

29 Repatriation file of Benjamin Arthur Hubbard, C3951, AA[NSW], Detailed Medical History of an Invalid, CM Form, D.2, 9 February 1916; Form U, 29 February 1916.

30 Col. R. J. Millard, diary, 18 May 1915, AWM 1DRL 499.

31 Repatriation file of Lawrence Henry Cooper Riggs, M9710, AA[NSW], Medical Report on an Invalid, Army Form B-179, 23 March 1916; Form U, 19 February 1917.

32 Hubbard, repatriation file, Notice, 28 August 1919.

33 *SMH*, 27 April 1925.

34 Ibid.

35 'In Memory of the Landing of the AIF, April 25, 1915', *Smith's Weekly*, 26 April 1919. For a similar though less effusive example, see the description that appeared in *Lone Hand*, 1 March 1919, cited in Carmel Shute, 'Sexual Mythology, 1914–1918', p. 19. See also Grimshaw *et al.*, *Creating a Nation*, pp. 218–19. The quote reads, in part: 'The Australian comes out of this great war looking the most virile thing on earth. The tasks other men could not do, he went into with a laugh, and though the laughter died in the bitter strain of the front trenches in the rush across "no man's land" . . . his achievements remain.'

36 Ibid.

37 *Reveille*, 1 November 1932, p. 13.

38 1st Battalion AIF Association, AWM/PR 84/239, item 3; Committee minutes for 1 March 1948, 5 March 1951, 24 March 1958, 14 February 1938.

[39] *Reveille*, 29 February 1932. These names have been cross-checked with the nominal roll provided in *First Battalion* to determine the ranks held on return to Australia.

[40] Total members of the Battalion Association numbered 903. The total number of men that served the Battalion, according to the nominal roll, is 6221. The unknown figure represents names on the Battalion Association membership listing whose rank could not be definitely determined against the nominal roll, the most common reason being that first and second name data matched more than one record. These have been ignored in the computation of the Battalion Association as a percentage of the total Battalion. It is presumed they would be equitably distributed through the rank categories.

[41] Richard White, 'Motives for Joining up: Self-sacrifice, Self-interest and Social Class, 1914–18', p. 15. See Table 1 for comparison of professions between officers and men.

[42] Information on McConnel is drawn from a questionnaire sent to his daughter, Mrs Barbara Fitzherbert, Sydney. Details of his wedding and house rental are contained in his family memoirs held by Mrs Fitzherbert, pp. 82, 90.

[43] Mant's actions were mentioned by three interviewees, Ms J. Stacy, Mrs B. Fitzherbert and one anonymous.

[44] The nominal roll contains 6221 names. If the 1165 dead are subtracted the total number of men who survived is 5056. The 903 Association members represent 17.85 per cent. A variation of these figures might also be used if a figure of approximately 500 was subtracted from the total survivors to account for the originals and reinforcements that were transferred from the 1st Battalion to form the 53rd Battalion in February 1916. This would increase the proportion of Association members to 19.82 per cent. However, as these men did serve, in most cases, with the 1st Battalion, the first figure is preferred.

[45] A short biography of Fred Kelly appears in Tony Stephens, *The Last Anzacs: Gallipoli, 1915*; see also *Weekend Australian*, 26–27 April 1997.

[46] Leonard Beckett and Emanuel Polglase were both 1st Battalion soldiers who were members of the Limbless Soldiers' Association, and Jack Hayes was a member of the Marrickville Anzac Memorial Club. Information obtained from questionnaires sent to Len Beckett and William Polglase whose fathers served in the 1st Battalion.

[47] Information about the Marrickville Club and Jack Hayes' involvement supplied in an interview with his son.

[48] G. L. Kristianson, *The Politics of Patriotism: The Pressure Group Activities of the Returned Servicemen's League*, pp. 36, 67.

[49] King, On the Definition of 'Digger', p. 318; White, *Inventing Australia.*, pp. 137–9; Garton, *Cost of War*, pp. 51–69.

[50] *The First at War: The Story of the 2/1st Australian Infantry Battalion, 1939–45, The City of Sydney Regiment*, p. 548.

[51] *Reveille*, 1 September 1935, p. 5.

[52] Pte A. C. Traill, letter, 16 May 1918.

[53] Eric Leed, *No Man's Land: Combat and Identity in World War I*, p. 205.

[54] Ibid., p. 204.

[55] Ibid., p. 194. Bill Gammage also addresses the theme of the subordination of individuality to the industrialisation and increased authority of the war: 'Australians and the Great War', pp. 32–4.

[56] For an Australian context to these themes see Raymond Evans, *The Red Flag Riots: A Study of Intolerance*, pp. 187–9.

57 Ibid., p. 196. The experience of Australia's First World War and Vietnam veterans certainly fits Leed's model. Richard White has referred to the 'schizophrenic' post-war image of the Great War soldier: *Inventing Australia*, p. 137.

58 The Battle of Long Tan has been the subject of a number of books and articles in recent years. See for example, Ian McNeill, *To Long Tan: The Australian Army and Vietnam War, 1950–1966*; Lex McAulay, *The Battle of Long Tan*; Terry Burstall, *The Soldiers' Story: The Battle of Xa Long Tan, Vietnam, 18 August 1966*.

59 Paul Fussell, *The Great War and Modern Memory*, pp. 21–2.

60 Mercer, diary, 26 December 1917, p. 19.

61 Butler, *Official History of the Australian Medical Services, 1914–18*, vol. III, Table 4, p. 912.

62 Ibid., vol. II, p. 499.

63 Ibid.

64 Gnr E. J. Pitcher to Pte F. Buchan, 23 December 1917 in possession of Mr Bruce Buchan, Melbourne. For a discussion on the prevalence of malingering in the AIF see Joanna Bourke, '"Swinging the lead": malingering, Australian soldiers, and the Great War', pp. 10–18.

65 Archie Barwick, Diary No. 8, 7 January 1917, pp. 27–8. To signal a 'washout' a person would raise their arms and wave from side to side. See J. M. Arthur and W. S. Ramson (eds), *W. H. Downing's Digger Dialect*, p. 232.

66 Barwick, Diary No. 16, 24 December 1918.

67 McConnel, family memoirs, held by Mrs Barbara Fitzherbert, Sydney, p. 123.

68 Ibid., pp. 123–4, emphasis added.

69 Personnel dossier, James Molloy, AA[ACT].

70 See graph of 'Military Prisons in the Field' showing number of men per thousand in prison, AWM 27/363/9. Australians represented 8.1 per thousand, Canadian/NZ/South Africans 1.2, and British 0.8.

71 Record of sentences served by prisoners at Detention Barracks, Lewes, 16 November 1917/23 January 1920, AWM 25/231/5.

72 Clark, *The Waratahs*, p. 24.

73 Personnel dossier, Leo Galli, AA[ACT]. Letter from Lt Paine to Maj. Leicester, OIC, A Company, 26 May 1915. Also on file, statement of case of Pte Galli, undated.

74 King, On the Definition of 'Digger', pp. 33–50.

75 George L. Mosse, *Fallen Soldiers: Reshaping the Memory of the World Wars*, p. 106.

76 It is a view that continues to find currency and one evident in the title of Garrie Hutchinson's book, *An Australian Odyssey: From Gaza to Gallipoli*. 'The fact that Gallipoli, Egypt, Turkey, ancient Greece and Troy are all in the same part of the world is more than a coincidence for me. It is why I am here, and why Australians are at home here. Our story is part of the great collection of stories told in this area from back beyond the Bible.' For Hutchinson, Bean's story of the Australian soldier is the 'primary Australian story'. These quotes cited in a book review by Michael McGirr, 'Pilgrim on a War Footing', *Age*, 20 April 1997.

77 *Australian Chivalry*.

78 My thanks to Heather Cooper, Sydney, for drawing my attention to this controversy and providing assorted clippings of the *Evening News, SMH, Daily Telegraph, Daily Mail*, and *Sun* (early June 1925).

79 Interview (name withheld), Sydney.

[80] Judith A. Allen, *Sex and Secrets: Crimes Involving Australian Women since 1880*, pp. 131–56.

[81] Interview (name withheld), Sydney.

[82] Obituary in *The Union Recorder:* Sydney University Journal, 17 March 1938.

[83] Obituary in *Reveille*, 1 February 1938.

[84] Questionnaire completed by Susan Conrade, NSW.

[85] The lack of contemporary influence of Bean's official histories is raised in Michael McKernan, 'Writing about War', p. 13.

[86] Interview (name withheld).

Conclusion

[1] Jane Ross, *The Myth of the Digger: The Australian Soldier in Two World Wars*, pp. 60–1.

[2] Bill Rawling, *Surviving Trench Warfare: Technology and the Canadian Corps, 1914–1918*.

Bibliography of works cited

Primary Sources

Australian Archives

Canberra: Series B2455, Personnel dossiers for 1st Australian Imperial Forces ex-service members. These records include a soldier's attestation papers (which provides details of age, residential address, next-of-kin, religion, previous military experience, height, weight and marital status); Army Form B.103: Casualty Form—Active Service and statement of service (which provide details of wounds, sickness, hospitalisation, crimes committed and punishments incurred); assorted correspondence (usually particular to aspects of service noted on the B.103 and enquiries from family members to military authorities about the whereabouts or health of soldier relations).

Sydney: Repatriation Department (later Department of Veterans' Affairs) personnel case files. These files generally comprised two folders: an 'R' file (Repatriation), which dealt with a soldier's general relationship with the Department—claims, complaints, employment etc.; the 'M' file (Medical or sometimes 'C' Clinical record) dealt exclusively with medical assessments, diagnosis and treatments.

Australian War Memorial

AWM 4	AIF unit war diaries
AWM 8	AIF embarkation rolls
AWM 9	AIF nominal rolls
AWM 10	AIF HQ (London) A Registry, files and register of file titles
AWM 25	Written records, 1914–18
AWM 26	Operations files
AWM 27	Subject classified files

AWM 30   Prisoner of war statements
AWM 38   Bean, C. E. W., papers
AWM 43   Biographical and other research files
AWM 51   Ex-confidential records, 1913–54
AWM   1st Battalion AIF Association membership rolls
AWM   Personal records, 1st Battalion
AWM   Birdwood papers, 3DRL 3376
          Dunlop, Pte A. C., PR 00676
          Gates, Pte F. J., 1DRL 307
          Leslie, Lt G. H., PR 88/67
          Mackay, Lt-Gen. Sir Iven, 3DRL 6850
          McDonald, Lt C. J., 2DRL 146
          Millard, Col. R. J., 1DRL 499
          Mulholland, Capt. D. V., 2DRL 40

MITCHELL LIBRARY, STATE LIBRARY OF NEW SOUTH WALES

Barwick, Sgt A. A., MSS 1493/1
Cave, Cpl H. J., ML MSS 1224
Horton, Cpl D., ML MSS 1991
Larkin, Sgt E. R., MLA 2660
Lee, C., ML MSS 1132
Luders, L.Cpl. E. M., ML MSS 2782, item 1
Harold Mercer Papers, ML MSS 1143
Vial, Sgt J. J., ML Doc 1287
Ward, Sgt Eric H., ML Doc 1300

VARIOUS

Backhouse, Lt A., *Sydney Mail*
Bartley, Sgt H. H., *Delegate Argus*
Buchan, Pte F. J., Private collection
Davey, R. S., (unconfirmed 1Bn), *Henty Observer*
Dinning, Sgt L. L., Private collection
Hayes, Sgt J., Private collection
Higbid, Sgt A. D., *Globe and Sunday Times War Pictorial*
Kirby, Sgt J. H., *Dan Dorigo Gazette and Guy Fawkes Advocate*
Knight, Sgt M., MSB 176, MS 10143, La Trobe Collection, State Library of Victoria
McLeod, L.Cpl D. F., *Sydney Mail*
Mitchell, Pte Alan, *The King's School Magazine*
Montague, Lt H. L., *St George Call*
Moore, Sgt O. W., *Town and Country*
Murphy, Sgt-Maj. T., *Anzac Memorial*
Newton, Cpl E., *Sydney Mail*
O'Leary, Pte J., *Globe and Sunday Times War Pictorial*
Peel, Pte J., *Globe and Sunday Times War Pictorial*
Reid, Pte J., Private collection

Selman, Sgt A. R., *Globe and Sunday Times War Pictorial*
Selman, Pte J., *Globe and Sunday Times War Pictorial*
Sharpe, Pte H., *Evening News/Town and Country*
Simms, Pte W., *Sydney Morning Herald*
Vickery, Dvr E. C., Private collection
Wilkinson, Lt T. R. B., *Sydney Mail*

INTERVIEWEES AND CORRESPONDENTS

Anonymous (2)
Beckett, Mr L.
Conrade, Mrs S. C.
Cooper, Mrs H.
Evans, Mr W.
Fitzherbert, Mrs B.
Joyce, Miss N.
Polglase, Mr W.
Prince, Mrs J.
Stacy, Ms J.
Wayland, Mrs M.

OFFICIAL SOURCES

Bean, C. E. W., *Official History of Australia in the War of 1914–18: The Story of Anzac*, vol. I, Angus & Robertson, Sydney, 1941 [1921].
—— *Official History of Australia in the War of 1914–18: The Story of Anzac*, vol. II, Angus & Robertson, Sydney, 1936 [1924].
—— *Official History of Australia in the War of 1914–18: The AIF in France 1916*, vol. III, Angus & Robertson, Sydney, 1936 [1929].
—— *Official History of Australia in the War of 1914–18: The AIF in France 1917*, vol. IV, Angus & Robertson, Sydney, 1933.
—— *Official History of Australia in the War of 1914–18: The AIF in France 1918*, vol. V, Angus & Robertson, Sydney, 1937.
—— *Official History of Australia in the War of 1914–18: The AIF in France 1918*, vol. VI, Angus & Robertson, Sydney, 1942.
Butler, A. G., *Official History of the Australian Army Medical Services, 1914–1918*, vol. II, Australian War Memorial, Canberra, 1943.
—— *Official History of the Australian Army Medical Services, 1914–1918*, vol. III, Australian War Memorial, Canberra, 1943.
Commonwealth of Australia, Parliamentary Papers, General, Session 1914.15.16.17, No. 42, vol. II.
Commonwealth of Australia, Parliamentary Papers, General 2, Session 1914–1917, Interim Report, Further Interim Report, and Report on Liverpool Military Camp, New South Wales, by His Honour Mr Justice Rich.
Commonwealth Parliamentary Papers, Repatriation Department Interim Report to 30th June 1919, 1917–19, vol. IV, Melbourne 1919.

Edmonds, J., *Military Operations: France and Belgium, 1916*, vol. 2, Macmillan, London, 1938.

—— *Military Operations: France and Belgium, 1917*, Macmillan, London, 1938.

Scott, Ernest, *Official History of Australia in the War of 1914–18: Australia During the War*, vol. XI, Angus & Robertson, Sydney, 1938.

Secondary Sources

BOOKS AND ARTICLES

Adam-Smith, P., *The Anzacs*, Nelson, Melbourne, 1978.

Aiken, Alex, *Courage Past: A Duty Done*, George Outram and Co. Ltd., Glasgow, 1971.

Allen, Judith A., *Sex and Secrets: Crimes Involving Australian Women since 1880*, Oxford University Press, Melbourne, 1990.

Alomes, S., and Jones, C. (eds), *Australian Nationalism: A Documentary History*, Angus and Robertson, Sydney, 1991.

Andrews, E. M., *The Anzac Illusion: Anglo-Australian Relations during World War I*, Cambridge University Press, Melbourne, 1993.

Anonymous, 'Review of Joan Beaumont's *Gull Force*', *Sabretache*, October–December 1991.

Arthur, J. M., and Ramson, W. S. (eds), *W. H. Downing's Digger Dialect*, Oxford University Press, Melbourne, 1990.

Ashworth, Tony, *Trench Warfare, 1914–1918: The Live and Let Live System*, Macmillan Press, 1980.

Association of First Infantry Battalions, Editorial Committee, *The First at War: The Story of the 2/1st Australian Infantry Battalion, 1939–45, The City of Sydney Regiment*, 1987.

Aston, Sir George (ed.), *The Study of War: For Statesmen and Citizens*, Longmans, Green and Co., London, 1927.

Asprey, Robert B., *The German High Command at War: Hindenburg and Ludendorff and the First World War*, Warner Books, London, 1994 [1991].

Austin, Ron, *The White Ghurkas: The Australians at the Second Battle of Krithia, Gallipoli*, R. J. & S. P. Austin, McCrae, 1989.

—— *Cobbers in Khaki: The History of the 8th Battalion, 1914–1918*, Slouch Hat Publications, Rosebud, Vic., 1997.

Australian Dictionary of Biography, vol. 10, *1891–1939*, Melbourne University Press, 1986.

Australian Imperial Force, *Staff, Regimental, Gradation Lists of Officers* for 1914 and 1915.

Bank of New South Wales, *Roll of Honour*, Sydney, 1921.

Australian War Memorial, *Australian Chivalry*, Lee-Pratt Press, Melbourne, 1933.

—— 'Collection Notes: A New Gallipoli Diary', *Journal of the Australian War Memorial*, no. 16, April 1990.

Barnett, Correlli, *Britain and Her Army, 1509–1970: A Military, Political and Social Survey*, William Morrow & Company, New York, 1970.

Barrett, John, 'No Straw Man: C. E. W. Bean and Some Critics', *Australian Historical Studies*, vol. 23., No. 89, April 1988.

Barter, Margaret, *Far above Battle: The Experience and Memory of Australian Soldiers in War, 1939–1945*, Allen & Unwin, Sydney, 1994.

Baynes, John, *Morale: A Study of Men and Courage*, Leo Cooper, London, 1987 [1967].

—— *Far from a Donkey: The Life of General Sir Ivor Maxse, KCB, CVO, DSO*, Brassey's, London, 1995.

Bean, C. E. W., *Letters From France*, Cassell and Company Ltd, Melbourne, 1917.

—— 'Sidelights of the War on Australian Character', *Royal Australian Historical Society Journal*, vol. XIII, pt. IV, 1927.

—— *Anzac to Amiens: A Shorter History of the Australian Fighting Services in the First World War*, Australian War Memorial, Canberra, 1946.

—— *Two Men I Knew: William Bridges and Brudenell White: Founders of the AIF*, Angus & Robertson, Sydney, 1957.

—— *On the Wool Track*, rev. edn, Angus and Robertson, Sydney, 1970.

Beaumont, J. (ed.), *Australia's War, 1914–18*, Allen & Unwin, 1995.

Belford, Capt. W., *Legs-Eleven: Being the Story of the 11th Battalion (AIF) in the Great War of 1914–1918*, Imperial Printing Company Limited, Perth, 1940.

Blackmore, Kate, 'The Australian Repatriation Process', in Smart and Wood (eds), *An Anzac Muster*.

Blair, D. J., 'The Glorification of Australian Masculinity and the Reshaping of Australia's Great War Experience', *Sabretache*, April/June 1994.

Blake, Robert (ed.), *The Private Papers of Douglas Haig, 1914–1919*, Eyre & Spottiswoode, London, 1952.

Blaxland, G., *Amiens 1918*, Frederick Muller, London, 1968.

Bourke, Joanna, ' "Swinging the lead": Malingering, Australian Soldiers, and the Great War', *Journal of the Australian War Memorial*, no. 26, April 1995.

—— 'Shell Shock and Australian Soldiers in the Great War', *Sabretache*, July–September 1995.

Bourne, Peter, 'From Boot Camp to My Lai', in Richard A. Falk (ed.), *Crimes of War*, New York, 1971.

Brugger, S., *Australians and Egypt, 1914–1919*, Melbourne University Press, 1980.

Cecil, Hugh, and Liddle, Peter (eds), *Facing Armageddon*, Leo Cooper, London, 1996.

Chapman, Ivan, *Iven G. Mackay: Citizen and Soldier*, Melway Publishing, Melbourne, 1975.

Charlton, Peter, *Pozières 1916: Australians on the Somme*, Methuen Haynes, Sydney, 1986.

Chateris, Brig.-Gen. J., *At GHQ*, Cassell and Company, London, 1931.

Clancy, Jack, 'Images of Australia in World War I: The Film, the Mini-Series and Historical Representation', in Smart and Wood (eds), *An Anzac Muster*.

Clark, Alan, *The Waratahs: South Coast Recruiting March, 1915*, self-published, Nowra, NSW, 1994.

Clark, C. M. H., *A History of Australia*, vol. VI: ' *The old dead tree and the young tree green*', 1916–1935, Melbourne University Press, 1987.

Cochrane, Peter, *Simpson and the Donkey: The Making of a Legend*, Melbourne University Press, 1992.

—— 'What is History? A Reply to Tom Curran', *Quadrant*, December 1996.

Connor, John, 'The British Part in Making the Anzac Legend', paper presented at the Australian Historical Association Conference, Hobart, 29 September 1999.

Cooksley, Jon, *PALS: The 13th and 14th Battalions, York and Lancaster Regiment: A History of the Two Battalions raised by Barnsley in World War One*, Wharncliff Publishing, Barnsley, 1986.

Corfield, Robin, *Hold Hard, Cobbers*, vol. 1: *1912–1930: The Story of the 57th and 60th and 57/60th Australian Infantry Battalions, 1912–1990*, 57/60th Battalion (AIF) Association, 1992.

Coulthard-Clark, Chris, *The Diggers: Makers of the Australian Military Tradition*, Melbourne University Press, 1993.

Curran, Tom, *Across the Bar: The Story of 'Simpson', The Man with the Donkey: Australia and Tyneside's Great Military Hero*, Ogmios Publications, Brisbane, 1994.

—— 'The True Heroism of Simpson: A Reply to Peter Cochrane', *Quadrant*, April 1997.

Cutlack, F. M. (ed.), *War Letters of General Monash*, Angus & Robertson, Sydney, 1934.

Damousi, J., and Lake M. (eds), *Gender and War: Australians at War in the Twentieth Century*, Cambridge University Press, Melbourne, 1995.

Dawes, J. N. I., and Robson, L. L., *From Citizen to Soldier: Australia before the Great War, Recollections of Members of the First AIF*, Melbourne University Press, 1977.

Dawson, Graham, 'Playing at War: An Autobiographical Approach to Boyhood Fantasy and Masculinity', *Oral History*, vol. 18, no. 1, Spring 1990.

Deery, Phillip, Labor Interlude in Victorian Politics: The Prendergast Government, 1924, BA Hons thesis, La Trobe University, 1972.

Dennis, P., Grey, J., Morris, E., and Prior, R., *The Oxford Companion to Australian Military History*, Oxford University Press, Melbourne, 1995.

Denton, Kit, *Gallipoli: One Long Grave*, Australians at War Bicentennial Series, Time–Life Books Australia and John Ferguson, Sydney, 1986.

Dinter, Elmar, *Hero or Coward: Pressures Facing the Soldier in Battle*, Frank Cass, 1985.

Dupuy, R. E., and T. N., *The Encyclopedia of Military History from 3500 BC to the present*, Jane's Publishing Company, London, 1980.

Dupuy, T. N., *Understanding War: History and Theory of Combat*, Paragon House Publishers, New York, 1987.

Echuca–Moama RSL Citizens Club, *Newsletter Souvenir*, 19 May 1995.

Eddy, J., and Schreuder, D., *The Rise of Colonial Nationalism: Australia, New Zealand, Canada and South Africa First Assert their Nationalities, 1880–1914*, Allen & Unwin, Sydney, 1988.

Ellis, Anthony, 'The Impact of War and Peace on Australian Soldiers, 1914–20', paper presented at the Australian War Memorial History Conference, 8–12 February 1983.

Ellis-Davidson, H. R., *Gods and Myths of Northern Europe*, Penguin, 1964.

Elshtain, Jean Bethke, *Women and War*, University of Chicago Press, Chicago, 1987.

Ely, R., 'The First Anzac Day: Invented or Discovered?', *Journal of Australian Studies*, no. 17, November 1985.

Evans, Raymond, *The Red Flag Riots: A Study of Intolerance*, University of Queensland Press, 1988.

Farrall, Lois, *The File on Fred: A Biography of Fred Farrall*, High Leigh Publishing Company, Carrum, Vic., 1992.

Fewster, Kevin, 'Ellis Ashmead Bartlett and the Making of the Anzac Legend', *Journal of Australian Studies*, no. 10, June 1982.

—— 'The Wazza Riots', *Journal of the Australian War Memorial*, no. 4, April 1984.

Field, Laurie, *The Forgotten War: Australia and the Boer War*, Melbourne University Press, 1979.

Field, M. D., 'Information and Authority: The Structure of Military Organization', *American Sociological Review*, vol. 24, no. 1, February 1959.

Firkins, Peter, *The Australians in Nine Wars: Waikato to Long Tan*, Pan Books, London, 1973.

Flaherty C., and Roberts, M., 'The Reproduction of ANZAC Symbolism', *Journal of Australian Studies*, no. 24, May 1989.

Floud, R., Wachter, K., and Gregory, A., *Height, Health and History: Nutritional Status in the United Kingdom, 1750–1980*, Cambridge University Press, 1990.

Fuller, J. G., Popular Culture and Troop Morale in the British and Dominion Forces, 1914–1918, PhD Thesis, King's College, 1988.

Fussell, Paul, *The Great War and Modern Memory*, Oxford University Press, London, 1975.

Gammage, W., *The Broken Years: Australian Soldiers in the Great War*, Penguin, Ringwood, Vic., 1975.

—— 'Australians and the Great War', *Journal of Australian Studies*, no. 6, June 1980.

—— 'The Crucible: The Establishment of the Anzac Tradition, 1899–1918', in McKernan and Brown (eds), *Australia: Two Centuries of War and Peace*.

—— The Genesis of the Anzac Ethos: Australian Infantry in France and Belgium during the Great War; and Some Attitudes and Values Relating to the Military Experience of the First AIF, BA Hons thesis, Australian National University, 1965.

Garton, Stephen, *The Cost of War: Australians Return*, Oxford University Press, Melbourne, 1996.

—— 'Return Home: War, Masculinity and Repatriation', in Damousi and Lake (eds), *Gender and War*.

Gawenda, Michael, 'History matters, so let's never forget it', *Age*, 6 May 1996.

Gerster, Robin, *Big-Noting: The Heroic Theme in Australian War Writing*, Melbourne University Press, 1992, [1987].

Gliddon, Gerald, *'When The Barrage Lifts': A Topographical History and Commentary on the Battle of the Somme, 1916*, Gliddon Books, Norwich, 1987.

Graham, D., *'Sans Doctrine*: British Army Tactics in the First World War', in Travers and Archer (eds), *Men at War*.

Grant, Ian, *Jacka, VC: Australia's Finest Fighting Soldier*, Macmillan Company and Australian War Memorial, 1989.

Graves, Robert, *The Greek Myths*, vol. 1, Penguin, 1975 [1955].

Griffith, Paddy, *Battle Tactics of the Western Front: The British Army's Art of Attack, 1916–18*, Yale University Press, London, 1996.

Grimshaw, P., Lake, M., McGrath, A., and Quartly, M., *Creating a Nation, 1788–1990*, McPhee Gribble Publishers, Melbourne, 1994.

Hagopian, Patrick, 'Oral Narratives: Secondary Revision and the Memory of the Vietnam War', *History Workshop Journal*, no. 32, Autumn 1991.

Hamilton, Sir Ian, *Ian Hamilton's Despatches from the Dardanelles etc.*, George Newnes, 1917.

Harris, Jose, *The Penguin Social History of Britain; Public Lives, Public Spirit: Britain, 1870–1914*, Penguin, London, 1993.

Hickey, Michael, *Gallipoli*, John Murray, London, 1995.

Higonnet, J., and Weitz, Michel (eds), *Behind the Lines: Gender and the Two World Wars*, Yale University Press, New Haven and London, 1987.

Hirst, John, 'Is Feminist History Bunk?', *Weekend Australian*, 4–5 March, 1995.

Holmes, Richard, *Firing Line*, Jonathan Cape, London, 1985.

Horner, David, 'Military History in Australia', in Smith (ed.), *Australians on Peace and War*.

Hughes, Colin, *Mametz: Lloyd George's 'Welsh Army' at the Battle of the Somme*, Orion Press, 1979.

Inglis, Ken, 'The Anzac Tradition', *Meanjin Quarterly*, vol. 24, no. 1, March 1965.

—— 'The Australians at Gallipoli', parts I–II, *Historical Studies*, April, October 1970.

—— *The Rehearsal: Australians at War in the Sudan, 1885*, Rigby, Sydney, 1985.

—— 'Review of Geoffrey Moorhouse's *Hell's Foundations*', *Journal of the Australian War Memorial*, No. 22, April 1993.

James, Robert Rhode, *Gallipoli: A British Historian's View*, Public lecture delivered at the University of Melbourne, 24 April 1995, published by the History Department, University of Melbourne, 1995.

Johnston, Mark, *At the Front Line: Experiences of Australian Soldiers in World War II*, Cambridge University Press, Melbourne, 1996.

Keegan, John, *The Face of Battle: A Study of Agincourt, Waterloo, and the Somme*, Penguin Books, 1978 [1976].

Kent, David, 'The Anzac Book and the Anzac Legend: C. E. W. Bean as Editor and Image-maker', *Historical Studies*, vol. 21, 1985.

—— 'Troopship Literature: A Life on the Ocean Wave, 1914–19', *Journal of the Australian War Memorial*, no. 10, April 1987.

—— 'The Anzac Book: A Reply to Denis Winter', *Journal of the Australian War Memorial*, no. 17, October 1990.

—— 'Bean's "Anzac" and the Making of the Anzac Legend', *Kunapipi*, vol. 18, nos. 2–3, 1996.

Kerr, Greg, *Lost Anzacs: The Story of Two Brothers*, Oxford University Press, Melbourne, 1997.

Keys, Sir William, 'The RSL View', in Smith (ed.), *Australians on Peace and War*.

King, Terry, On the definition of 'Digger': Australia and its Returned Soldiers, 1915–1920, PhD thesis, La Trobe University, 1988.

Kingsley, Charles, *Westward Ho!*, Heron Books, London, [1855].

Kristianson, G. L., *The Politics of Patriotism: The Pressure Group Activities of the Returned Servicemen's League*, Australian National University Press, Canberra, 1966.

Laffin, John, *Digger: The Story of the Australian Soldier*, Cassell & Company, 1959.

—— *Western Front, 1916–1917: The Price of Honour*, Time-Life Books and John Ferguson, Sydney, 1987.

—— *Western Front, 1917–1918: The Cost of Victory*, Time–Life Books and John Ferguson, Sydney, 1988.

—— *British Butchers and Bunglers of World War One*, Macmillan, South Melbourne, 1989.

—— *Guide to Australian Battlefields of the Western Front, 1916–1918*, Kangaroo Press and Australian War Memorial, 1992.

Lahey, John, 'The World's Most Democratic Army', 75th Gallipoli anniversary souvenir in the *Age*, 20 April 1990.

Lake, Marilyn, 'Women, Gender and History', *Australian Feminist Studies*, nos. 7–8, Summer 1988.

—— 'Birth of History', *Weekend Australian*, 18–19 March 1995.

Leed, Eric, *No Man's Land: Combat and Identity in World War I*, Cambridge University Press, London, 1979.

Liddle, Peter, *Men of Gallipoli: The Dardanelles and Gallipoli Experience, August 1914 to January 1916*, Newton Abbot, Devon, 1988.

—— *The Soldier's War, 1914–18*, Blandford Press, London, 1988.

—— *The 1916 Battle of the Somme: A Reappraisal*, Leo Cooper, London, 1992.

Liddle, P., and Richardson, M., 'Voices from the Past: An Evaluation of Oral History as a Source for Research into the Western Front Experience of the British Soldier, 1914–18', *Journal of Contemporary History*, vol. 31, no. 4, October 1996.

Lindstrom, R., Stress and Identity: Australian Soldiers during the First World War, MA thesis, Melbourne University, 1985.

—— The Australian Experience of Psychological Casualties, 1915–1939, PhD thesis, Dept of Humanities, Victoria University of Technology, 1997.

Lloyd, Clem, and Rees, Jaqui, *The Last Shilling: A History of Repatriation in Australia*, Melbourne University Press, 1994.

MacKenzie, C., *Gallipoli Memories*, Cassell, London, 1929.

MacKenzie, J. J., A Disabling Minority: Mutiny in the First Battalion AIF, September 1918, BA Hons thesis, Australian Defence Force Academy, 1988.

Maddocks, G., *Liverpool Pals: 17th, 18th, 19th and 20th Battalions, The King's (Liverpool) Regiment*, Leo Cooper, London, 1991.

Marwick, Arthur, *The Nature of History*, 3rd edn, Macmillan, 1989.

Masefield, John, *Gallipoli*, Heinemann, London, 1916.

McAulay, Lex, *The Battle of Long Tan*, Hutchinson, Hawthorn, Vic., 1986.

McCarthy, D., *Gallipoli to the Somme: The Story of C. E. W. Bean*, John Ferguson, Sydney, 1983.

McInnes, C., and Sheffield, G. D., *Warfare in the Twentieth Century: Theory and Practice*, Unwin Hyman, London, 1988.

McKernan, M., *The Australian People and the Great War*, Collins, Sydney, 1984 [1980].

—— 'Writing about War', in McKernan and Browne (eds), *Australia: Two Centuries of War and Peace.*

—— 'Review of *The Oxford Companion to Australian Military History*', *Eureka Street*, vol. 6, no. 1, January–February 1996.

McKernan, M., and Browne, M. (eds), *Australia: Two Centuries of War and Peace*, Australian War Memorial and Allen & Unwin, Canberra, 1988.

McLachlan, Noel, 'The Divisive Digger', *Meanjin Quarterly*, vol. 27, 1968.

McNeill, Ian, *To Long Tan: The Australian Army and Vietnam War, 1950–1966*, Allen & Unwin and Australian War Memorial, 1993.

McQueen, H., *Gallipoli to Petrov: Arguing with Australian History*, Allen & Unwin, Sydney, 1984.

McQuilton, John, 'A Shire at War: Yackandandah, 1914–18', *Journal of the Australian War Memorial*, no. 11, October 1987.

Middlebrook, M., *The Kaiser's Battle: 21 March 1918: The First Day of the German Spring Offensive*, Allen Lane, London, 1978.

Millar, John, D., A Study in the Limitations of Command: General Sir William Birdwood and the AIF, 1914–1918, PhD thesis, University of New South Wales, 1993.

Millington, Bob, 'Are We in Danger of Forgetting our History?', *Have a Go: News Victoria*, April 1996.

Monash, Sir John, *The Australian Victories in France in 1918*, rev. edn, Lothian Book Publishing Co., Melbourne and Sydney, 1923 [1920].

Moorhouse, G., *Hell's Foundations: A Town, its Myths and Gallipoli*, Sceptre, 1993 [1992].

Morton, Desmond, *When Your Number's Up: The Canadian Soldier in the First World War*, Random House of Canada, Toronto, 1993.

Mosse, George L., *Fallen Soldiers: Reshaping the Memory of the World Wars*, Oxford University Press, New York, 1990.

Moyer, Laurence, *Victory Must Be Ours: Germany in the Great War, 1914–1918*, Hippocrone Books, New York, 1995.

Murphy, Sgt-Maj. T., 'A Soldier's Diary' in *Anzac Memorial*, Returned Soldiers Association, Sydney, 1917.

New South Wales, Parliament, *Unveiling of Permanent Memorial in the New South Wales Legislative Chamber*, Commemorative booklet, November 1915.

Norman, Terry, *The Hell They Called High Wood: The Somme 1916*, Patrick Stephens, 1984.

North, John, *Gallipoli: The Fading Vision*, Faber & Faber, London, 1936.

Oman, Sir Charles, 'A Defence of Military History' in Aston (ed.), *The Study of War.*

Orr, Philip, *The Road to the Somme: Men of the Ulster Division Tell Their Story*, Blackstaff Press, Belfast, 1987.

O'Ryan, Maj.-Gen. J. F., *The Story of the 27th Division*, vol. 1, Wynkoop Hallenbeck Crawford Co., New York, 1921.

Palmer, Vance, *The Legend of the Nineties*, Melbourne University Press, 1980 [1954].

Paterson, A. B., *Happy Despatches*, Sydney, 1934.

Pederson, Peter, *Monash as Military Commander*, Melbourne University Press, 1985.

—— 'The AIF on the Western Front: The Role of Training and Command', in McKernan and Browne (eds), *Australia: Two Centuries of War and Peace*.

Powell, Sian, 'Larrikin Spirit of Anzac Heroes Inspires Another Generation', *Australian*, 25 April 1996.

Prior, R., and Wilson, T. *Command on the Western Front: The Military Career of Sir Henry Rawlinson, 1914–18*, Blackwell, Oxford, 1992.

—— *Passchendaele: The Untold Story*, Yale University Press, London, 1996.

Pugsley, C., *Gallipoli: The New Zealand Story*, Sceptre, Auckland, 1990 [1984].

—— *On the Fringe of Hell: New Zealanders and Military Discipline in the First World War*, Hodder & Stoughton, Auckland, 1991.

Rawling, Bill, *Surviving Trench Warfare: Technology and the Canadian Corps, 1914–1918*, University of Toronto Press, 1992.

Rickard, John, *Australia: A Cultural History*, Longman Cheshire, Melbourne, 1988.

Roberts, Chris, 'The Landing at Anzac: A Reassessment', *Journal of the Australian War Memorial*, no. 22, April 1993.

Robertson, John, *Anzac and Empire: The Tragedy and Glory of Gallipoli*, Hamlyn Australia, 1989.

Robson, L. L., *The First AIF: A Study of its Recruitment*, Melbourne University Press, 1970.

—— 'The Anzac Tradition', transcript from an ABC School Broadcast, March 1972.

—— Book review, *Meanjin Quarterly*, October 1974.

—— 'The Origin and Character of the First AIF, 1914–1918: Some Statistical Evidence', *Historical Studies*, vol. 15, 1973.

—— 'Images of the Warrior: Australian-British Perceptions in the Great War', *Journal of the Australian War Memorial*, no. 1, October 1982.

—— 'The Australian Soldier: Formation of a Stereotype', in McKernan and Browne (eds), *Australia: Two Centuries of War and Peace*.

—— (ed.), *Australian Commentaries: Select Articles from the 'Round Table', 1911–1942*, Melbourne University Press, 1975.

Ross, Jane, *The Myth of the Digger: The Australian Soldier in Two World Wars*, Hale & Iremonger, Sydney, 1985.

Serle, G., 'The Digger Tradition and Australian Nationalism', *Meanjin Quarterly*, vol. 24, no. 2, June 1965.

Scott, Joan, 'Rewriting History', in Higonnet and Weitz (eds), *Behind the Lines*.

Sheffield, G. D., '*Blitzkrieg* and Attrition: Land Operations in Europe 1914–45', in McInnes and Sheffield, *Warfare in the Twentieth Century*.

—— The Effect of War Service on the 22nd Battalion Royal Fusiliers (Kensington) 1914–18, with Special Reference to Morale, Discipline, and the Officer–Man Relationship, MA thesis, University of Leeds, School of History, 1984.

—— 'The Effect of the Great War on Class Relations in Britain: The Career of Major Christopher Stone DSO MC', *War and Society*, vol. 7, no. 1, May 1989.

—— *Leadership and Command: The Anglo-American Military Experience Since 1861*, Brassey's, London, 1997.

Shortis, Stephen, "Colonial Nationalism": New South Welsh Identity in the mid-1880s', *Journal of the Royal Australian Historical Society*, pt 1, vol. 59, March 1973.

Shute, Carmel, 'Sexual mythology, 1914–1918', *Hecate*, vol. 1, no. 1, 1975.

Simkins, Peter, *Kitchener's Army: The Raising of the New Armies, 1914–16*, Manchester University Press, 1988.

—— *World War I, 1914–1918: The Western Front*, Tiger Books International, London, 1994 [1991].

—— 'Everyman at War: Recent Interpretations of the Font Line Experience', in Brian Bond (ed.), *The First World War and British Military History*, Clarendon Press, Oxford, 1991.

Smart, J., and Wood, T. (eds), *An Anzac Muster: War and Society in Australia and New Zealand 1914–18 and 1939–45*, Monash Publications in History: 14, 1992.

Smith, Hugh (ed.), *Australians on Peace and War*, Australian Defence Force Academy, 1986.

Smith, Leonard V., *Between Mutiny and Obedience: The Case of the French Fifth Infantry Division During World War I*, Princeton University Press, 1994.

Smith, Lt.-Col. N. C., *The Red and Black Diamond: The History of the 21st Battalion, 1915–1918*, self-published, 1997.

Solarno, E. John (ed.), *Drill and Field Training*, John Murray, London, 1915.

Stacy, B. V., Kindon, F. J., and Chedgey, H. V., *The History of the First Battalion, AIF, 1914–1919*, First Battalion AIF Association, 1931.

Stanley, Peter, 'Paul the Pimp Re-considered: Australian "G" Staffs on the Western Front and the "Kiggell anecdote" ', paper presented at the Australian War Memorial History Conference, 6–10 July 1987.

Steel, N., and Hart, P., *Defeat at Gallipoli*, Macmillan, London, 1994.

Stephens, Tony, *The Last Anzacs: Gallipoli, 1915*, Allen & Kemsley, Sydney, 1996.

Stouffer, S., *The American Soldier: Combat and its Aftermath*, vol. 2, Princeton University Press, 1949.

Tate, Brian, 'The Gallipoli Samurai', manuscript, East Ballina, NSW.

Taylor F. W., and Cusack T. A., *Nulli Secundus: A History of the Second Battalion, AIF, 1914–1919*, Sydney, 1942.

Terraine, John, *To Win a War: 1918, The Year of Victory*, Sidgewick & Jackson, London, 1978.

Thomson, Alistair, 'Review of Kevin Fewster, *Gallipoli Correspondent: The Frontline Diaries of C. E. W. Bean*', *Historical Studies*, vol. 21, 1984.

—— '"Steadfast Until Death"? C. E. W. Bean and the Representation of Australian Military Manhood', *Historical Studies*, vol. 23, no. 93, October 1989.

—— *Anzac Memories: Living with the legend*, Oxford University Press, Melbourne, 1994.

Travers, T., and Archer, C. (eds), *Men at War: Politics, Technology and Innovation in the Twentieth Century*, Precedent, Chicago, 1982.

Travers, T. H. E., 'From Surafend to Gough: Charles Bean, James Edmonds, and the Making of the Australian Official History', *Journal of the Australian War Memorial*, no. 27, October 1995.

Turner, P. W., and Haigh, R. H., *Not for Glory: A Personal History of the 1914–18 War*, Robert Maxwell, London.

Vader, John, *ANZAC: The Story of the Anzac Soldier*, New English Library, London, 1971 [1970].

Van Creveld, Martin, *Command in War*, Harvard University Press, London, 1985.

von Clausewitz, Carl, *On War*, Pelican, 1968.

von Schmidt, Eric, 'How is the Alamo Remembered?', *Smithsonian*, vol. 1, no. 12, March 1986.

Wallace, R. L., *The Australians at the Boer War*, Australian War Memorial and Australian Government Publishing Service, Canberra, 1976.

Ward, Russel, *The Australian Legend*, Oxford University Press, Melbourne, 1965.

Welborn, Suzanne, *Lords of Death*, Fremantle Arts Centre Press, 1982.

White, Richard, *Inventing Australia: Images and Identity, 1688–1980*, Allen & Unwin, Sydney, 1981.

—— 'Motives for Joining up: Self-sacrifice, Self-interest and Social Class, 1914–18', *Journal of the Australian War Memorial*, no. 9, October 1986.

Wigmore, Lionel, *They Dared Mightily*, Australian War Memorial, Canberra, ACT, 1963.

Wilcox, Craig, Australia's Citizen Army, 1889–1914, PhD, ANU, 1993.

—— 'False Start: The Mobilisation of Australia's Citizen Army, 1914', *Journal of the Australian War Memorial*, no. 26, April 1995.

Wiley, Bell I., *The Life of Johnny Reb: The Common Soldier of the Confederacy*, Louisiana State University Press, Baton Rouge 1978 [1943].

—— *The Life of Billy Yank: The Common Soldier of the Union*, Louisiana State University Press, Baton Rouge 1978 [1952].

Wilkes, G. A., *A Dictionary of Australian Colloquialisms*, Oxford University Press, Melbourne, 1990.

Williams, Charles, *Bradman*, Little, Brown and Company, London, 1996.

Williams, J., Discipline on Active Service: The 1st Brigade, First AIF, 1914–1919, LitB thesis, Dept of History, Australian National University, 1982.

—— 'The First AIF Overseas', paper presented at the Australian War Memorial History Conference, 8–12 February 1983.

Williams, John F., *The Quarantined Culture: Australian Reactions to Modernism, 1913–1939*, Cambridge University Press, 1995.

Wilson, Trevor, *The Myriad Faces of War: Britain and the Great War, 1914–1918*, Polity Press, 1986.

Winter, Denis, *Death's Men: Soldiers of the Great War*, Allen Lane, London, 1978.

—— 'The Anzac Book': A Re-appraisal', *Journal of the Australian War Memorial*, April 1990.

—— *Making the Legend: The War Writings of C. E. W. Bean*, University of Queensland Press, 1992.

—— *25 April 1915: The Inevitable Tragedy*, University of Queensland Press, 1992.

Wintringham, Tom, *The Story of Weapons and Tactics: from Troy to Stalingrad*, Freeport, NY, 1971 [1943].

Wren, Eric, *Randwick to Hargicourt: History of the 3rd Battalion, AIF*, Ronald G. MacDonald, Sydney, 1935.

Index

Where rank is cited the last known rank attained is used.
Asterisks (*) indicate those killed in action or who died of wounds